Recent Policy Issues
in Environmental and
Resource Economics

Contributions to Economics

continued on page 194

Peter Michaelis · Frank Stähler (Eds.)

Recent Policy Issues in Environmental and Resource Economics

With 19 Figures
and 20 Tables

Physica-Verlag

A Springer-Verlag Company

Series Editors
Werner A. Müller
Martina Bihn

Editors
Prof. Dr. habil. Peter Michaelis
Fachhochschule Anhalt
Department of Economics
Strenzfelder Allee 28
D-06406 Bernburg, Germany

PD Dr. Frank Stähler
Institute of Economic Theory
University of Kiel
Wilhelm-Seelig-Platz 1
D-24098 Kiel, Germany

ISBN 3-7908-1137-8 Physica-Verlag Heidelberg New York

Cataloging-in-Publication Data applied for
Die Deutsche Bibliothek – CIP-Einheitsaufnahme
Recent policy issues in environmental and resource economics: with 20 tables / Peter Michaelis, Frank Stähler (eds.). – Heidelberg: Physica-Verl., 1998
  (Contributions to economics)
  ISBN 3-7908-1137-8

© Physica-Verlag Heidelberg 1998
Printed in Germany

Softcover design: Erich Kirchner, Heidelberg

SPIN 10687634   88/2202-5 4 3 2 1 0 – Printed on acid-free paper

Contents

List of Contributors

Johannes Heister, S-2-129, ENVGC - Climate Change, The World Bank, 1818 H Street, N.W., Washington, D.C. 20433, U.S.A., jheister@worldbank.org

Gernot Klepper, Kiel Institute of World Economics, D-24100 Kiel, Germany, gklepper@ifw.uni-kiel.de

Peter Michaelis, Fachhochschule Anhalt, Department of Economics, Strenzfelder Allee 28, D-06406 Bernburg, Germany, michaelis@serviwi.wi.fh-anhalt.de

Christian M. Scholz, Kiel Institute of World Economics, D-24100 Kiel, Germany, christian.scholz@ifw.uni-kiel.de

Frank Stähler, Institute of Economic Theory, University of Kiel, Wilhelm-Seelig-Platz 1, D-24098 Kiel, Germany, fstaehler@econ-theory.uni-kiel.de

1. Introduction

Peter Michaelis and Frank Stähler

This book deals with recent policy issues in environmental and resource economics. To collect articles on recent policy issues is of course always also a question of taste. This volume tries to represent a broad range of papers which covers the double dividend hypothesis, the role of non-profit organizations for environmental policies, trade implications and international environmental agreements. It consists of two parts, a part on domestic policy issues and a part on international policy issues. A separate part on international policy issues would not have been on the agenda when this volume would have been published two decades ago. But international and global environmental problems are different from purely national problems and deserve a special approach.

However, also domestic policies face new challenges. One new focus of domestic policies is the discussion on the relationship between environmental benefits and other policy objectives. '*Some Remarks on the Double Dividend Hypothesis*' by Christian Scholz deals with this discussion. In opposition to a number of recent papers it is found that the possibility for a double dividend depends largely on the substitutability characteristics of taxed commodities. It is found that a double dividend is possible, if the following conditions are met. First, the initial tax system has to be inefficient from a non-environmental point of view. Second, it is possible to raise the tax on the externality creating commodity and in exchange to reduce the tax on a commodity that is a gross substitute for the externality creating commodity. Third, under the existing distortionary tax system the commodity whose tax is reduced is relatively difficult to substitute through other taxed commodities and hence easier to substitute through the untaxed numeraire.

'*Selling the Greenpeace Car*' by Peter Michaelis deals with competition between profit-maximizing firms and non-profit organizations. The non-profit organization is a supplier which does not maximize profits but which aims at minimizing ecological impacts. The paper takes the Greenpeace car as an example since Greenpeace has announced to market a car which consumes less fuel than the conventional cars. The paper shows that an equilibrium in this market exists only under certain conditions. It is shown that the product supplied by the non-profit organization will cause less ecological damage and will be more expensive than the product supplied by profit maximizing firms.

'*Stock-dependent Uncertainty and Optimal Resource Exploitation*' by Frank Stähler and Peter Michaelis discusses the role of stock-dependent uncertainty for optimal resource exploitation. It considers the case that the probability of a certain event depends not only on current actions but on the sum of all past actions. These stock-dependent risks imply an intertemporal effect. In the paper, this problem is analyzed using the example of the exploitation of a non-renewable, exhaustible common-pool resource. The paper discusses resource extraction policies under endogenous closure risks which depend on the accumulated stock of extracted resources. It turns out that the optimal time path of resource extractions requires a tax rate which surmounts both the no-risk and second-best tax which tackles the problem by a mere evaluation of the expected exhaustibility stock.

'*Trade Implications of Environmental Taxes*' by Gernot Klepper begins the analysis of recent international policy issues. It develops a simple analytic framework in which the impact of different environmental taxes on the international division of labor can be illustrated. It shows that even in this simple framework numerous different configurations have to be distinguished. It discusses also empirical studies on environmental policies and the possibilities for mitigating the impact of these taxes on the international competitiveness of industrial sectors.

'*The International Dimension of Sustainability Policies*' by Gernot Klepper and Frank Stähler deals with the international aspects of environmental policies which intend to guarantee a sustainable development. It discusses some of the rather rare concrete definitions of sustainability in the context of open economies, and it shows the international repercussions of these policies which have been ignored so far. In particular, the authors demonstrate that any sustainability policy which intends to compensate resource extraction should not accumulate physical capital because physical capital accumulation may lead to increased resource extraction in the long run. This effect is substantially stronger when resources are traded.

'*Who Will Win the Ozone Game?*' by Johannes Heister presents an analysis of the Montreal Protocol on Substances that Deplete the Ozone Layer. It advances the view that the Developing World did not exploit its relatively strong bargaining position in negotiations over side-payments and that the concessional ten-year grace period for less developed countries is a cause of instability. The paper derives conditions under which side-payments and sanctions can produce stable cooperation, and it compares the non-cooperative outcome with the Nash bargaining solution of a hypothetical cooperative game.

The last two papers entitled '*On the Economics of International Environmental Agreements*' and '*Managing Global Pollution Problems by Reduction and Adaptation Policies*' by Frank Stähler deal also with international environmental problems. The first paper demonstrates that partial cooperation with respect to the use of an international environmental resource can be supported even when countries are able to break an agreement. It assumes that cooperation starts with two countries. However, broader cooperation is shown to be possible when these two countries compensate a third country for extra reduction efforts. The paper discusses also a reversible and an irreversible technology option, and it demonstrates that compensating a third country for the introduction of an irreversible technology may be profitable for the donors even if this technology incurs higher costs than a reversible one. The second paper questions the standard results of an international non-cooperative reduction game and considers scope effects between reduction and adaptation policies. In particular, it demonstrates that scope effects can result in positively sloped reaction curves. The paper discusses also the role of different conjectures and corner solutions. It concludes that, compared to the well-known standard results, all these effects imply ambiguous theoretical results.

PART ONE

Domestic Policy Issues

2. Some Remarks on the Double Dividend Hypothesis

Christian M. Scholz

1. INTRODUCTION[1]

In an influental paper on environmental tax reforms Bovenberg, De Mooij (1994) come to the result that „environmental taxes typically exacerbate, rather than alleviate, preexisting tax distortions". Especially, these authors show that a revenue neutral environmental tax reform that increases a tax on a polluting consumption good and cuts the labor income tax, reduces labor supply. Fullerton (1997) and Schöb (1997) have shown that when a different normalization of the Bovenberg, De Mooij model is chosen, environmental taxes do not need to exacerbate preexisting tax distortions. This paper extends the analysis of Fullerton (1997) and Schöb (1997) to show that the choice of the numeraire leads also to different conclusions regarding the efffects of environmental tax reforms on labor supply.

In the discussion of environmental taxation there has been a considerable confusion about the effects of environmental tax reforms. Especially, the debate focuses on whether it could be possible that an environmental tax reforms yields next to environmental benefits also non-environmental benefits. The non-environmental benefits are defined in various ways. The most frequently used definitions focus on the non-environmental dividend in terms of the reduction of the overall distortion of the tax system and on the increase in employment.

A tax reform that yields environmental and non-environmental benefits is said to yield a double dividend.[2] The question of the existence of a double

---

1   This paper is a revised version of Scholz (1996).

2   The term double dividend was introduced by Pearce (1991).

dividend gains importance when designing environmental tax reforms. The public and academic interest in the double dividend results from the argument that the magnitude of environmental benefits is largely unknown due to missing markets for environmental quality [See Goulder (1995)]. When a tax reform yields only environmental benefits it is not guaranteed that the net welfare effect is still positive. Therefore, in order to guarantee positive welfare effects, an environmental tax reform must yield a double dividend.

However, the papers of Bovenberg, De Mooij (1994), Bovenberg, van der Ploeg (1994), find that the double dividend hypothesis is subject to serious doubt. These authors find that as long as the uncompensated elasticity of household labor supply is positive, in a model with a dirty consumption good causing a negative externality, a tax reform that aims at raising the tax on the dirty consumption good and reducing the labor income tax will increase preexisting tax distortions and reduce employment, [Bovenberg, De Mooij (1994), p. 1085]. Nothing is wrong with this result in the chosen framework of the respective papers, but it seems that it might be misinterpreted. This paper emphasizes that at least theoretically the prospects of positive employment effects of environmental tax reforms are not as pessimistic as the mentioned papers might suggest. It will be shown that a different choice of the taxes involved in an environmental tax reform can lead to a double dividend, in the sense of a reduction of distortions and also increased employment.[3] Therefore, this paper puts more emphasis on the importance of choice of tax rates involved in an environmental tax reform.

2.   THE FRAMEWORK

Tax reforms have the feature of changing a vector composed of price vector q^0 and income vector I^0, from $\left(q^0; I^0\right)$ to $\left(q^1; I^1\right)$. Using the indireutility function $W(q; I)$ it is easy to express the resulting welfare change as $W\left(q^0; I^0\right) - W\left(q^1; I^1\right)$. But since utility functions are ordinal and not cardinal, there is not a unique number that represents this welfare change. For this reason Hicks (1943) introduced the concepts of compensating variation and equivalent variation. As shown in Mayshar (1990) both measures are equal when only marginal variations are considered. Consider the indirect utility function of a representative household:

---

[3]   That a reduction of the overall level of distortion is possible follows of course from the work of Fullerton (1997) and Schöb (1997). However, when the working paper version of this paper was written, these papers had not been known to the author.

$$W(q; I - T; z) = \max_{x}\{u(x; z): I - T \geq qx\}, \tag{1}$$

where $u(x; z)$ denoted a concave and continuously differentiable utility function. x denotes the $(n + 1) \times 1$ vector of private commodities, with x_0 as the numeraire. $q = p + t$ denotes consumer price vector, p the producer price vector and t the $(n \times 1)$ tax vector. x_i, p_i, q_i and t_i denote the ith element of the vectors x, p, q and t, respectively. T denotes lump-sum taxes, and z denotes environmental quality, i. e. $\partial u(x; z)/\partial z = u_z > 0$, which is a public good. In order to simplify the analysis we follow a large part of the literature and assume weak separability in the utility function between environmental quality z and the vector of private commodities x, hence $\partial x/\partial z = 0$. It is also assumed that environmental quality depends on the consumption of the commodity x_d, which is an element of the vector x, in the following way:

$$z = e(x_d(q, I - T)), \text{ with } e' < 0. \tag{2}$$

Therefore, equation (2) describes a consumption externality. Thus, the government can change the provision of z only via induced changes of dirty consumption x_d. This means that the government has to change taxation in order to change environmental quality z. The revenue constraint of the government is:

$$R = T + \sum_{i=1}^{n} t_i x_i(q, I - T), \tag{3}$$

where R denotes government revenue and t_i commodity tax i. Note that x_0 is untaxed. Consider a change in the tax rate t_k. Assuming a linear transformation curve, i.e. constant producer price vector p, differentiating (1), while leaving the utility level constant, one can express the marginal costs of raising t_k in terms of income I in the following way:

$$\frac{dI}{dt_k} = x_k(q, I - T) - \frac{u_z(x, z)}{\lambda} e' \frac{\partial x_d(q, I - T)}{\partial t_k}, \tag{4}$$

where use of Roy´s identity $x_k = -W_{q_k}/W_I$ has been made and $\lambda = W_I$ is the marginal household utility of income. (4) gives the marginal compensating variation in lump-sum income I that is necessary to fully compensate the household for raising t_k. Differentiating (3) one gets:

$$R_k = \frac{dR}{dt_k} = x_k(q, I-T) + \sum_{i=1}^{n} t_i \frac{\partial x_i(q, I-T)}{\partial t_k}.$$

We get the marginal social cost of public funds of t_k as defined in Schöb (1995) by dividing (4) through the marginal government revenue R_k:

$$\frac{dI/dt_k}{R_k} = MSCF_k = MCF_k - MEI_k = \frac{x_k}{R_k} - \frac{1}{R_k}\frac{u_z}{\lambda}e'\frac{\partial x_d}{\partial t_k},$$

where MCF_k denotes the private marginal cost of public funds of t_k as defined commonly in modern public finance, e. g. Mayshar (1990), and MEI_k denotes the marginal environmental impact of t_k. $MSCF_k$ measures the welfare costs of a tax increase per unit of additional government revenue raised by the marginal increase in t_k. Expressing the welfare costs per unit of additional government revenue allows the comparison of welfare costs of different tax rates. If $MSCF_k$ is negative, raising t_k yields a welfare gain, since lump sum income could be taken away from the household without changing its pretax utility level.

The measure MCF_k gives the welfare costs that result from a change in consumption of commodity k. MCF_k denotes therefore the marginal private welfare costs of t_k.

The measure MEI_k gives the marginal welfare costs that are associated with a change in environmental quality. MEI_k denotes therefore environmental benefits, note that this benefit is negative if $\partial x_d/\partial t_k > 0$, i.e. commodity k and d are gross substitutes. MEI_k has to be subtracted from MCF_k since a positive environmental benefit reduces the marginal welfare costs of raising t_k. This definition of $MSCF$ allows us to separate the environmental benefits and the private benefits of a tax reform. Closely related to $MSCF$ is the marginal social excess burden $MSEB$. The $MSEB$ wants to compensate the household only over the additional revenue that the government raises by a tax change. Differentiating (1) while leaving the utility level constant gives:

$$MSEB_k = x_k - R_k - \frac{u_z}{\lambda}e'\frac{\partial x_d}{\partial t_k}. \tag{5}$$

Note that $MSEB_k = (MSCF_k - 1)R_k$. With this framework one can analyze the welfare costs of environmental tax reforms.

3. ENVIRONMENTAL TAX REFORM AND THE DOUBLE DIVIDEND

In this section environmental tax reforms are considered in which the government raises an environmental tax t_d on the externality creating dirty consumption good x_d and in exchange adjusts another tax t_c, such that the tax revenue R remains constant. Throughout the analysis it is assumed that the marginal revenue of a tax is always positive, which is the normal case. The marginal social excess burden that results when in exchange for raising an environmental tax t_d a distortionary tax t_c is reduced, is derived from totally differentiating (1), with $dT=0$:

$$W_{q_d} dt_d + W_{q_c} dt_c + W_I dI + W_z dz = 0. \tag{6}$$

Note that revenue neutrality means $R_d dt_d + R_c dt_c = 0$. Under consideration of (2), equation (6) can be rearranged to give:

$$\frac{dI}{dt_d} = x_d - x_c \frac{R_d}{R_c} - \frac{u_z}{\lambda} e' \left(\frac{\partial x_d}{\partial t_d} - \frac{\partial x_d}{\partial t_c} \frac{R_d}{R_c} \right). \tag{7}$$

This expression can be rewritten as:

$$\frac{dI}{dt_d} = R_d \left[\left(MEI_c - MEI_d \right) + \left(MCF_d - MCF_c \right) \right]. \tag{8}$$

Equation (8) says that the described environmental tax reform will yield a welfare gain if the expression on the right hand side is negative, or in other words:

$$MSCF_d < MSCF_c.$$

In the literature it is usually stated that there is uncertainty about the environmental benefits. An environmental tax reform yields environmental benefits as long as:

$$MEI_c < MEI_d,$$

which is equivalent to:

$$\frac{1}{R_c}\frac{\partial x_d}{\partial t_c} > \frac{1}{R_d}\frac{\partial x_d}{\partial t_d}. \tag{9}$$

From (9) it can be seen that environmental benefits are always be positive, if $\partial x_d/\partial t_c > 0$. As pointed out by Schöb (1995), a sufficient condition for achieving environmental benefits is that an environmental tax reform reduces only taxes on commodities that are gross substitutes for the dirty commodity. This means that as long as the commodities c and d are gross substitutes an environmental tax reform will yield an environmental benefit.

Under the assumption that an environmental tax reform reduces taxes on commodities that are gross substitutes for the dirty consumption good, the environmental benefits are guaranteed to be positive. There is uncertainty about the magnitude of the environmental benefit, such that it is not known if the environmental benefits outweigh possible decreases in non-environmental welfare. The uncertainty stems from the term:

$$MEI_k = \frac{1}{R_k}\frac{u_z}{\lambda}e'\frac{\partial x_d}{\partial t_k}.$$

Since there is no market for environmental quality, u_z/λ cannot be observed. Also e' is not known in a lot of cases due to informational lacks. All that is known with certainty of the expressions u_z/λ and e' are the signs.

Under the assumption that environmental tax reforms reduce taxes on commodities that are gross substitutes for the dirty consumption good a necessary and sufficient condition for a double dividend is:

$$MCF_d < MCF_c. \tag{10}$$

That is, the specified environmental tax reform will yield a double dividend if the marginal cost of public funds are higher for the tax rate that is about to be reduced. Substituting the demand functions into (10) gives after some manipulations:

$$MCF_d - MCD_c = x_d x_c\left(\sum_{i=1}^{n}\frac{t_i}{q_i}\varepsilon_{ci} - \sum_{i=1}^{n}\frac{t_i}{q_i}\varepsilon_{di}\right), \tag{11}$$

where use of the symmetry of the Slutzky matrix has been made. ε_{ji} denotes the compensated demand elasticity of commodity j with respect to commodity price i. If expression (11) is negative and commodity c is a gross substitute for the dirty commodity d then an environmental tax reform that raises the environmental tax t_d and reduces the tax t_c will yield a double dividend. For a value added tax with $t_i = p_i\tau_i$ and $q_i = (1+\tau_i)p_i$ expression (11) gives the following condition for a double dividend under the assumption that commodity c is a gross substitute for commodity d:

$$MCF_d - MCD_c = \sum_{i=1}^{n} \frac{\tau_i}{1+\tau_i}(\varepsilon_{ci} - \varepsilon_{di}) < 0. \tag{12}$$

Expression (12) shows that the double dividend depends on initial tax rates and on compensated demand elasticities. In order to yield a double dividend the government has to reduce taxes on commodities c that are relatively more difficult to substitute through other taxed commodities. Commodity d should be easier to substitute through other taxed commodities relative to c. Since $\sum_{i=1}^{n} \varepsilon_{ci} = -\varepsilon_{c0}$ one can interpret (12) that the commodity whose tax is reduced should in average, where the weights are $\tau_i/(1+\tau_i)$, be a better Hicksian substitute for the numeraire relative to the dirty commodity.

4. AN IMPORTANT SPECIAL CASE: THE BOVENBERG, DE MOOIJ MODEL

An important special case of the result obtained above is described in the contributions of Bovenberg, De Mooij (1994), Bovenberg, van der Ploeg (1994).[4] To these two contributions we refer to as the Bovenberg, De Mooij model.

The Bovenberg, De Mooij model assumes the existence of only three goods, a clean consumption good, x_c, a dirty consumption good, x_d, that creates a negative externality and leisure, x_l, where the maximum value of leisure is assumed to be unity. In addition to these assumptions Bovenberg, De Mooij assume the following special utility function:

$$u(x_c; x_d; x_l; z) = u\big(M\big(x_l; H(x_c; x_d)\big); z\big). \tag{13}$$

As before, environmental quality z is weakly separable from the private commodities. In addition, the consumption goods x_c and x_d are weakly

---

4   In this section a simplified version of these models is presented that nevertheless captures the main features of the mentioned models.

separable from leisure x_l. The subutility functions M and H are homothetic. The indirect utility function of the representative household is:

$$
V^i(q_c; q_d; q_l; C; z) =
$$
$$
\max_x \left\{ u(x_c; x_d; x_l; z) : C + q_l \geq q_c x_c + q_d x_d + q_l x_l \right\}. \tag{14}
$$

As before the consumer prices are the sum of the producer price and the tax, i.e. $q_j = p_j + t_j$, where $j = c; d$, for the consumer good prices and for the wage $q_l = p_l + t_l$. It is assumed that $p_i = 1$, with $i = c, d, l$. Under this assumption follows $t_i = \tau_i$, $i = c, d, l$. The tax revenue of the government is:

$$
R = \sum_{j=c;d} \tau_j x_j(q_c; q_d; q_l; C) + \tau_l \left(1 - x_l(q_c; q_d; q_l; C)\right). \tag{15}
$$

Due to the choice of p_i, $i = c, d, l$, we can choose a commodity as a numeraire, simply by setting its respective tax rate equal to zero. For the choice of the numeraire we consider two cases. The first case follows the Bovenberg, De Mooij model and chooses the clean consumption good as the numeraire, i. e. $\tau_c = 0$. In a second case we consider $\tau_l = 0$, that is we choose leisure as the numeraire. The easiest way to derive the effects on labor supply and on the consumption of the dirty good is to do a comparative static analysis. In order to do this we log-linearize the budget constraint of the household, and the government and the supply and demand functions of the household. The results are derived in the appendix and summarized in the next table:

Table 1:   Log-linearized Bovenberg, De Mooij model

Labor supply	$-\dfrac{x_l}{1-x_l}\tilde{x}_l = -\theta\left(\dfrac{\tau_l}{1-\tau_l}\tilde{\tau}_l + \dfrac{\tau_d}{1+\tau_d}s_d^H\tilde{\tau}_d \right.$ $\left. + \dfrac{\tau_c}{1+\tau_c}\left(1 - s_d^H\right)\tilde{\tau}_c\right)$
Demand for x_c	$\tilde{x}_c = \tilde{x}_d + \sigma_{cd}\left(\dfrac{\tau_d}{1+\tau_d}\tilde{\tau}_d - \dfrac{\tau_c}{1+\tau_c}\tilde{\tau}_c\right)$

Government budget constraint	$\tilde{G} = \left(\tilde{\tau}_c + \tilde{x}_c\right)s_c^G + \left(\tilde{\tau}_d + \tilde{x}_d\right)s_d^G$ $+ \left(\tilde{\tau}_l - \dfrac{x_l}{1-x_l}\tilde{x}_l\right)\left(1 - s_c^G - s_d^G\right)$
Household budget constraint	$-\dfrac{\tau_l}{1-\tau_l}\tilde{\tau}_l = \left(\tilde{x}_c + \dfrac{\tau_c}{1+\tau_c}\tilde{\tau}_c\right)\left(1 - s_d^H\right)$ $+ \left(\tilde{x}_d + \dfrac{\tau_d}{1+\tau_d}\tilde{\tau}_d\right)s_d^H + \tilde{x}_l\dfrac{x_l}{1-x_l}$

A tilde denotes a relative change, i. e. $\tilde{x} = dx/x$. The variable s_i^H with $i{=}c, d$ denote shares of household expenditure for the clean and the dirty consumption good. The variable and s_i^G with $i{=}c, d$ denotes the share of government revenue from the taxation of the clean and the dirty consumption good, respectively. The variable θ denotes the uncompensated elasticity of labor supply. The variable σ_{cd} denotes the elasticity of substitution between the consumption goods x_c and x_d.

In the two following sections the effects of the respective tax reforms on labor supply, on the consumption of the dirty good, and hence on environmental welfare and on private welfare are analyzed.

4.1. Environmental tax reform in the Bovenberg, De Mooij model

In this section the government increases the environmental tax τ_d and adjusts the tax on labor income τ_l, such that government revenue remains constant. This section reproduces the effects of this tax reform on labor supply, on the consumption of the dirty good, and hence on environmental welfare, and on private welfare. Substituting the demand for x_c equation into the government and household budget constraint one can derive from table 2 the following system of equations under the assumption that x_c is the numeraire:[5]

$$
\begin{pmatrix}
\dfrac{x_l}{1-x_l} & 0 & -\theta\dfrac{\tau_l}{1-\tau_l} \\[2ex]
\dfrac{x_l}{1-x_l} & 1 & \dfrac{\tau_l}{1-\tau_l} \\[2ex]
-\dfrac{x_l}{1-x_l}\left(1-s_d^G\right) & s_d^G & \left(1-s_d^G\right)
\end{pmatrix}
\begin{pmatrix}
\tilde{x}_l \\[2ex]
\tilde{x}_d \\[2ex]
\tilde{\tau}_l
\end{pmatrix}
$$

$$
=
\begin{pmatrix}
\theta\dfrac{\tau_d}{1+\tau_d}s_d^H\tilde{\tau}_d \\[2ex]
-\left[\left(1-s_d^H\right)\sigma_{cd}+s_d^H\right]\dfrac{\tau_d}{1+\tau_d}\tilde{\tau}_d \\[2ex]
-s_d^G\tilde{\tau}_d+\tilde{G}
\end{pmatrix}
$$

(16)

Under the assumption that a ceteris paribus increase of government expenditure requires an increase in the wage income tax τ_l, all other taxes constant, in order to maintain a balanced budget, i. e. $\tilde{\tau}_l/\hat{G}>0$, one can derive that the determinant of the matrix in (16) has to be positive:[6]

$$
Det=\frac{x_l}{1-x_l}\left(1-\theta\frac{\tau_l}{1-\tau_l}-\frac{s_d^G}{1-\tau_l}\right)>0.
$$

Therefore, it follows from Cramer's rule that:[7]

---

5   Note that this implies $\tau_c=s_c^G=0$.

6   The sign of the determinant is also determined in this way in Bovenberg, De Mooij (1994) and also in Scholz (1998).

7   It might be helpful for the reader to note that

$$\frac{\tilde{x}_l}{\tilde{\tau}_d} = \frac{1}{Det}\theta\sigma_{cd}\frac{\tau_l}{1-\tau_l}\frac{\tau_d}{1+\tau_d}\left(1-s_d^H\right)s_d^G,\tag{17}$$

$$\frac{\tilde{x}_d}{\tilde{\tau}_d} = -\frac{1}{Det}\frac{x_l}{1-x_l}\left(1-\theta\frac{\tau_l}{1-\tau_l}\right)\frac{\tau_d}{1+\tau_d}\left(1-s_d^G\right)\left(1-s_d^H\right)\sigma_{cd}.\tag{18}$$

Hence, for a positive elasticity of labor supply, i.e. $\theta > 0$, the households choose more leisure and as a consequence employment decreases after the environmental tax reform, specified above. If the determinant is positive, it can be seen from (18) that the demand for dirty consumption will decrease as a consequence of the environmental tax reform. Therefore, the environmental tax reform will lead to an increase in environmental welfare, but a decrease in employment. Hence, there is no double dividend in the Bovenberg, De Mooij model. This result is valid as long as the initial tax rates and the uncompensated elasticity of labor supply are positive.

To check whether there exists also a private dividend according to expression (12) the compensated elasticities are needed. These are taken from the table in the appendix and inserted in the terms of expression (12). In order to reduce the distortion of the tax system, the following condition needs to be fulfilled:[8]

$$MCF_d - MCD_l = \frac{\tau_d}{1+\tau_d}\sigma_{cd}s_c^H < 0\tag{19}$$

The inequality of (19) is only fulfilled in this tax reform if $\tau_d < 0$. Therefore, there is no private dividend. The price of the dirty consumption good and the price of leisure increases through the tax changes. In order to yield a double dividend, labor has to be the better Hicksian substitute for the clean good, compared to the dirty good. With the specified utility function from above, the dirty consumption good is the better Hicksian substitute for the clean

---

$$\frac{\tau_d}{1+\tau_d}\left(1-s_d^G\right)s_d^H - \frac{\tau_l}{1-\tau_l}s_d^G = \frac{\tau_l}{1-\tau_l}s_d^G - \frac{\tau_l}{1-\tau_l}s_d^G = 0.$$

[8]   In deriving inequality (19) it is important to remember that an increase in τ_l functions like a subsidy for leisure. Therefore (12) changes slightly in the context of labor taxation to

$$MCF_d - MCD_l = \frac{\tau_l}{1-\tau_l}\left(\frac{x_l}{(1-x_l)}\varepsilon_{ll}^c + \varepsilon_{dl}^c\right) + \frac{\tau_d}{1+\tau_d}\left(-\frac{x_l}{(1-x_l)}\varepsilon_{ld}^c\right.$$
$$\left. -\varepsilon_{dd}^c\right) < 0$$

consumption good. Hence, in the Bovenberg, De Mooij model a double dividend, neither in the sense of less distortion nor in the sense of more employment, can be achieved, if in exchange for raising the environmental tax, the labor tax is reduced.

The reason for the failure of the double dividend hypothesis in this model is that the government is unable to reduce the labor tax sufficiently, if it has to maintain an unchanged revenue. This is because raising the environmental tax will cause substitution away from the dirty consumption good to the untaxed clean consumption good. Thus the decrease in demand for dirty consumption will not only improve environmental quality, but also erode the tax base of the government. This effect, that Bovenberg, De Mooij (1994) call the tax base erosion effect, is responsible for the inability of the government to reduce the labor tax sufficiently.

Another interpretation of this result that follows the optimal taxation literature is offered by Schöb (1997). As was shown above, an environmental tax reform yields a private dividend when the tax system approaches the optimal tax system that neglects the environmental externality. As is known from Sandmo (1975), however, assuming the above form of utility function implies that the dirty and the clean consumption good should be taxed at equal rates. But the tax reform considered in the Bovenberg, De Mooij model raises the dirt tax and leaves the tax rate of the clean consumption good unchanged. Therefore, it deviates further from the optimal tax system that neglects the externality. This must decrease private welfare and at the same time it also decreases labor supply, because the real wage of the households decreases.

4.2. An alternative environmental tax reform in the Bovenberg, De Mooij model

The reason for the failure of the double dividend hypothesis in the Bovenberg, De Mooij model, is the assumption that dirty and clean consumption are closer Hicksian substitutes than labor and clean consumption. To strengthen this point, let us consider a simple modification of the environmental tax reform in the Bovenberg, De Mooij model. Instead of reducing the tax on labor income the tax on the clean consumption good is reduced, while labor becomes the untaxed commodity. After substituting the government budget constraint into the household budget constraint one can derive the equilibrium condition for the commodity market. After substituting the demand equation for the clean consumption good into this equation and into the government budget constraint one can derive from table 2 the following system of equations under the assumption that x_l is the numeraire:

$$
\begin{pmatrix}
\dfrac{x_l}{1-x_l} & 0 & -\theta\tau_c\dfrac{x_c}{1-x_l} \\[2ex]
-\dfrac{x_l}{1-x_l} & -\left(\dfrac{x_d}{1-x_l}+\dfrac{x_c}{1-x_l}\right) & \dfrac{x_c}{1-x_l}\dfrac{\tau_c}{1+\tau_c}\sigma_{cd} \\[2ex]
0 & 1 & \left(1-\sigma_{cd}\dfrac{\tau_c}{1+\tau_c}\right)s_c^G
\end{pmatrix}
\begin{pmatrix}
\tilde{x}_l \\[1ex]
\tilde{x}_d \\[1ex]
\tilde{\tau}_c
\end{pmatrix}
$$

$$
=
\begin{pmatrix}
\theta\tau_d\dfrac{x_d}{1-x_l}\tilde{\tau}_d \\[2ex]
\dfrac{x_c}{(1-x_l)}\sigma_{cd}\dfrac{\tau_d}{1+\tau_d}\tilde{\tau}_d+\dfrac{G}{(1-x_l)}\tilde{G} \\[2ex]
-\left(s_d^G+\sigma_{cd}\dfrac{\tau_d}{1+\tau_d}s_c^G\right)\tilde{\tau}_d+\tilde{G}
\end{pmatrix}
$$

(20)

The determinant, which under the assumption of $\tilde{\tau}_c/\tilde{G}>0$ has to be negative, is:

$$
Det=\frac{x_l}{1-x_l}\frac{x_c}{1-x_l}\left[\frac{\tau_c-\tau_d}{G}x_d\left(\frac{\tau_c}{1+\tau_c}\sigma_{cd}-1\right)-(1-\theta\tau_c)\right]<0. \quad (21)
$$

One can derive:

$$
\frac{\tilde{x}_l}{\tilde{\tau}_d}=\frac{1}{Det}\theta\sigma_{cd}\frac{x_d}{1-x_l}\frac{x_c}{G}\frac{\tau_c}{1+\tau_c}\frac{\tau_d}{1+\tau_d}(\tau_c-\tau_d), \quad (22)
$$

$$
\frac{\tilde{x}_d}{\tilde{\tau}_d}=\frac{1}{Det}\frac{x_l}{1-x_l}\frac{\tau_d}{1+\tau_d}\frac{\tau_c}{1+\tau_c}\sigma_{cd}\frac{x_c}{G}[1-\theta\tau_c]. \quad (23)
$$

Leisure demand decreases, and thus, labor supply increases if $\tau_d<\tau_c$. The demand for the dirty consumption good always decreases if $1>\theta\tau_c$. For $\tau_d<\tau_c$, a sufficiently large σ_{cd}, and positive marginal tax revenues this is always the case. Therefore, there exists a double dividend in the form of more employment if initially the tax on the dirty consumption good is below the tax on the clean consumption good and the mentioned asumptions are met. However, for a small σ_{cd} and a large θ it is possible that there is more employment, but also more demand for the dirty consumption good.[9] For $\tau_d < \tau_c$, a small σ_{cd} and a large θ the positive income effect is so large that the substitution effect that reduces the demand for x_d is overcompensated through the labor income increase. Then the demand for both consumption commodities increases. This would, however, mean that condition (9) is violated. Especially, with positive marginal tax revenues it means that either the demand curve for the dirty consumption good has a positive slope or that the dirty consumption good is not a gross substitute, but a gross complement for the clean consumption good.

A non-environmental dividend is reached if inequality (12) is fulfilled. Substituting the relevant compensated demand elasticities into (12) yields:

$$MCF_d - MCD_c = \frac{1}{1+\tau_c}\frac{1}{1+\tau_d}\sigma_{cd}(\tau_d - \tau_c) < 0 \qquad (24)$$

The conditions for an employment increase and a reduction of the distortion of the tax system are the same, i.e. $\tau_d < \tau_c$.

This result emphasizes two aspects: First, the welfare costs of an environmental tax reform can be influenced substantially by the initial tax rates, as Bovenberg, De Mooij (1994) have noticed. Second, compared to the original Bovenberg, De Mooij analysis the modified analysis shows that the employment effects and the welfare costs of an environmental tax reform can be influenced by the choice of tax rates to be reduced.

If the tax system is initially efficient from a non-environmental point of view, i. e. $\tau_d = \tau_c$, the non-environmental welfare costs of the environmental tax reform are zero. This result shows that non-environmental welfare costs depend largely on how far the initial tax system is away from non-environmental efficiency.

5.   CONCLUSIONS

The above analysis underlines that an environmental tax reform yields a double dividend if the tax on a commodity is reduced that is a better substitute for the numeraire than the dirty good and the numeraire. In this case the tax base erosion effect can be limited such that the government is able to sufficiently reduce the tax on the other good, so a double dividend is possible. In this case there will be still substitution away from the dirty good. But at the same time there will be substitution from the dirty good to the good whose tax is reduced. This limits and possibly erases the tax base erosion effect. Definitely, one cannot say that „environmental taxes *typically* exacerbate,

---

[9]   This point is emphasized by Weinbrenner (1997).

rather than alleviate, preexisting tax distortions" when revenues are used to cut preexisting distortionary taxes. It all depends on which tax rates are cut and on the initial tax system. The above analysis shows that there will be a double dividend if the tax system approaches to the tax system that is efficient from a non-environmental point of view and the commodities with reduced taxes are gross substitutes to the dirty goods.

In general there will be a double dividend if the following conditions are met. First, the initial tax system has to be inefficient also from a non-environmental point of view.[10] Second, it is possible to raise the tax on the externality creating commodity and in exchange to reduce the tax on a commodity that is a gross substitute for the externality creating commodity. Third, under the existing distortionary tax system the commodity whose tax is reduced is relatively difficult to substitute through other taxed commodities and hence easier to substitute through the untaxed numeraire. If the last two conditions are met, the tax base erosion effect that results from raising the tax on the externality creating commodity will be eliminated such that the government is able to sufficiently reduce another distorting tax.

REFERENCES

Bovenberg, A.L. and R.A. De Mooij (1994), Environmental Levies and Distortionary Taxation, *American Economic Review (Papers and Proceedings)*, 94: 1085-1089.

Bovenberg, A.L. and R.A. De Mooij (1995), Environmental Taxation and the Double-Dividend: The Role of Factor Substitution and Capital Mobility, Discussionpaper prepared for the SFB-Workshop 1995: Environmental Policy in Open Economies, June 5-7, 1995, in Konstanz .

Bovenberg, A.L. and F. van der Ploeg (1994), Environmental Policy, Public Finance and the Labour Market in a Second-Best World, *Journal of Public Economics*, 55: 349-390.

Fullerton, D. (1997), Environmental Levies and Distortionary Taxation: Comment, *American Economic Review*, 87: 245-250.

Goulder, L.H. (1995), Environmental Taxation and the Double Dividend: A Reader's Guide, *International Tax and Public Finance*, 2: 157-184.

Hicks, J.R. (1943), The Four Consumers' Surpluses, *Review of Economic Studies*, 11: 31-41.

Mayshar, J. (1990), On Measures of Excess Burden and their Application, *Journal of Public Economics*, 43: 263-289.

Pearce, D. (1991), The Role of Carbon Taxes in Adjusting to Global Warming, *Economic Journal*, 101: 938-948.

---

10   A similar result is found in Bovenberg, De Mooij (1995).

Sandmo, A. (1975), Optimal Taxation in the Presence of Externalities, *Swedish Journal of Economics*, 77: 86-98.

Schöb, R. (1995), Ökologische Steuersysteme. Umweltökonomie und optimale Besteuerung, Campus Verlag, Frankfurt a. M.

Schöb, R. (1997), Environmental Taxes and Pre-Existing Distortions: The Normalization Trap, *International Tax and Public Finance*, 4: 167-176.

Scholz, C.M. (1996), A Note on the Double Dividend Hypothesis, Kiel Working Paper, The Kiel Institute of World Economics.

Scholz, C.M. (1998), Involuntary Unemployment and Environmental Policy: The Double Dividend Hypothesis: A Comment, *Scandinavian Journal of Economics*, forthcoming.

Weinbrenner, D. (1997), A Comment on the Impact of the Initial Tax Mix on the Dividends of an Environmental Tax Reform, Volkswirtschaftliche Diskussionsbeiträge, University of Siegen.

APPENDIX

The following table can be found in Bovenberg, van der Ploeg (1994). The derivation of the compensated elasticities can be found in Scholz (1996).

Table 2: Compensated demand elasticities for the Bovenberg De Mooij model.

ε_{ij}^{c}	q_c	q_d	q_l
x_c	$-s_d^H(\sigma_{cd}-\sigma_{Hl}x_l)-\sigma_{Hl}x_l$	$s_d^H(\sigma_{cd}-\sigma_{Hl}x_l)$	$\sigma_{Hl}x_l$
x_d	$s_c^H(\sigma_{cd}-\sigma_{Hl}x_l)$	$s_d^H(\sigma_{cd}-\sigma_{Hl}x_l)-\sigma_{cd}$	$\sigma_{Hl}x_l$
x_l	$\sigma_{Hl}(1-x_l)s_c^H$	$\sigma_{Hl}(1-x_l)s_d^H$	$-\sigma_{Hl}(1-x_l)$

3. Selling the Greenpeace Car. On Competition Between Firms and Non-profit Organisations

Peter Michaelis

---

1. INTRODUCTION

Recently, GREENPEACE has announced plans to market a „green" car which consumes less fuel and causes less ecological damage compared to conventional cars. From an economic point of view, the introduction of a „green" car constitutes a problem of horizontal product differentiation because the ecological characteristics of cars are usually negatively correlated with other desirable features like, e.g., cubic capacity and maximum speed. The standard approach for analysing this class of problems is based on Hotellings (1929) famous paper „Stability in competition" where two firms compete on a market for a distinct product differentiated by a single characteristic. The problem is modelled as a non-cooperative two stage game. In the second stage firms play a game in prices given the choices of product varieties made in the first stage. In the first stage firms chose product varieties expecting to receive the Nash equilibrium profits of the price game played in the second stage.[1] Assuming a uniform distribution of preferences in the product space and linear disutility caused by differences between available product varieties and individual preferences, Hotelling (1929) derives the so-called *Principle of Minimum Differentiation* which claims that in equilibrium both firms will supply (nearly) identical varieties.

---

[1] This structure of the game is natural since firms may decide on price in the short run and on variety in the long run.

However, D'Aspremont et al. (1979) show that the price subgame in Hotelling's model fails to have a (pure strategy) equilibrium if the product varieties are relatively close together. Since this flaw in Hotelling's argumentation
was detected several variations of his model have arisen that attempt to over-
come the non-existence of a subgame perfect equilibrium. For example,
D'Aspremont et al. (1979) show that an equilibrium always exists if one assumes quadratic disutility, Economides (1984) shows that the region of existence of equilibrium is enlarged if a finite reservation price is imposed, and
Wauthy (1996) shows that introducing capacity constraints may restore the
existence of equilibrium.

All of the above contributions assume that both suppliers aim at maximising
profits. In contrast to this, GREENPEACE can be understood as a non-profit
organisation (NPO) which aims at minimising ecological impacts.[2] Hence, the
recent plans of GREENPEACE to market a „green" car give rise to the following questions: Under which conditions exists an equilibrium in Hotelling's
duopoly if one assumes that one of the players is a NPO ? And, whenever it
exists, what are its properties of the equilibrium, or, with other words, how
green will the „green" car be and how much will it cost ?

The remainder of the paper is organised as follows: Section 2 introduces
the modified version of the Hotelling's (1929) original model, Sections 3 and
4 analyse the equilibrium in the price game and the variety game, respectively, Section 5 presents some comparative statics and Section 6 summarises
the main results.

2.   THE MODEL

Assume there are only two suppliers of cars. Supplier $i=1$ is a profit maximising firm, whereas supplier $i=2$ is a NPO which aims at minimising ecological impacts. Let p_i denote the price and $\alpha_i \in [0,1]$ denote the degree of
environmental friendliness of the respective car $(\alpha_2 > \alpha_1)$. Per unit cost of
production are given by a twice differentiable cost function $c_i(\alpha_i)$ with
$\partial c_i / \partial \alpha_i > 0$ and $\partial^2 c_i / \partial \alpha_i^2 > 0$. Choices are made in stages. In the first
stage, both suppliers decide on the product variety α_i; in the second stage,
given the choices of product qualities each supplier decides on the price p_i.

There are n consumers each of them buys exactly one car for which she has
to pay the price p_i plus a sales tax τ_i that is differentiated according to the
environmental characteristics of the chosen car: $\tau_i = \tau(1-\alpha_i)$. Preferences are
symmetric and single peaked, the consumers are uniformly distributed on the

---

2   On the economics of non-profit organisations see, e.g., Holtmann (1988) and
         West (1989).

product space [0,1]. In order to decide from which supplier to buy each consumer j compares the price (including sales tax) with the disutility caused by the difference between α_i and her most preferred variety α^j. Consumer j buys the car that minimises the sum of $p_i + \tau(1-\alpha_i)$ and disutility $|\alpha^j - \alpha_i|$ weighted by an uniform coefficient $\delta > 0$. If $k \in [1,n]$ is the consumer at the margin for whom $\delta|\alpha^k - \alpha_1| + p_1 + \tau(1-\alpha_1) = \delta|\alpha^k - \alpha_2| + p_2 + \tau(1-\alpha_2)$ and if $\alpha_2 \geq \alpha^k \geq \alpha_1$, then each consumer to the left of k buys from supplier 1, whereas each consumer to the right of k buys from supplier 2. Hence, the market share of supplier 1, $x_1(\cdot)$, is given by:

$$x_1(\alpha_1,\alpha_2,p_1,p_2) = \frac{1}{2\delta}\left[\delta(\alpha_1+\alpha_2)+p_2-p_1-\tau(\alpha_2-\alpha_1)\right]. \qquad (1)$$

One important qualification, however, should be emphasised. As noted above, equation (1) is only valid if α^k is located within the range $[\alpha_1, \alpha_2]$. For $\alpha^k < \alpha_1$ the non-profit organisation would take over the whole market, whereas for $\alpha^k > \alpha_2$ the profit maximising firm would become the only supplier. The following analysis concentrates on an interior equilibrium with both firms producing at positive levels. A condition for the existence of such an interior solution is derived below.

3.   EQUILIBRIUM IN THE PRICE GAME

In the second stage of the game the environmental characteristics α_i are already fixed and the suppliers have to choose a price p_i. Concerning the non-profit organisation it is natural to assume that it has to balance its budget, i.e. $p_2^*(\alpha_1,\alpha_2) = c_2(\alpha_2)$. For an interior solution with the private firm's profit function is given by:

$$\pi_1(p_1|p_2,\alpha_1,\alpha_2) = \frac{n}{2\delta}\left[\delta(\alpha_1+\alpha_2)+p_2-p_1-\tau(\alpha_2-\alpha_1)\right]\left[p_1-c_1(\alpha_1)\right]. \quad (2)$$

Differentiating $\pi_1(\cdot)$ with respect to p_1 and inserting $p_2^* = c_2(\alpha_2)$ yields the profit maximising price $p_1^*(\alpha_1,\alpha_2)$ as well as the corresponding market share $x_1^*(\alpha_1,\alpha_2)$ which can be derived from (1):

$$p_1^*(\alpha_1,\alpha_2) = \frac{1}{2}\left[\delta(\alpha_1+\alpha_2)+c_2(\alpha_2)+c_1(\alpha_1)-\tau(\alpha_2-\alpha_1)\right], \qquad (3)$$

$$x_1^*(\alpha_1,\alpha_2) = \frac{1}{4\delta}\left[\delta(\alpha_1+\alpha_2)+c_2(\alpha_2)-c_1(\alpha_1)-\tau(\alpha_2-\alpha_1)\right]. \qquad (4)$$

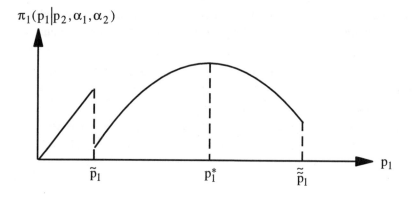

Figure 1:   *Shape of the private firm's profit function in the price game*

Equations (3) and (4), however, apply only to an *interior* equilibrium with both firms producing at positive levels. Alternatively to the pricing policy described by (3), the private firm has also the option to take over the whole market by reducing p_1 marginally below $\tilde{p}_1 := p_2 - (\delta + \tau)(\alpha_2 - \alpha_1)$ such that $\alpha^k > \alpha_2$. Hence, $\pi_1(\cdot)$ exhibits a discontinuity at $p_1 = \tilde{p}_1$ and there exist two local maxima. In order to guarantee an *interior* equilibrium, the model has to satisfy the condition $\pi_1(p_1^*) \geq \pi_1(\tilde{p}_1)$ such that p_1^* is the global maximum as assumed in Fig. 1.[3] From equations (1) to (4), the two local maxima of $\pi_1(\cdot)$ can be calculated as

$$\pi_1(p_1^*) = \left[n/8\delta \right]\left[\delta(\alpha_1 + \alpha_2) + c_2(\alpha_2) - c_1(\alpha_1) - \tau(\alpha_2 - \alpha_1) \right]^2, \tag{5}$$

$$\pi_1(\tilde{p}_1) = n\left[c_2(\alpha_1) - c_1(\alpha_1) - (\delta + \tau)(\alpha_2 - \alpha_1) \right]. \tag{6}$$

Combining together yields the condition for an internal equilibrium in the price game:

$$\left[\delta(\alpha_1 + \alpha_2) + c_2(\alpha_2) - c_1(\alpha_1) - \tau(\alpha_2 - \alpha_1) \right]^2 \geq$$
$$8\delta\left[c_2(\alpha_2) - c_1(\alpha_1) - (\delta + \tau)(\alpha_2 - \alpha_1) \right]. \tag{7}$$

If α_1 and α_2 are sufficiently close together condition (7) is satisfied since the RHS converges to zero whereas the LHS is still positive. If α_1 and α_2 are

---

3   Note that a second discontinuity exists at $p_1 = p_2 + (\delta + \tau)(\alpha_2 - \alpha_1)$ where the market share of the private firm is about to drop to zero (see Figure 1).

relatively far apart the existence of an internal equilibrium in the price game depends on the cost function $c_i[\alpha_i]$ as well as on the magnitude of δ and τ. In general, the existence of an internal equilibrium is the more likely the lower are the production cost compared to δ and τ. Assuming quadratic cost $c_i[\alpha_i] = c\alpha_i^2$ with $c>0$, condition (7) is always satisfied if $c \leq (\delta+\tau)/2$ such that $\pi_1(\tilde{p}_1) \leq 0$. For larger magnitudes of c an internal equilibrium in the price game is only guaranteed if the product varieties chosen in the first stage of the game are located within a certain existence region described by condition (7). The main results of the present Section are summarised in the following Proposition:

> *Proposition 1.* Assume linear disutility and constant per unit produc-
> tion cost of $c_i[\alpha_i] = c\alpha_i^2$. An internal equilibrium in the price game
> exists if and only if product varieties are located in the existence
> region $R \equiv \{ \alpha_1,\alpha_2 \in [0,1] | [c(\alpha_2^2 - \alpha_1^2) + \delta(\alpha_1 + \alpha_2) - \tau(\alpha_2 - \alpha_1)]^2 \geq$
> $8\delta[c(\alpha_2^2 - \alpha_1^2) - (\delta + \tau)(\alpha_2 - \alpha_1)] \}$, and, whenever an equilibrium
> exists, it is uniquely determined by the prices $p_1^* = [\delta(\alpha_1 + \alpha_2) +$
> $c(\alpha_1^2 + \alpha_2^2) - \tau(\alpha_2 - \alpha_1)]/2$ and $p_2^* = c\alpha_2^2$.

4.   EQUILIBRIUM IN THE VARIETY GAME

In the first stage of the game both suppliers choose a product variety $\alpha_i \in [0,1]$. The private firm seeks at maximising profits given the optimal choice of p_1 in the second stage of the game. Assuming quadratic production cost the profit function for an interior equilibrium in the price game can be rewritten as $\pi_1(\alpha_1,\alpha_2) = [n/8\delta][\delta(\alpha_1 + \alpha_2) + c(\alpha_2^2 - \alpha_1^2) - \tau(\alpha_2 - \alpha_1)]^2$. Differentiating with respect to α_1 yields the private firm's optimal choice:

$$\alpha_1^* = (\delta+\tau)/2c. \tag{8}$$

As indicated by (8), the optimal choice of the private firm is independent of the product variety supplied by the NPO and an internal solution to the location game (i.e., $\alpha_1^* < 1$) is only possible if $c > (\delta+\tau)/2$.

The optimal choice of the NPO depends on the assumed utility function. If the NPO is only interested in minimising the ecological impacts of the supplied car, it will choose $\alpha_2^* = 1$. Inserting $\alpha_1^* = (\delta+\tau)/2c$ and $\alpha_2^* = 1$ into condition (7) yields $(\delta-\tau+2c)^4 \geq 32c\delta(\delta+\tau-2c)^2$. Hence, if the NPO solely aims at maximising α_2, a subgame perfect equilibrium exists if, and only if δ, c and τ satisfy the condition $(\delta-\tau+2c)^4 \geq 32c\delta(\delta+\tau-2c)^2$ and, whenever an equilibrium exists, it is uniquely determined by the product varieties $\alpha_1^* = (\delta+\tau)/2c$ and $\alpha_2^* = 1$ and by the corresponding equilibrium prices $p_1^* = [\delta(2\delta+\tau+2c)+(\delta+\tau)^2 +4c^2 - \tau(4c-\delta-\tau)]/8c$ and $p_2^* = c\alpha_2^{*\,2}$.

The above strategy of maximising α_2, however, might be unsuitable for the NPO since it does not account for the number of products sold. Hence, it might lead to a situation where the NPO sells a „super green" car for only a negligible number of buyers.

A more sophisticated strategy would therefore aim at maximising a utility function $u(\alpha_1,\alpha_2)$ which might be specified as a weighted average of product characteristic and market share, i.e. $u(\alpha_1,\alpha_2) = z \cdot \alpha_2 + (1-z) \cdot [1- x_1^*(\alpha_1,\alpha_2)]$ with $0<z<1$. By substituting $x_1^*(\alpha_1,\alpha_2)$ according to (4), this utility function can be rewritten as:

$$u(\alpha_1,\alpha_2)=z\alpha_2 +(1-z)\left[1-\frac{1}{4\delta}\Big[\delta(\alpha_1+\alpha_2)+c(\alpha_2^2-\alpha_1^2)-\tau(\alpha_2-\alpha_1)\Big]\right]. \quad (9)$$

Differentiating $u(\alpha_1,\alpha_2)$ with respect to α_1 yields the product variety chosen by the NPO:

$$\alpha_2^* = \frac{(5z-1)\delta+(1-z)\tau}{2c(1-z)}. \quad (10)$$

Equation (10) shows that the impact of z on the equilibrium outcome is ambiguous. The following analysis concentrates on the symmetrical case $z=0.5$, i.e., the NPO assigns equal weights to market share and product characteristic. For $z=0.5$ equation (10) reduces to $\alpha_2^* =(3\delta+\tau)/2c$. In this case, an internal equilibrium in the 'location' game (i.e., $\alpha_1^* < \alpha_2^* \leq 1$) requires $c \geq (3\delta+\tau)/2$. Moreover, subgame perfectness requires condition (7) to be satisfied such that the existence of a corresponding internal equilibrium in the price subgame is guaranteed. Inserting $\alpha_1^* = (\delta+\tau)/2c$ as well as $\alpha_2^* =(3\delta+\tau)/2c$ into (7) yields $[(4\delta^2+\delta\tau)/c]^2 \geq 8\delta^3/c \Rightarrow c \leq (4\delta+\tau)^2/8\delta$. Hence, an internal subgame perfect equilibrium exists if and only if the cost parameter falls into the interval $[(3\delta+\tau)/2, (4\delta+\tau)^2/8\delta]$. As can easily be verified, this interval is not empty if $\tau^2+(8\delta-4)\tau+4\delta^2 \geq 0$. Proposition 2 summarises the main results of the present Section:

Proposition 2: Assume linear disutility and constant per unit production cost of $c_i[\alpha_i] = c\alpha_i^2$. For the NPO's utility function $u(\alpha_1,\alpha_2) = 0.5\alpha_2 + 0.5\ [1 - x_1^*(\alpha_1,\alpha_2)]$, an internal subgame perfect equilibrium exists if, and only if $[(3\delta+\tau)/2] \leq c \leq [(4\delta+\tau)^2/8\delta]$, and, whenever it exists, it is uniquely determined by product varieties $\alpha_1^* = (\delta+\tau)/2c$ and $\alpha_2^* = (3\delta+\tau)/2c$ and by the corresponding pair of equilibrium prices $p_1^* = (9\delta^2 + 4\delta\tau + \tau^2)/4c$ and $p_2^* = (3\delta+\tau)^2/4c$.

5. COMPARATIVE STATICS

In this Section it is assumed than an interior subgame perfect equilibrium according to Proposition 2 exists and it is asked how the equilibrium changes if the government marginally increases the tax rate τ.

Due to $\alpha_1^* = (\delta+\tau)/2c$ and $\alpha_2^* = (3\delta+\tau)/2c$ the effect on the supplied product varieties is straight forward: With an increasing tax rate the private firm as well as the NPO will increase the absolute degree of environmental friendliness of the cars supplied to the market. This effect is the stronger the lower the cost parameter c is. A similar result holds concerning the equilibrium prices: An increase in τ leas to an increase in both p_1^* and p_2^*. However, the *ratio* between these two prices does not remain unchanged. Comparing p_1^* and p_2^* reveals that the „green" car will be more expensive than the conventional car, but the difference in prices is the smaller the higher the tax rate is.

Finally, by inserting α_1^* and α_2^* into equation (4) the market shares in equilibrium can be calculated as $x_1^* = (4\delta+\tau)/4c$ and $x_2^* = (4c - 4\delta - \tau)/4c$.

Hence, an increase in the tax rate τ leads to an increase in the *private firm's* market share and therefore also to an increase in its equilibrium profits.

6. SUMMARY

The present paper has investigated a special variation of Hotelling's duopoly with horizontal product differentiation where one of two the players is a non-profit organisation (NPO) which aims at minimising the ecological impacts of the product supplied. The ecological impacts in turn depend on the chosen product variety $\alpha_i \in [0,1]$. Preferences are symmetric and single peaked, the consumers are uniformly distributed on the product space, and the disutility of distance in the product space is assumed to be linear. Per unit cost of production are constant but their magnitude varies according to the chosen product variety. Moreover, the model assumes that the government introduces a differentiated sales tax which depends on the ecological impacts of the product under consideration.

The main results are as follows: For given product varieties α_i an equilibrium in prices p_i does only exist if the product varieties are located within a certain existence region. Moreover, if the NPO aims at maximising a specific utility function which is composed of its market share and the degree of environmental friendliness of the product supplied, a subgame perfect equilibrium in product varieties is guaranteed if and only if per unit production cost fall into a certain interval which depends on the tax rates as well as on the disutility of distance in the product space. Whenever such an equilibrium exists, it can be uniquely determined by product characteristics α_1^* and α_2^* and a corresponding pair of prices p_1^* and p_2^*. In equilibrium, the product supplied by the NPO will cause less ecological damage and will be more expensive than the product supplied by the profit maximising firm. Moreover, a marginal increase in tax rates will induce both suppliers to increase the price and to decrease the ecological damaged caused by the chosen product varieties.

REFERENCES

D'Aspremont, C., J. Jaskold Gabszewicz and J.F. Thisse (1979), On Hotelling's 'Stability in Competition', *Econometrica* 47:1145-1150.

Economides, N. (1984), The Principle of Minimum Differentiation Revisited, *European Economic Review* 24:345-368.

Holtmann, A. (1988), Theories of Non-Profit Institutions, *Journal of Economic Surveys* 2: 29-45.

Hotelling, H. (1929), Stability in Competition, *Economic Journal* 39:41-57.

Wauthy, X. (1996), Capacity Constraints may Restore the Existence of an Equilibrium in the Hotelling Model, *Journal of Economics* 64:315-324.

West, E. (1989): Nonprofit Organizations: Revised Theory and New Evidence, *Public Choice* 63:165-174.

4. Stock-dependent Uncertainty and Optimal Resource Exploitation

Frank Stähler and Peter Michaelis

1. INTRODUCTION[1]

The probability that an agent takes a certain action or a certain event occurs depends often on the actions taken by some agents. If this probability depends not only on current actions but on the sum of all past actions, these stock-dependent risks imply an intertemporal effect. In the present paper, we analyse this problem using an example concerning the exploitation of a non-renewable, exhaustible common-pool resource. The paper discusses resource extraction policies under endogenous closure risks which depend on the accumulated stock of extracted resources. The notion of closure risks means that a certain resource may be no longer available although its physical stock was not completely extracted. Closure risks mirror two different, important phenomena which have not yet been considered in the literature in the context of stock dependency.

First, closure risks may originate from threshold effects. If a resource stock falls short of a certain level, this resource may have lost its quality and may have become useless for production and consumption. Alternatively, resource extraction may add to the stock of an environmental bad, and when this stock reaches a certain level, resource extraction has to be phased out completely in order to avoid an environmental disaster. The accumulation of greenhouse gases which is due to the production and burning of fossil fuels is

---

1   We wish to thank Kai Konrad for useful comments on a predecessor of this paper. The usual disclaimer applies.

an example. When the threshold is not known, we face a typical stock-dependent risk.

Second, closure risks may be due to potential political actions. Suppose for example that a certain common-pool resource in a foreign country is exploited by several domestic resource producers. In addition to exhaustibility, this resource may have an intrinsic value for the foreign country, and foreign policy makers may prohibit exploitation when a certain stock level is reached. When the level which implies policy intervention is not known, we face a typical stock-dependent risk as well.

In order to put our paper into the context of the literature on exhaustible resources and uncertainty, it should be emphasised that closure risks as modelled below are driven by the accumulated stock of already extracted resources. Without this stock externality, managing resource extractions under uncertainty would resemble the well-known standard problem of resource exploitation under the risk of expropriation [see, e.g., Long (1975)] and our paper would add nothing new to the literature. Additionally, we do not assume that the physical stock size is uncertain [see Gilbert (1976), Loury (1976)]. Hence, uncertainty applies only on the future availability of the resource. Compared to the famous problem of *'eating a cake of unknown size'* [see, e.g., Kemp and Long (1980)], eating a piece of cake does not only imply a smaller cake in physical terms but also an increased risk that the cake will be stolen.

The paper is organised as follows. Section 2 introduces our model and determines the (myopic) laissez-faire level of resource extractions. Section 3 contrasts this solution with the optimal time path and discusses the properties of an optimal tax scheme on resource extractions. Section 4 closes the paper with a summary of the main results and a discussion of possible extensions and alternative applications of our model.

2.   THE MODEL

We assume that the economy needs a constant flow of materials W° for production. These materials may be provided by the resource under consideration and an alternative technology which does not employ resources (e.g. a recycling technology). Resource extraction involves *constant* extraction costs q. The total resource stock is given by W_0. We assume that the risks that the resource is closed depends on past extraction policies. The accumulated stock of extracted resources is denoted by S and the probability of closure is given by the continuous probability function $P(S)$ with

$$P(0) = 0, \quad P(\Omega_0) \le 1 \text{ and } dP(S)/dS = p(s) \ge 0, \tag{1}$$

where $p(S)$ is the corresponding density function. Equation (1) indicates that the closure probability, i.e. the probability that resources do not provide materials any longer, depends on the accumulated stock. It should be noted that (1) does not require that the closure probability equals unity if the resource limit W_0 is reached. Instead, (1) may allow resource producers to use W_0 completely if they are lucky. A specific probability function with $P(W_0) < 1$ is:

$$P(S) = 1 - e^{-\pi S} \quad \text{with} \quad p(S) = \pi e^{-\pi S}. \tag{2}$$

In Section 3, this specific function will be used for deriving some conclusions which we cannot arrive at for the general case.

Alternative provision of materials is possible through a technology which does not use resources. This technology is assumed to have increasing marginal costs. For the sake of simplicity, we assume a quadratic cost function

$$C = \frac{\gamma}{2} (W^\circ - \dot{S})^2 \quad \text{with} \quad \gamma > 0 \tag{3}$$

where $\dot{S}$, the first derivative of the stock S with respect to time, indicates resource extraction. We further assume that the number of resource producers is sufficiently large such that each individual producer does not take into account the risk-increasing effects as well as the resource depleting effects of his policy. The producers may even know that their production increases the closure risk and deplete the common-pool resource. But any *individual* denial on resource extractions merely generates strong positive externalities for the other producing firms. Thus, the *individual benefits* of reducing exploitation fell extremely short of the corresponding *individual costs*. Consequently, a sufficiently large number of unregulated individual producers neglects exhaustibility constraints and closure risks. Then, perfect competition makes resource producers charge q and resource users balance marginal costs of employing the alternative technology with the pure extraction costs q, $q < g \ W^\circ$. Consequently, resource extractions $\dot{S}(t)$ are constant over time until the resource is closed or is completely exploited:

$$\dot{S}_m(t) = W° - \frac{q}{\gamma} = const. \tag{4}$$

This solution, however, cannot be optimal not only because it neglects the exhaustibility constraint but also because it does not take into account the closure risks.

3. OPTIMISING RESOURCE EXTRACTION

In the following subsection 3.1 we derive the conditions for an optimal solution in the presence of stock-dependent closure risks. However, in the general case, interpreting these conditions turned out to be extremely difficult. In subsections 3.2 and 3.3 we therefore provide two additional solutions which relate a) to the well-understood case of no risks and b) to a simplified second-best policy which relies on evaluating an 'expected closure stock'. These two additional solutions are then used as point of reference for analysing the behaviour of the optimal time path.

3.1 The case of stock-dependent risks

We assume that the regulating authority is risk-neutral and minimises the expected costs of providing materials. Additionally, we assume that future costs and benefits are discounted by a constant non-zero discount rate r. Since the alternative technology does not stand at risk, we can adopt the dual problem of maximising the expected profits of resource exploitation. Thus, using the definition

$$F(\dot{S}, S, t) := e^{-rt} \left[1 - P(S(t)) \right] \left[\frac{\gamma}{2} W°^2 - \frac{\gamma}{2} (W° - \dot{S}(t))^2 - q\dot{S}(t) \right],$$

the socially optimal time path of resource extractions is given by the solution of the following maximisation problem:

$$\tag{5}$$

$$\max_{S(t),T^*} \int_0^{T^*} F(\dot{S}, S, t)dt \quad s.t.: S(0)=0, \ S(T^*)=\Omega_o, \ P(0)=0 \ and \ P(\Omega_o) \le 1$$

The corresponding Euler equation yields:[2]

$$\dot{S}(t) = W^\circ - \frac{q}{\gamma} + \frac{\ddot{S}(t)}{r} - \frac{p(S(t))}{2r[1 - P(S(t))]}\dot{S}(t)^2. \tag{6}$$

Unfortunately, equation (6) does not generally fulfil the second-order-conditions because the second derivative of the integrand with respect to the stock, i.e. $F_{SS} = - \text{e}^{-rt} \, dp/dS\{W^{\circ 2} - (\gamma/2)[W^\circ - q\dot{S}(t)] - q\dot{S}(t)\}$, is only negative if dp/dS is positive. A negative dp/dS, however, is a necessary condition which is not sufficient to guarantee the concavity condition of an always positive $F_{\dot{S}\dot{S}}F_{SS} - F_{\dot{S}S}^2$. This is no minor requirement because it rules out many well-known density functions which exhibit a descending branch in the relevant range of stocks between 0 and W_0 like, e.g., the normal distribution with a density function's maximum below W_0. However, the second derivative of the integrand with respect to resource extractions, i.e.

$F_{\dot{S}\dot{S}} = -e^{-rt}[1 - P(S(t))]\gamma$, is clearly non-positive and ensures that (6) meets

the Legendre condition for local concavity [see, e.g., Chiang (1992)]. Hence, (6) turns out to represent at least a locally optimal plan, and we assume that it is the only locally optimal plan and therefore the globally optimal plan as well. Moreover, we can prove that the myopic path does not represent a local optimum since any marginal restriction on resource extractions shows up to improve on the myopic outcome (the corresponding proof is available upon request). The remaining set of conceivable solutions, i.e. zero extractions and extractions which are W°, can be disregarded for obvious reasons. This line of reasoning holds also for the specific probability function (2) because of
$dp/dS = -\pi^2 e^{-\pi S} < 0.$

The differential equation (6) is not very convenient since the term which contains $p(S(t))$ prevents to solve it explicitly. This term signals that present resource extractions deteriorate the risks of future extraction options. A free T^* and a fixed closure stock induce the transversality condition that all expected opportunities should be exploited at time T^* which can be satisfied only by the condition $\dot{S}(T^*) = 0$. Hence, the optimal time path of resource extractions approaches zero when the resource will be completely exploited.

---

[2]   Compared to the Hamiltonian approach, the Euler equation turned out to be more suitable for the problem at hand.

3.2   The case of no risk

Now suppose alternatively that risks are absent and consider regulation policies which aims at exploiting the limited common-pool resource efficiently. This assumption lets the risk term in (6) vanish:

$$\dot{S}(t) = W^\circ - (q/\gamma) + (\ddot{S}(t)/r). \qquad (6')$$

Condition (6') represents a solvable second-order inhomogenous differential equation which has the following solution (note that $1 - e^{rt}$ is unambiguously negative):

$$S(t) = \left[1 - e^{rt}\right]\left[W^\circ - \frac{q}{\gamma}\right]\frac{e^{-rT}}{r} + \left[W^\circ - \frac{q}{\gamma}\right]t. \qquad (7)$$

Differentiating (7) with respect to t provides the time path of resource extractions, $\dot{S}(t)$, and its curvature:

$$\dot{S}(t) = \left[1 - e^{r(t-T)}\right]\left[W^\circ - (q/\gamma)\right] > 0, \qquad (8a)$$

$$\ddot{S}(t) = -re^{r(t-T)}\left[W^\circ - (q/\gamma)\right] < 0, \qquad (8b)$$

$$\dddot{S}(t) = -r^2 e^{r(t-T)}\left[W^\circ - (q/\gamma)\right] < 0. \qquad (8c)$$

Comparing the unregulated path (4) with (8a) reveals that the latter path implies lower extractions at every moment of time. Thus, (8a) takes into account the resource-depleting effect but assumes that closure risks are absent for every level of accumulated stocks. Moreover, as can be seen from (8b) and (8c), the first and second derivatives with respect to time are negative. The description of the no-risk path is completed by equalising $S(T)$ and Ω_0 according to (7).

3.3   The case of an expected closure stock

Now suppose that the regulating agency pursues a simplified second-best policy by evaluating an 'expected closure stock'. The line of reasoning goes as follows: The regulating agency knows that resource extractions add to the risks that the resource will be closed. Hence, it knows that resource producers are likely to face a stop of extraction policies before the resource is depleted in physical terms. The second-best policy determines the initially expected closure stock,

$$\hat{\Omega}(0) := \int_0^{\Omega_0} \left[1 - p(S)\right] S \, dS , \tag{9}$$

and introduces a policy which ensures that resource extractions are zero when the expected closure stock is reached. The second-best path is given by the solution of the maximisation problem:[3]

$$\tag{10}$$

$$\max_{S(t),\hat{T}} \int_0^{\hat{T}} e^{-rt} \left[\frac{\gamma}{2} W^{o^2} - \frac{\gamma}{2} \left(W^o - S(t)\right)^2 - q\dot{S}(t) \right] dt \quad \text{s.t. } S(0)=0, \ S(\hat{T})=\hat{\Omega}(0).$$

Maximising the expected utility according to (10) is obviously only a second-best treatment of the problem at hand as it transforms the risk effect of accumulated stocks into *physical terms*: $\hat{\Omega}(0)$ gives the lower expected closure stock and resource extractions are phased out when $\hat{\Omega}(0)$ is reached although the probability that the resource is still open is positive. For example, using the specific probability function (2), the initially expected closure stock is given by $\hat{\Omega}(0) = \Omega_0 - (1 - e^{\pi\Omega_0})$

It should be stressed that (10) serves only as a reference case for comparison with the optimal solution. Especially, it should be noted that (10) involves *dynamic inconsistency* because the evaluation of the expected closure stock changes in the course of time, i.e. $\hat{\Omega}(t) > \hat{\Omega}(0)$ for $S(t) > 0$. Consequently, the above second-best policy relies on an *open-loop assumption* in that policies depend only on time and neglect feedback effects.

The Euler equation which solves (10) is identical with condition (6') derived in the last subsection. As the resource stock is not exploited completely in physical terms, however, the determination of $\hat{T}$ changes the

---

[3]   In order to avoid confusion with time derivatives, the different paths are not yet distinguished by additional scripts. The only exception is the end of the planning horizon: T relates to the case of no risk, T^* relates to the case of stock-dependent risks, and $\hat{T}$ relates to the above case of an expected closure stock.

resulting time path compared to the case of no risk. In particular, for $\hat{\Omega}(0) \leq \Omega_o$ the following relationship holds:

(11)

$$S(\hat{T}) = \left[1 - e^{r\hat{T}}\right]\left[W^\circ - \frac{q}{\gamma}\right]\frac{e^{-rT}}{r} + \left[W^\circ - \frac{q}{\gamma}\right]\hat{T} = \hat{\Omega}(0) \quad \Leftrightarrow \quad \hat{T} \leq T \ .$$

Differentiating (8a) to (8c) with respect to T reveals that a lower T which is due to a lower Ω_0 decreases extractions and makes the slope of the extraction path more declining and more concave (see Figure 1):

$$\partial \dot{S}(t) / \partial T = T \, e^{r(t-T)}\left[W^\circ - (q/\gamma)\right] \quad > 0, \qquad (12a)$$

$$\partial \ddot{S}(t) / \partial T = T \, r \, e^{r(t-T)}\left[W^\circ - (q/\gamma)\right] \quad > 0, \qquad (12b)$$

$$\partial \dddot{S}(t) / \partial T = T \, r^2 e^{r(t-T)}\left[W^\circ - (q/\gamma)\right] > 0. \qquad (12c)$$

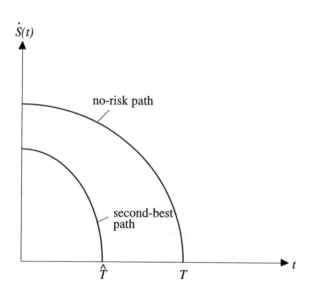

Figure 1:   No-risk path and second-best path.

3.4   Analysing the behaviour of the optimal time path

In this subsection, the no-risk path and the second best path will serve as reference cases for analysing the behaviour of the optimal path. First, assume that the optimal path intersects both the no-risk and the second-best path. Let the optimal path variables be denoted by a star and both the no-risk and the second-best variables use no scripts. Intersection of these paths means equalising (6) and (6') which yields:[4]

$$\ddot{S}^* = \ddot{S} + \frac{p(S^*)}{2r\left[1 - P(S^*)\right]}S^{*2} > \ddot{S}. \tag{13}$$

Condition (13) reveals that the first derivative of the optimal path, $\ddot{S}^*$, exceeds the first derivative of both the no-risk and the second-best path at the point of intersection. This condition, however, assumes intersection but does not prove it. Comparing the optimal path and the *no-risk path*, an easy line of reasoning proves the existence of an intersection: In both cases, the resource is planned to be exploited completely in physical terms. Thus, the area below the no-risk path and the optimal path must be of identical size. Moreover, as (6) and (6') differ, both paths must differ. An identical area and different paths, however, are only possible if both paths intersect. As intersection implies (13), the optimal path must intersect the no-risk path with a lower slope than the no-risk path as it is indicated in Figure 2:

Figure 2 demonstrates that the optimal path must start below the no-risk path, that only one intersection is possible and that the optimal path plans to use the resource not shorter than the no-risk path. The start below and the unique intersection follow from (13), and the longer use follows from (13) together with the condition that the areas below both paths must be of equal size. In economic terms, the introduction of risks makes the regulating agency more reluctant with respect to resource extractions in the beginning because the negative intertemporal externality is taken into account. The more patient the regulating agency is, i.e. the lower r, the lower is the start level of extraction policies.

---

4   Remember that both the no-risk and the second-best path satisfy condition (6').

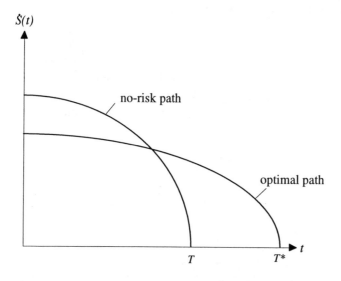

Figure 2:   *No-risk path and optimal path.*

Figure 2, however, assumed a concave shape of the optimal path. This shape is an arbitrary assumption which cannot be justified on the basis of (6). Rearranging (6) and differentiating with respect to time gives

$$
(14)
$$

$$
\ddot{S}^* = \dot{S}^* \left[r + \frac{p(S^*)\dot{S}^*}{1 - P(S^*)} \right] + \frac{\dot{S}^{*3}}{2\left[1 - P(S^*)\right]^2} \left[\frac{dp(S^*)}{dS}\left[1 - P(S^*)\right] + \left[p(S^*)\right]^2 \right]
$$

the sign of which is undetermined due to the second term on the RHS. However, in the close neighbourhood of the terminal date T^*, for which the transversality condition $\dot{S}^*(T^*) = 0$ holds, the second term on the RHS vanishes and (14) indicates that $\ddot{S}^*$ has the same sign as $\dot{S}^*$. Consequently, the shape is either increasing and convex or decreasing and concave. Because the assumptions with respect to the probability function imply a steady and differentiable resource extraction path, it must be decreasing and concave in the close neighbourhood of T^*, since an increasing, convex shape would conflict with $\dot{S}^*(T^*) = 0$. Moreover, an increasing, convex shape would imply a maximum and consequently $\ddot{S}^* \times \ddot{S}^* < 0$ in its close neighbourhood. This, however, conflicts with the observation that $\ddot{S}^*$ has the same sign as $\ddot{S}^*$.

For the specific probability function (2), the decreasing, concave shape is guaranteed because $\dddot{S}^* = \ddot{S}^*[r + \pi \dot{S}^*]$ holds. In this case, the line of reasoning which proved the concave shape in the close neighbourhood of T^* applies on the *whole* optimal path. The shape of the path depicted in Figure 2 therefore relies on the specific probability function (2). In the general case, the shape may be either convex or concave except for the close neighbourhood of the terminal date T^*.

Now, we turn to a comparison of the optimal path and the second-best path. We start by using the specific probability function (2) for which $p(S)/[1 - P(S)] = \pi$ holds. As the area below the second-best path falls short of the area below the optimal path, either the optimal path lies above the second-best path or starts below the second-best path and intersects the second-best path once.[5] Let the second-best variable be denoted by "$\wedge$". If both paths intersect at time t, the following condition holds:

$$(15)$$

$$\ddot{S}^*(\tau) = \hat{\ddot{S}}(\tau) + \frac{\pi}{2}\hat{\dot{S}}(\tau)^2 = \frac{\pi}{2}\left[1 - e^{r(\tau-\hat{T})}\right]^2\left[W^\circ - \frac{q}{\gamma}\right]^2 - r\,e^{r(\tau-\hat{T})}\left[W^\circ - \frac{q}{\gamma}\right]$$

$$= \left[W^\circ - \frac{q}{\gamma}\right]\left\{\frac{\pi}{2}\left[1 - 2e^{r(\tau-\hat{T})} + e^{2r(\tau-\hat{T})}\right]\left[W^\circ - \frac{q}{\gamma}\right] - re^{r(\tau-\hat{T})}\right\}.$$

Condition (15) uses (8a) and (8b) with $\hat{T}$ substituted for T. Integration of (15) gives resource extractions at τ which - by assumption - must be equal for both paths:

$$(16)$$

$$\dot{S}^*(\tau) = \left[W^\circ - \frac{q}{\gamma}\right]\left\{\frac{\pi}{2}\left[\tau - \frac{2e^{r(\tau-\hat{T})}}{r} + \frac{e^{2r(\tau-\hat{T})}}{2r}\right]\left[W^\circ - \frac{q}{\gamma}\right] - e^{r(\tau-\hat{T})}\right\}$$

$$= \left[1 - e^{r(\tau-\hat{T})}\right]\left[W^\circ - \frac{q}{\gamma}\right] = \hat{\dot{S}}(\tau).$$

---

[5]   If the second case holds, the line of reasoning which gives this result is quite similar to comparing the optimal path and the no-risk path. Additionally, $\Omega_0 > \Omega(0)$ implies that the optimal path induces a later terminal date.

Next, (16) can be rearranged and be written as an implicit function:

$$\Phi(\tau,\pi)=\left[W^{\circ}-\frac{q}{\gamma}\right]\left[\tau-\frac{2e^{r(\tau-\hat{T})}}{r}+\frac{e^{2r(\tau-\hat{T})}}{2r}\right]-\frac{2}{\pi}\overset{!}{=}0 \tag{17a}$$

$$\frac{\partial\Phi(\tau,\pi)}{\partial\tau}=\frac{\dot{S}^{*}(\tau)^{2}}{W^{\circ}-\frac{q}{\gamma}}\cdot\frac{\pi}{2}>0, \tag{17b}$$

$$\frac{\partial\Phi(\tau,\pi)}{\partial\pi}=\frac{2}{\pi^{2}}>0, \tag{17c}$$

$$\Phi(0,\pi)=\left[W^{\circ}-\frac{q}{\gamma}\right]\frac{1}{2r}e^{-r\hat{T}}\left[e^{-r\hat{T}}-4\right]-\frac{2}{\pi}<0. \tag{17d}$$

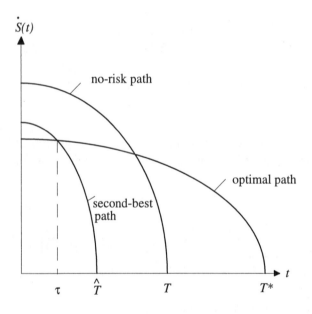

Figure 3:   *No-risk path, second-best path and optimal path.*

(17d) shows that $\tau=0$ cannot solve the implicit function $\Phi(\tau,\pi)$, and (17b) shows that $\Phi(\tau,\pi)$ is increased by an increasing τ. This proves that the optimal path starts below the second-best path because a start above the second-best path would imply a negative τ which contradicts $\partial\Phi/\partial\tau>0$ and $\Phi(0,\pi)<0$. As the optimal path aims at using the whole resource stock, a start below the second-best path further implies an intersection with this path for a positive τ. For a specific probability function like (2), all three paths are shown in Figure 3. Here, it should be noted that (17) implies $d\tau / d\pi < 0$, i.e. the higher the risk parameter p is, the earlier occurs the intersection between the optimal path the second-best path.

The above line of reasoning has used the specific probability function (2) for determining the relationship between the optimal path and the second-best path. Other or more general probability functions, however, produce the same qualitative results if they satisfy the following condition (18), where Π $(S):=p(S)/[1 - P(S)] \geq 0$ denotes the probability term which is a constant π in the case of probability function (2):

$$(18)$$

$$\frac{d\Pi(S)}{dS} = \frac{\frac{dp(S)}{dS}\left[1 - P(S)\right] + \left[p(S)\right]^2}{\left[1 - P(S)\right]^2} \overset{!}{\geq} 0$$

$$\Leftrightarrow \frac{\left[p(S)\right]^2}{1 - P(S)} \geq \frac{dp(S)}{dS} \quad \text{for all } S \leq \Omega_o.$$

Since $\Phi(\tau,\pi)$ is still negative for $\tau = 0$ if $\Pi(S)$ is substituted for π, the optimal path starts always below the second-best path. Whether $\partial\Phi / \partial\tau > 0$ also holds, depends on (18) because the sign of

$$\frac{\partial\Phi\left[\tau, \Pi\left(S(\tau)\right)\right]}{\partial\tau} = \frac{\partial\Phi\left[\tau, \Pi\right]}{\partial\tau} + \frac{2}{\Pi\left(S(\tau)\right)^2} \frac{\partial\Pi(S)}{\partial S} \cdot \frac{\partial S}{\partial\tau}$$

depends on $\partial\Pi(S)/\partial S$. If condition (18) holds, $\partial\Phi\left[\tau, \Pi\left(S(\tau)\right)\right]/\partial\tau$ is unambiguously positive. For all other cases, however, the sign of $\partial\Phi\left[\tau, \Pi\left(S(\tau)\right)\right]/\partial\tau$ is ambiguous.

Whether a higher closure risk lets the intersection date τ be realised earlier, depends on (18), too. A higher risk is associated with an increased stock of accumulated resource extractions. If (18) holds, $[\partial\Phi\left[\tau, \Pi(S)\right]/\partial\Pi(S)]\cdot$ $[\partial\Pi(S)/\partial S] \geq 0$ indicates that the same qualitative result is implied by the more general probability function under consideration .[6] In any case, Figure 3 gives the relations between the different paths although the exact curvature of the optimal path is undetermined.

3.5   Implementing optimal resource extraction policies

Section 2 has assumed a sufficiently large number of resource producers who would not take into account the risk-increasing effect of resource extractions. The present section discusses how to charge resource extractions by a tax in order to cover both the exhaustibility rent and the risk-increasing externality. As a reference case, we start with the no-risk path. Suppose, the regulating authority introduces a tax on resource extractions the rate of which is given by $\mu(t)$. In this case, profit maximisation by the resource producer to:

$$\dot{S}_m(t)=W^\circ-\frac{q+\mu(t)}{\gamma} \ . \tag{4'}$$

Equalising (4') and (8a) yields the tax rate for the no-risk case:

$$\mu(t)=e^{r(t-T)}\left[\gamma\,W^\circ-q\right] \ . \tag{19}$$

Analogously, the tax rate for the second-best case, $\hat{\mu}(t)$, can be calculated as:

$$\hat{\mu}(t)=e^{r\left(t-\hat{T}\right)}\left[\gamma\,W^\circ-q\right] \ . \tag{20}$$

Conditions (19) and (20) induce a progressive tax scheme because both paths imply overproportionally decreasing resource extractions. Moreover, the *optimal* tax in the case of stock-dependent risks is also a progressive one if probability function (2) holds, because (2) was shown to imply a concave resource extraction path.

Assuming a concave shape of the optimal time path of resource extractions, the corresponding tax rate, $\mu^*(t)$, follows a scheme which is shown in reference to the other taxes in Figure 4. Consequently, our model does not merely provide a rationale for taxing resource extraction with an

---

[6]   Note that (18) does not make the optimal path concave in every case because a positive second RHS-term in (14) does not resolve ambiguity.

increasing rate for a certain class of probability functions which satisfy condition (18). It also demonstrates that optimal policies may imply an even more rigid taxation scheme at the beginning of the time horizon if resource extractions do not only exploit an exhaustible resource but also increase the risks of closure as well. However, as the optimal path aims at using the resource longer than the other two paths, the tax falls short of the other taxes after the respective paths have intersected the optimal path.

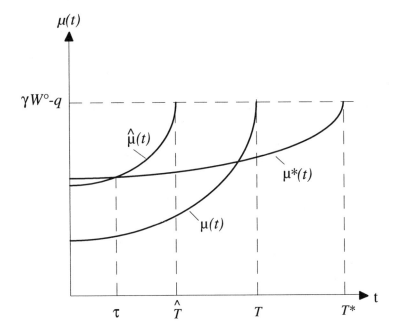

Figure 4:   *Taxes on resource extractions for different paths.*

4.   CONCLUDING REMARKS

In the present paper, we have analysed stock-dependent risks using an example concerning the optimal management of extractions of a non-renewable, exhaustible common-pool resource. The paper has demonstrated that a rationale for taxing resource extractions beyond charging pure exhaustibility rents exists when closure risks are endogenous in that they depend on the stock of extracted resources. It turned out that the optimal time path of resource extractions requires a tax rate which surmounts both the no-risk and second-best tax which tackles the problem by a mere evaluation of the expected closure stock.

Of course, the structure of our model can be used for analysing a large number of real world-problems which involve stock-dependent risks. For example, a firm's risk to be regulated may depend on the sum of its profits realised in the past. In this case, there is no restriction on profits such as a limited stock but increasing profits today implies a higher risk of being regulated for all future periods. Oligopolistic market structures initiated a differential game if potential regulation covered the whole industry because every individual firm's profits increase regulation risks for all firms in the industry. In any case, the firms can be expected to underexploit their market power compared to the no-risk case if regulation lowered their individual profits.

Obviously, stock-dependent risks result in changed activity patterns of agents who are endangered by these risks and who are able to reduce these risks. It may therefore pay for a regulating authority to build up a reputation which is materialised by the subjective probability beliefs of agents. In particular, a regulating authority has not to regulate all activities but to make potentially regulated agents believe both that regulation of activities will sometimes be introduced and that the chances to be regulated depend on the sum of all past activities which give rise to potential regulation. Compared to regulation risks which depend only on current actions, the intertemporal link involves a more severe threat, and intertemporal reoptimisation leads to a more significant change of plans at the beginning of the planning horizon.

REFERENCES

Chiang, A.C. (1992), Elements of dynamic optimization, McGraw Hill, New York.

Gilbert, R.J., (1976), Optimal Depletion of an Uncertain Stock, IMSSS Technical Report No. 207, Stanford University.

Kemp, M.C. and N.V. Long (1980), Eating a cake of unknown size: pure competition versus social planning, in M.C. Kemp and N.V. Long (eds.), *Exhaustible resources, optimality and trade*, North Holland, Amsterdam.

Long, N.V. (1975), Resource extraction under the uncertainty about possible nationalization, *Journal of Economic Theory*, 10: 42-53.

Loury, G.C. (1976), The Optimal Exploitation of an Unknown Reserve, Discussion paper, Economics Department, Northwestern University.

PART TWO

International Policy Issues

5. Trade Implications of Environmental Taxes

Gernot Klepper

1. INTRODUCTION

There is little disagreement about the need for tighter policy measures to avoid a further environmental degradation. It is also widely accepted that economic instruments will achieve this objective in a wide range of circumstances more efficiently than other policy measures. Still, there is concern over side effects of such environmental policies, because they might negatively affect employment in the economy, they might create undesirable distributive impacts, and they might disturb international trade relations by changing the competitiveness of export industries. The aim of this paper is to review the potential impact of environmental taxes on trade flows on a conceptual as well as on an empirical level.

Trade policy and environmental policy have been distinct subjects for a long time — in policy as well as in a theoretical analysis. In the past few years, the debate about the rounding up of the Ururguay-Round on trade liberalization in connection with the increasing awareness about the deterioration of local as well as global environmental media has united the two policy arenas. A major effort in empirically investigating the impact of trade liberalization on environmental quality has been undertaken by the World Bank (Low 1992). The reverse relationship, i.e. the impact of environmental policy on the international division of labor, has not been paid as much attention although the topic has become a research subject much earlier.

The early empirical research on the impact of environmental policy on trade has generally found little evidence for a measurable relationship such that this topic has not been followed on a wider scale. Only the recently emerging global problem of controlling emissions of greenhouse gases has led economists to focus again on the interaction of international trade issues and environmental policies. Although the main reason for this interest came from the presence of transfrontier externalities requiring coordinated policy approaches, it became clear that even coordinated climate policies may result in drastic changes in the international division of labor and that these effects depend on the particular form in which these policies were implemented.

The positive analysis of the effects of environmental policies on trade are in fact independent of whether the emissions are trans-frontier or local externalities. It is therefore of interest in itself to analyse these trade effects for all types of environmental policies. In a first best world of policy choice the environmental policy should always be introduced at the source of the externality, i.e. charges or taxes should be imposed directly upon the emissions or the environmental services. Yet, in reality many factors can prevent the imposition of first best policies and environmental taxes are supplemented by command and control measures or the taxes are imosed upon products or processes related to the emissions in a more or less direct way.[1] These types of second-best environmental policies may have quite different impacts upon trade than the emission taxes.

One of the major problems of measuring the relationship between environmental taxes and trade has been in the past and presently still is the fact that environmental taxes are generally low — in most cases quite below their optimal level — thus making it impossible to deduct with statistical methods the impact of optimally set environmental taxes on trade volumes and trade structure. At best one can find the impact of the observable low taxes, but extrapolating these effects to higher — and presumably optimal tax levels — would only be sensible if taxes and trade effects had a linear relationship. Many studies have therefore concentrated on simulation models in order to assess not yet implemented taxes at or near their optimal levels.

This paper first develops a very simple analytical framework in which the impact of different environmental taxes on the international division of labor can be illustrated. It consists of a simple 2x2x2 Heckscher-Ohlin trade model in which the positive analysis of environmental taxes is assessed. Even in this simple framework numerous different configurations can be distinguished. The technical details are given in the Appendix where the results of the model are also illustrated graphically. The positive analysis in this simple model is followed by a number of possible extensions. The second part is devoted to a

---

[1]   See OECD (1989, 1991, 1993).

discussion of empirical studies on environmental policies from which conclusions about the specific topic of this paper can be deducted. Although no empirical study specifically on this subject has been done, details from several studies can be used to draw at least some tentative conclusions for the theme at hand.

The paper continues with a short discussion of issues which dominate the policy debate as far as trade effects of environmental taxes are concerned. The widespread fear of leakage of emissions as well as of the relocation of industries into unregulated regions is confronted with the available evidence. The difference between short-run and long-run effects of environmental taxes is discussed. Finally, the problem of the distributional effects of introducing environmental taxes is taken up. The income effect of these tax revenues can have an important impact on the resource allocation as well as on the regional distribution of gains and losses of environmental policies. The final chapter discusses the possibilities for mitigating the impact of environmental taxes on the international competitiveness of industrial sectors and assesses their likely environmental consequences. The paper ends with some conclusions.

2. ANALYTICAL FRAMEWORK

2.1 Trade and the Environmental Taxes — The Basic Relationship

The impact of environmental policy in general — and of environmental taxes in particular — on the international division of labor depends even in a relatively simple framework on a large number of factors. Disentangling these different aspects requires an analysis on a relatively abstract level before the more practical issues can be discussed. This part therefore develops a theoretical framework in which the impact of environmental taxes on trade can be assessed. The results of trade models incorporating environmental issues vary with the exact specification of the situation under consideration. Without an explicit recognition of these different subgroups of possible situations the allocative effects as well as the welfare and distributional impacts of environmental policy can not be assessed. Therefore, some important cases will be discussed here before the impact of different environmental taxes on trade will be analysed.

It is, of course, necessary to define precisely, what is meant by the "environment". The environment is a resource which can be used in the production or consumption process either by dicharging emissions into it or by using the resource directly as an input in these processes, thus in both cases diminishing the size or the quality of the resource. The environment could — in addition to being a by-product in production or consumption processes —

have positive welfare through its mere existence. In the latter case the choice of an environmental tax needs to recognize not only the scarcity of the resource extracted from the stock as an productive input but also the utility of the stock itself. A further factor might be that the stock of the environment may have some positive external effect on the production process. The environmental tax should therefore be seen as an instrument which determines the amount of resource use and the quality and size of the resource stock in an optimal way, i.e. by internalizing all the just mentioned externalities. In this paper the stock effects are ignored since taking account of them would be beyond the scope of this paper.

At least in a simple model, the environmental tax set by the government to achieve a desired resource use is no different from a command and control approach where the resource itself is allocated by the government, except for the possible income effect of the tax revenue. It is implicitly assumed in most models that the use of the environmental resource creates some spillover effects, i.e. the use of the environment produces externalities, thus rendering government intervention necessary. Without such externalities the environment as a resource reduces to a "normal" resource extraction problem which could be allocated under private ownership without efficiency problems.

It is well known from trade theory that there is a difference whether the country under consideration is a relatively small country, i.e. it can not influence world market prices, or a large one, i.e. its actions influence the terms of trade. Another dichotomy of equal importance comes from the nature of the environmental effect to be investigated. If the use of the environmental resource affects the utility functions of the individuals of the domestic country only, then there are no spillovers of pollution or resource use. On the other hand, if such transborder effects are present, then the optimal policy choice will be different. In addition, it will differ depending on whether the country follows an egoistic policy of maximizing national welfare or whether it maximizes global welfare.

Another issue related to the use of the environment concerns the question whether the environmental effect occurs during the production or the consumption of a particular commodity and where the environmental tax is levied. Internal efficiency would require to locate the economic instrument, i.e. the tax, as close to the source as possible.[2] Hence, emissions in the production process should be taxed directly at the emitting source, and environmental impacts during consumption should be taxed at the emitting household. In many cases a direct taxing of emissions is impossible or too costly due to monitoring, control, or other problems. In these cases taxes can be imposed upon the product either at the domestic producer level, at the retail

---

[2]   See OECD (1991).

level which is already quite close to the consumer, or at the point of consumption. This makes an important difference since the environmental tax on externalities in the production process would be levied only on domestic production, whereas an environmental tax for correcting consumption externalities would need to be levied on domestic consumption, i.e. domestic production minus exports plus imports. Consequently, the impact of these two different taxes on the international division of labor can vary considerably.

A final distinction common in trade models is the one determining comparative advantage in Heckscher-Ohlin models, i.e. the relative endowment with the different factors of production, one of which being the environment. A permutation of all these cases produces a considerable number of combinations which need to be investigated. In order to facilitate the presentation, they are summarized below and each situation is given a letter such that, e.g. case (L,I,K,C) describes the case of a large country with transfrontier externalities through consumption which is relatively scarcely endowed with the environment, i.e. relatively well-endowed with capital and/or labor. Some of the different possible configurations are given in the following list:

- Small country (S) — large country (L);
- no transfrontier pollution (N) — transfrontier pollution (I);
- relatively scarcely endowed with environment (K) — rel. well-endowed with environment (E);
- tax on — domestic production (P) — on consumption (C) — on emissions (X).

The most important cases will be discussed in the following by using a Heckscher-Ohlin trade model framework where the international division of labor is driven by comparative advantage through differences in the resource endowments. The technology and homothetic preferences are assumed to be identical between countries for the moment, and the country has balanced trade. Deviations from these assumptions will be discussed subsequently.

The basic difference between the small and the large country case is that in the former the imposition of an environmental tax will not influence relative world market prices, whereas in the latter case it will. E.g., a carbon tax unilaterally imposed by Belgium will not change the world market prices for steel, but the same tax imposed by all OECD countries might do so. The implications of this distinction are important. If the environmental tax is imposed on emissions in a small country, consumer prices — which are determined by the perfectly elastic world market supply — will not change such that the only adaptation in the economy will take place within the sectoral production structure. In contrary, the same situation in the large country case will have repercussions on demand through the change in relative prices on the world market.

Distinguishing between transboundary and national pollution problems is important from a welfare standpoint and in terms of spillover effects of the reallocation of production among countries. Policies towards pollution which does not cross the frontiers will only indirectly change the environmental quality in the foreign country, whereas transfrontier pollution has direct spillovers as well as indirect ones through changes in trade flows. As long as only the allocation effects of an arbitrarily set environmental tax are considered a distinction between local and transfrontier pollution is not necessary. Choosing optimal tax rates or analyzing overall welfare effects, however, would require to distinguish between the two cases.

The relative factor endowments of countries determine their comparative advantage and the trade structure. Environmental policies which directly limit the use of the environment or which directly raise the costs of using environmental resources will consequently change the comparative advantage of that country. Hence, a relatively capital rich country by reducing the use of the environmental resource will even increase its comparative advantage in the production of goods which use capital intensively. In contrary, a country which is relatively well endowed with the resource "environment" would by imposing environmental policies reduce its comparative advantage and — in an extreme case — even reverse the comparative advantage.

The next three sections will summarize the results of a simple Heckscher-Ohlin model of trade for the case of an emission tax, a product tax which is levied on domestic production — in the following called a production tax -, and a tax which is levied at the retail level — in the following called a consumption tax. Other ways of introducing environmental taxes are conceivable but will not be discussed here.

2.1.1 Emission Taxes

A first best environmental tax is one which is directly levied at the emission which is to be controlled by the economic instrument. The emission can take place during the production of a commodity, during its transport, or during, resp. after, the consumption of a commodity. In the following only the case of an emission tax in the production process is considered. This seems to be the most frequent case, and it is tractable within the standard trade models.[3] Emissions are assumed to represent the factor input "environment". The imposition of an environmental tax on emissions during production in a small

---

3   Emission taxes in the consumption process would require an analysis of household consumption decisions, presumably within a household production function framework. This case is ignored as well as emission taxes on transport activities.

country increases the price of the factor "environment". Consequently the derived input demand for that factor falls and less of the factor "environment" will be used. The production of the "dirty" goods which use the environment intensively will therefore decrease and that of the emvironmentally friendly, i.e. capital/labor intensive, good will increase. This parallels the classical Rybczynski-effect of a change in the resource endowment, except that the factor price of the environment is set exogenously determining the quantity demanded of that factor whereas in the former the quantity is set and results in an endogenously determined factor price. If trade barriers do not exist the world market prices will govern consumer demand and the change in the production structure of the small country will therefore not influence output prices and demand. As a result of the tax the economy will move to a lower production possibility frontier and it will shift its production structure towards the low emission commodity.[4]

The effect of the emission tax on trade flows depends on the comparative advantage of the country under consideration. Suppose the country is relatively well-endowed with the factor environment, i.e. the country is an exporter of the environmentally intensive good and an importer of the capital/labor intensive good (case S,N,E,X). The environmental tax has reduced the relative production costs of the capital/labor intensive good leading to the above mentioned reallocation of production. But at the same time the lower factor endowment has induced a negative income effect such that the domestic demand for both goods will fall if they are normal goods. Consequently the country looses some of its comparative advantange and it looses real income such that imports as well as exports will fall. If the environmental tax is raised sufficiently far until the reduction in the production of the "dirty" commodity falls below domestic demand, then the comparative advantage — and the trade structure — will change towards the clean good becoming an export and the "dirty" good becoming an import good.

If the country, however, is an importer of the taxed product (case S,N,K,X) then the trade effect is different. Whereas there is little change in the production of the clean commodity, the environment-intensive good production falls strongly such that the gap between domestic demand and domestic production for this commodity widens even when the negative income effect is taken into account and if it is not too strong. The imports of the taxed commodity as well as the exports of the clean commodity are therefore likely to increase. This increase in trade volumes comes about through an increase in the comparative advantage of that country which has been forced upon it by the tax induced change in the resource endowments.

---

[4]   This is illustrated in Figures 1 and 2 in the Appendix.

2.1.2 Production Taxes

Emission control through taxes or charges can often not be performed at the emission source because monitoring is infeasible or too costly, or because the number of emission sources is large or non-stationary. In such cases product charges can act as an — often imperfect — substitute for emssion charges (OECD 1991, 1993a). They should also be applied if the product itself has some negative impact on environmental quality (ibd.). In all these cases the product charge remains a second best instrument which does not directly address the environmental damage but acts as a proxy for that damage thus leaving untaxed some other impacts of minor importance. The environmental impact of a product charge on the overall environmental quality is therefore not clearly predictable since the reallocation of the factors of production towards untaxed products also changes their emissions. This issue is ignored here since optimal taxes are not subject of this analysis. It has been noted that the trade effects of product charges may be quite different from emission charges or taxes (OECD 1993a). Yet they also require a different model.

The previous model with the environment — or more precisely, the environment's assimilative capacity for emissions — as a factor of production is inappropriate for modelling product or consumption taxes. Contrary to a partial equilibrium analysis which shows a reduction in the production and consumption of a taxed commodity and — in connection with this — a reduction of emissions, in a general equilibrium analysis of a perfectly competitive economy without factor market rigidities, a product tax at the producer or at the consumer level would have no influence on the full use of all available factors of production of which one would be emissions. The reallocation away from the environmentally intensive product would take place, but the factors becoming idle through this reduction would be used in the production of the capital/labor intensive product. Hence emissions would remain constant.

A meaningful simple model for analysing the effects of such taxes could consist of emissions being the joint product of the production process. Hence, an economy produces with some unspecified factors of production two different products which both have the same joint product, called "emission". Now suppose that the emission coefficient of one product is higher than that of the other. A second-best policy of taxing the "dirtier" product will then shift the production away from the commodity with a high emission coefficient to that with a low emission coefficient. This is illustrated in panel (a) of Figure 3 in the Appendix. The corresponding effect on total emissions is shown in panel (b) of Figure 3. In the particular situation chosen, total emissions increase as the economy moves from specializing in the product with a high emission coefficient to the product with the low emission coefficient, but the opposite is also possible and in general more likely.

Suppose now that the taxation of emissions is not feasible for whatever reason such that a policy of taxing the product at the producer level (case S,N,K/E,P) is chosen. In this case the imports are not taxed whereas the exports of domestic producers are subject to the tax.[5] If domestic production is taxed and imports are not taxed then the elastic world market supply will determine domestic consumer prices and producer prices net of taxes need to adjust to them. The domestic producers will shift production from the high to the low emission product because its relative price has risen. Thus the production tax has forced producer to switch to the low emission commodity while it leaves consumer prices untouched. Consumers will adjust their consumption bundle only because their real income has changed due to the change in the production structure.

The change in the trade structure and trade volumes again depends on the country's comparative advantage. Suppose case S,N,E,P, i.e. the country is an exporter of the high emission commodity. Since the economy has moved away from the production of the commodity in which it has a comparative advantage, trade volumes will shrink if both goods are normal goods. The terms-of-trade remain constant by the assumption of a small country. The trade effects of the production tax are therefore quite similar to the emission tax. Only the emissions are more effectively reduced by the emission tax which directly affects the environmental resource through the change in the resource price.[6]

The opposite effect on trade volumes can arise, if at the same original allocation the emission intensive commodity is an importable. Then the reallocation of production will increase trade volumes. i.e. more of the emission-intensive good will be imported.[7] In summary, the effect of an environmental tax on emission-intensive domestic production or products will change trade volumes as expected. If the tax is on the importable trade volumes increase, if it is on the exportable trade volumes generally fall. Total emissions can fall or rise depending on the compound effect of the difference in emission coefficients, on the technical rate of substitution, on preferences, and on the tax rate.

---

[5]   This type of taxation resembles the case of an indirect tax under the country of origin principle. See Baldwin (1970) for such an analysis.

[6]   For a graphical presentation see the Appendix, Figure 4.

[7]   This only holds if the good with the low emission coefficient, i.e. good k, is not too inferior.

2.1.3 Consumption Taxes

A tax on consumption will by definition be a tax on domestic products only if they are sold domestically and on imports but not on exports, i.e. the domestic consumer price will rise and producer prices remain equal to world market prices. The domestic demand for the taxed product will fall and that for the substitute will rise. Domestic production remains unchanged. Hence, a second-best policy of emission control through a tax on the consumption of the "dirty" good has only a chance of becoming effective, if the externality is indeed a consumption and not a production externality because the production of the two goods will not change. In the case of a consumption externality total emissions will only fall if the relative domestic price of the high-emission to the low-emission good is smaller than the inverse ratio of the emission coefficients of those two goods.[8]

In a country which is well endowed with capital/labor, i.e. it is importing the environmentally intensive commodity (case S,N,K,C), imports as well as exports will decline at the same rate since the producer's terms-of-trade have not changed. If the tax rate is sufficiently high the direction of trade can change as soon as the domestic demand for the importable falls below domestic production — which is determined by the world market price — and that of the exportable rises beyond domestic production. This can easily happen despite the negative real income effect which is induced by the divergence between relative producer and consumer prices if the imports of the low emission commodity are low. Hence, if the externality is indeed a consumption externality then the negative environmental effect is exported. If the consumption tax is used for controlling production externalities but is levied at the retail level in order to also tax imports, it will have no environmental effectiveness since the lack in domestic demand is taken up by exports.[9]

If the comparative advantage of the economy is in the environmentally intensive good (S,N,E,C), domestic sales will decline but since the world market demand is perfectly elastic exports will increase by the same amount by which domestic sales have been reduced. At the same time imports of the low-emission commodity will increase. Hence, trade volumes will always increase in this case.

---

[8]   A graphical illustration of these cases can be found in Figures 6 and 7 of the Appendix.

[9]   See also chapter 5.

2.1.4 Terms-of-Trade Effects

If the emission, production, or consumption taxes are high enough to influence domestic production and/or consumption decisions and the country is
large enough that these decisions also influence world market prices, the
analysis of the domestic adjustments to internal price changes — as it has
been done in the small country case — needs to be supplemented by an
analysis of the repercussions through the world market. Unilateral policies in
a large country will influence supply and demand of tradable commodities on
the world market such that prices on these markets will also change. Consequently, the environmental tax will not only influence the allocation in the rest
of the world, but the repercussions in the world market will again change the
internal allocation in the taxing country. Again, the effects of imposing an
emission tax upon producers or consumers are presented first, followed by the
second-best options of production or consumption taxes.

Introducing an emission tax reduces the economic use of the resource endowment "environment". The corresponding rise in the relative world market
price of the commodity which requires the relatively high share of the factor
environment in production will induce domestic producers to exploit this increased price by producing more of that commodity at the expense of the
other commodity. The production effect of the terms-of-trade change will
therefore to some degree counteract the objective of the emission tax, i.e. to
move domestic production away from the environment-intensive commodity.
The difference is illustrated in Figures 1 and 2 of the Appendix where in both
figures point B represents the production point without terms-of-trade
changes and point C represents the production point after the terms-of-trade
effect.

The consumption, trade, and welfare effects depend on the comparative advantage of the economy. If the environment-intensive commodity is the exportable (case L,N,E,X) the terms-of-trade for the country improve such that
the tendency for a reduction in exports due to the higher production costs is
alleviated somewhat. Consumers experience an increase in real income
through the terms-of-trade change and thus reach a higher welfare surface
than under constant world market prices.[10] The opposite happens when the
emission-intensive commodity is the importable. Then the change in relative
prices amounts to a deterioration of the terms-of-trade. The increase in the
production of the importable high-emission commodity reduces the country's
comparative advantage thus leading to a reduction in trade volumes as well as
a further loss in welfare due to the income effect of the fall in the terms of
trade.

---

[10]   Points b and c in Figure 1 of the Appendix.

In the case of a production tax, similar effects of the terms-of-trade effect come into play although through different channels. The production tax on the high emission commodity will reduce the world supply of this commodity such that its relative price rises. At a given tax rate the price wedge between consumer prices, i.e. world market prices, and producer prices net of taxes can only be sustained if the producer price of the high emission commodity increases. Hence, the incentive effect of the production tax will be lowered somewhat through the terms-of-trade effect. Since in case L,N,E,P the terms-of-trade change in favour of the exportable there is a tendency for a higher trade volume and higher welfare as in the case of an emission tax case. When the comparative advantage is in the low emission product (case L,N,K,P) trade volumes shrink and welfare falls below that of the small country case.

Under a consumption tax there was no change in domestic production as long as the relative world market price was constant. The terms-of-trade effect will then induce a reallocation of resources towards the low emission commodity because the increased consumer price will reduce domestic demand for the high-emission product and increase it for the low-emission product. This corresponds to a parallel change in world supply and demand such that the relative world market price, i.e. the domestic producer price, for the high emission product falls. Hence, not only consumption — as in the small country case S,N,E/K,C — but also production shifts away from the high emission commodity. This production effect reduces the consumption induced expansion of trade when the high-emission commodity was exported (case L,N;E,C), firstly, because the country's comparative advantage in the high-emission product has deteriorated and, secondly, because the terms-of-trade effect goes hand in hand with a fall in real income.

If the country's comparative advantage is in the low-emission product the consumption tax on the high-emission product will through the terms-of-trade effect also force a specialization towards the low-emission product, i.e. it supports the commodity with the comparative advantage. Yet, at the same time the substution of consumer demand away from the emission-intensive commodity towards the low-emission commodity absorbs this additional production such that the trade volume shrinks. When the substitution effect in consumption is much stronger than the substitution effect in production the direction of trade can possibly change. In this case domestic production of the low-emission exportable will increase but it will also become an importable due to the change in domestic demand. Hence, a reduction in trade or even a change in the trade direction of a commodity needs not conicide with lower domestic production.

2.2 A Diagrammatic Summary

The different cases discussed so far have not been distinguished between national and transborder pollution problems. This has not been necessary because the analysis was not concerned with optimal tax levels but only with the effect of marginal changes in the tax rate on production, consumption, trade, and prices. In these cases the type of pollution does not make a difference. Transfrontier pollution would also need to be taken into account if the welfare effects of the tax were to be assessed. However, this would require to have available a technique for measuring not only the welfare effects of consuming products but also the welfare effects of the environmental externalities and the possible welfare of the environmental stock which is preserved. Such an analysis is beyond the scope of this paper.

By ignoring these distinctions between national and international pollution problems, one can summarize the other configurations — i.e. large vs. small country, factor endowments, and type of tax — in a tabular form. Table 2.1 presents the effects of the different types of environmental taxes on prices, production, consumption, and trade within a country which is relatively well endowed with capital/labour. The left-hand side of Table 2.1 presents the case where no terms-of-trade effects occur on the world market. The output price effects of the different taxes are shown in the first two rows. Under the emission tax no output price changes take place, whereas the product tax lowers relative producer prices without changing consumer prices and the consumption tax raises consumer prices without changing producer prices. This does not hold for a large country, because the world market price will change. Table 2.1 also shows that the trade effects depend on the particular type of tax chosen irrespectively of the presence of the terms-of-trade effect.

Table 2.1:   *Environmental Taxes in a Relatively Capital-Rich Country (a)*

	Small Country (No ToT-Effect)			Large Country (ToT-Change)		
	Emission Tax	Product Tax	Consump-tion Tax	Emission Tax	Product Tax	Consump-tion Tax
Relative Producer Price*	0	–	0	+	–	–
Relative Consumer Price*	0	0	+	+	+	+
Production (Env.–Intensive Com.)	–	–	0	–	–	–
Production (Cap.-Intens. Comm.)	+/–	+	0	(+)/–	+	+
Consumption (Env.-Intensive Com.)	–	–	–	–	–	–
Consumption (Cap.-Intensive Com.)	–	–	+	+/–	–	+
Imports (Env.-Intensive Com.)	+/–	+	–	(+)/–	+/–	–
Exports (Cap.-Intensive Com.)	+/–	+	–	+/–	+/–	–

* Price of the environment-intensive commodity relative to the capital-intensive commodity.
(a) 0 := no change; + := increase; – := decrease; +/– := uncertain effect; (+)/– := uncertain, but decrease likely. Both commodities are normal.

The same summary is given in Table 2.2 for the case in which the country is relatively well-endowed with the factor environment. In this case the price effects remain the same, but the adjustment of the economy in production, consumption and trade will be different.

Table 2.2:   *Environmental Taxes in a Relatively Environment-Rich Country (a)*

	Small Country (No ToT-Effect)			Large Country (ToT-Change)		
	Emission Tax	Product Tax	Consump-tion Tax	Emission Tax	Product Tax	Consump-tion Tax
Relative Producer Price*	0	–	0	+	–	–
Relative Consumer Price*	0	0	+	+	+	+
Production (Env.-Intensive Com.)	–	–	0	(+)/–	–	–
Production (Cap.-Intens. Comm.)	+/–	+	0	(+)/–	+	+
Consumption (Env.-Intensive Com.)	–	–	–	+/–	+/–	–
Consumption (Cap.-Intensive Com.)	–	–	+	+/–	+/–	+/–
Imports (Env.-Intensive Com.)	+/–	–	+	(+)/–	(+)/–	+/–
Exports (Cap.-Intensive Com.)	+/–	–	+	+/(–)	(+)/–	+/–

* Price of the environment-intensive commodity relative to the capital-intensive commodity.
(a) 0 := no change; + := increase; – := decrease; +/– := uncertain effect; (+)/– := uncertain, but decrease likely. Both commodities are normal.

The two tables reveal that one can not predict the trade impact of an environmental tax without explicitly stating the particular situation of the economy and the specific form in which the environmental tax is imposed. Trade volumes can increase or decrease depending on whether the comparative advantage of the taxing country in its export product has been strengthened or weakened. It is clear, however, that the consumer surplus of commodity consumption in general falls. But this is only a partial welfare measure since the gains in environmental quality are not taken into account.

2.3   Extensions to the Basic Relationship

The simple mechanics of the preceding paragraphs ignore several important relationships. In reality factors of production are not completely immobile. At the extreme, only the natural environment itself can be considered an immobile factor whereas labor and evidently capital are mobile factors of production. The classical trade models with mobile factors (e.g. Jones et al. 1986, Bhagwati/Srinivasan 1983) do not include an immobile factor. Kuhn and Wooton (1987) have added such an immobile factor and did investigate the impact of factor movements. Environmental taxes will then induce factor flows which in turn change the comparative advantage of the countries and as a consequence the sectoral production and trade structure. Environmental taxes which reduce the availability of the immobile factor environment by raising its price will then induce an outflow of the mobile factors since the larger immobile resource endowments in the rest of the world will secure a higher marginal product of the mobile factors than in the country from which the factors have emigrated.

Mobile factors of production would then strongly increase the adjustment cost to the imposition of environmental taxes since the reduced stock of the environment which is available for production purposes will also reduce the supply of other factors of production. This complementary relationship between the availability of the environment and other mobile factors of production introduces a strategic element into environmental policy by allowing a country to attract mobile factors of production by imposing lower environmental standards than the rest of the world.

If the 2x2x2 Heckscher-Ohlin model is extended to higher dimensions, the already ambiguous predictions become even more dependend on the particular situation in which the environmental tax is imposed. In a multi-factor, multi-commodity world the sectoral structure of trade can not predicted according to factor intensities, i.e. the good which uses the most abundant factor most intensively will not necessarily be exported any more. The trade flows are   rather   determined   by   the   factor   content   of   the   commodities

(Helpman/Krugman 1986). Consequently, a tax on emissions need not necessarily have a direct trade impact on the sector with the highest emission intensity. The only prediction which can be made is in terms of the factor content of trade; a prediction which is difficult to implement empirically because especially the factor endowment "environment" can hardly be measured with the necessary accuracy.

Environmental policies are not implemented in isolation from other policy objectives. The concern over the loss of international competitiveness of industries through environmental taxes or standards will also have industrial and trade policy aspects. Governments may therefore wish to consider industrial targeting goals and environmental goals simultaneously thus aiming at the achievement of two end with just one instrument. It is well known that such an approach in general yields suboptimal outcomes. Barrett (1992) has modelled the interaction between strategic trade policy considerations and environmental policy objectives.[11] By considering the trade effects of environmental regulations, governments will set environmental targets which are above or below the optimal level, i.e. the induced marginal abatement costs are below or above the marginal damage. The results depend on the particular set-up of the behaviour of governments and of firms. In the case of domestic monopolies, a unilaterally set environmental target by one country would result in a target which is below that which would be imposed for environmental reasons alone.[12] This also carries over to the case where both countries set their targets strategically. The resulting Nash-equilibrium has suboptimal environmental standards in both countries. This result, however, does not hold for olgopolistic market structures. In this case, predictions about the restrictiveness of the environmental standard can not be made. However, both countries have an incentive to cooperate and impose targets which are above environmentally optimal, independent from the market structure in the two countries.[13] All these results hold for firms competing in quantities. Under price competition (Bertrand behaviour) the noncooperative results are reversed.

Barrett's model has been extended by explicitly considering the strategic aspects of R&D in abatement technologies by David Ulph (1993). The strategic interaction of firms in abatement technologies which is added to the strategic gevernment behaviour increases the complexity of the model in such a way that no predictions about the optimal environmental policies can be

---

[11]   Barretts analysis is not for environmental taxes but for targets. This may make
       a difference because of the additional tax burden.

[12]   See Proposition 1 in Barrett (1992).

[13]   See Propositions 3 to 6 in Barrett (1992).

made. Despite the inconclusive results of these models, a comparison with the perfectly competitive non-strategic framework of a Heckscher-Ohlin model shows that higher environmental taxes need not result in a deterioration of the competitive position of the industry exposed to the tax. Moreover, in non-competitive markets a variety of effects can occur which mainly depend on the type of behaviour governing the firms in such industries and on the shape of the abatement cost function. Therefore, one can at least say that environmental taxes will not necessarily reduce the competitiveness of particular sectors of the economy. This is again a case where the inconclusive trade effects of the simple model of perfectly competitive markets are even less predictable in general.

A model which explicitly models locational choice of imperfectly competitive firms also produces results which can be opposite to the simple model presented above (Alistair Ulph 1993). The introduction of an environmental tax which usually is designed to raise producer prices might even lower these prices. This result again stems from the non-competitive market structure which is changed through the environmental tax and the subsequent locational decisions. Since the degree of competitiveness of a market depends on the locational decisions of firms, Ulph generates cases where low environmental taxes would lead to price increases and less competition whereas high taxes in the same situation can lead to lower prices and increased competition. In addition, the locational choice will increase leakage rates far beyond those in competitive models.

3. EMPIRICAL EVIDENCE

3.1 Statistical Ex-Post Evidence

Efforts to relate the theoretical results of the possible impact of environmental policies on the economy to empirical evidence have begun only recently. Empirical research on this issue is faced with a number of problems. First, as it has been shown above, the theoretical predictions about trade and allocation effects are not at all clear due to the complexity of the models. Secondly, the data basis for measuring the relationship between environmental intensity of production and trade patterns of goods and factors is still scarce.

The older empirical studies on the impact of environmental policy on trade are summarized by Dean (1992). The first studies (Walter (1973), U.S. Department of Commerce (1975), Yezer/Philipson (1974)) all come to the conclusion that the environmental policies did not have a significant effect on trade. However, their evidence was based on environmental regulations in the late 1960s which by now has been greatly intensified such that it is conceiv-

able that the potential for negative impacts on trade as they are voiced by
Walter (1973) could be observed for the 1980s.

Robison (1988) updates the study of Walter (1973) and determines the
"pollution content", i.e. the factor content of U.S. trade for the years 1973,
1977, and 1982 by using an input-output-analysis. Since such an approach
implicitly assumes a complete pass-through of abatement costs or taxes on
prices this estimate presents an upper bound on the potential general equilibrium effect which would also allow for alleviating reallocations of resources.
He finds that the pollution content of imports relative to exports has shifted
over the period under consideration towards pollution intensive imports thus
indicating a slight tendency towards a loss of competitiveness of pollution intensive sectors. This finding could not be reproduced for bilateral trade between the U.S.A. and Canada which could be explained by the fact that both
countries have changed their environmental policies in a comparable fashion
such that no changes in comparative advantage have occured. Robison also
computes from his data a kind of trade elasticity of abatement costs. An increase in abatement costs leading to a rise in prices of 1 % will on average
lead to a reduction of the trade volume in the merchandise sector of 2.69 %.
The highest reduction on the two-digit level of disaggregation was found in
copper with 7.08 %. If the reduction in trade is measured relative to domestic
consumption, the highest impact is just 0.8 % in the ferrous metal industry
(Robison 1988, p.195). Whether this change in the trade structure is
attributable to increased environmental regulations or to the secular trend
away from high-polluting sunset industries remains an open question.

There are some recent studies on the impact of environmental regulation on
competitiveness in connection with the debate on the North American Free
Trade Argeement (NAFTA) which can give some hints as to how large the
price effect of environmental taxes and other regulations could be today — at
least as far as the United States are concerned. Low (1992a) finds that in 1988
the abatement costs for the American industry overall amounted to a weighted
average of 0.54 % of total output. Even a disaggregation to the three-digit
level reveals that out of 123 three-digit industries only seven had pollution
abatement operating costs in excess of 2 % of output, and that the cement
industry shows the highest percentage with just 3.17 % pollution abatement
costs. Table 3.1 summarizes the abatement costs for the USA on the two-digit
level and distinguishes between internal operating costs and payments to the
government. Although it does not include taxes, fees, and the like, it still
gives an indication of the potential cost effect of taxes since the tax rate
would represent an upper bound on the marginal abatement cost. If the
marginal abatement costs would rise above the tax firms would prefer to pay
taxes instead of engaging in pollution abatement.

The pollution abatement operating costs in the USA which are presented here suggest that the impact of environmental taxes is practically negligible if one takes into account that many of the environmental regulations are not taxes but consist of other regulatory instruments. E.g., the payments to government in Table 3.1 which contribute on average roughly 10 % to total pollution abatement costs are most likely induced by legal requirements instead of taxes. In addition, the internal disposal costs for solid waste amounting to almost 4 billion US$ would need to be subtracted from those total operating costs which could possibly be induced by taxes such that the cost to output ratio could at most amount to 0.34 % on average. One can therefore hardly expect to identify with econometric methods the impact of environmental taxes on specific trade flows or on the trade structure in general because the potential impact of rising costs on supply prices would be too small and because the sectoral variation — although large in relative terms — is too small in absolute terms in order to have an impact on comparative advantage.

Similar results finds Tobey (1990) who identifies the most polluting three-digit industries in the USA in order to test the impact of different stringencies of the regulatory framework with respect to the environment in different countries upon the international division of labour. In his study pollution abatement costs are computed inclusive of indirect costs which are derived from the current input-output table. Even then the share of direct and indirect pollution abatement costs does not rise above 3 %. Tobey goes on and tries to perform several tests on trade flows in order to see whether there may be some impact of environmental controls on the comparative advantage of

Table 3.1:   *Pollution Abatement Operating Costs in the USA 1988 (mio. US$)*

SIC No.	Industry	Total Cost	Total Output	Cost/ Output in %	Payments to Government	Internal Operating Cost
20	Food & kindred products	1,160.1	351,514.9	0.33	398.6	761.5
21	Tobacco manufactures	37.6	2,831.8	0.16	6.1	31.5
22	Textile mill products	177.0	64,767.9	0.27	62.4	114.6
24	Lumber & wood products	236.1	72,065.4	0.33	20.2	215.9
25	Furniture and fixtures	118.4	39,226.1	0.30	11.1	107.3
26	Paper and allied products	1343.3	122,556.2	1.10	141.6	1,201.7
27	Printing and publishing	206.4	143,906.8	0.14	41.8	164.6
28	Chemicals & allied products	3,074.9	259,699.1	1.18	181.8	2,893.1
29	Petroleum and coal products	2,005.5	131,414.8	1.53	30.5	1,975.0
30	Rubber & misc. plastic prod.	278.0	94,200.2	0.30	50.7	227.2
31	Leather and leather products	23.1	9,663.7	0.24	7.8	15.3
32	Stone, clay and glass prod.	438.5	63,059.4	0.70	27.7	410.7
33	Primary metal industries	1,809.0	149,079.8	1.21	63.4	1,745.6
34	Fabricated metal products	761.9	158,833.8	0.48	73.1	688.9
35	Machinery, exc. electrical	429.7	243,260.8	0.18	56.6	373.1
36	Electric & electrical equipm.	659.3	186,950.8	0.35	86.0	573.2
37	Transportation equipment	974.5	354,047.8	0.28	82.6	891.9
38	Instruments & related prod.	197.7	114,528.4	0.17	23.1	174.6
39	Misc. manufacturing ind.	76.7	34,869.4	0.22	12.7	64.0
	Total	14,008.6	2,617,476.9	0.54	1,378.7	12,629.9

Source: Low (1992a).

the polluting sectors of the American economy. His findings support the suspicion that such a relationship can not be detected at the current degree of environmental regulation.[14]

The potential trade impact of environmental regulation was also calculated by Low (1992a) for the NAFTA between Mexico and the USA through a quite different procedure. Low calculates the tariff which would be necessary to equate pollution control costs between the two countries under the assumption that Mexico will not undertake any additional pollution control

---

[14] One could argue that the tests may be too crude to detect such relationships. The omitted variable test in which the trade equation is estimated without the factor environment assumes that the error term should reveal in a consitent manner exactly this omitted vaiable is probably to crude if one considers the small impact of the omitted variable relative to other error terms. Similar arguments can be given for the introduction of an index of environmental regulations for the size of the resource andowment. Tobey also gives some theoretical arguments why the effect under investigation could not be detected from the trade data.

following the introduction of the NAFTA. This exercise yields an average tariff rate of just 0.6 % for all imports and tariffs for specific polluting products. This artificial environmental tariff would in most cases lie far below the current tariffs.

A recent study on the impact of environmental policy on pollution intensity[15] did test the hypotheses that

"(1) industrial pollution intensity follows an inverse U-shaped pattern as development proceeds; and
(2) OECD environmental regulation has significantly displaced toxic industrial production toward less-regulated LDC's."[16]

The findings of Hettige, Lucas, and Wheeler (1992) can be summarized as follows: The inverse U-shaped relationship between toxic intensity per unit of GDP and per capita incomes holds, but it is — according to the authors — attributable to the structural change of high income economies away from manufacturing and towards services. This is supported by the fact that this relationship does not exist if toxic intensity is measured per unit of industrial output. This would indicate that — at least on this aggregate level — the introduction of environmental policies in higher income countries together with structural changes in the economy has not had a statistically significant effect on industrial abatement activities. Given this result and given the low cost estimates of industrial pollution control one can not expect measurable trade impacts to occur in the industrialized countries.

In order to test whether the structural change away from the manufacturing sector has dislocated manufacturing production into LDC's the authors have separated the data into three decades and found that in the 1980s which had experienced the advent of stricter regulations the toxic intensity in OECD countries grew slower than in LDC's — contrary to previous periods. Unfortunately, one can still not discern whether this shift is due to more intense regulation within the OECD countries or due to the rising income in LDC'S inducing a structural change away from agriculture towards manufacturing

The evidence from ex-post statistical analyses can apparently not clearly indicate a negative impact of environmental regulations on the competitiveness of high polluting sectors in industrialized countries. The studies on costs of environmental regulations relative to the value of the product seem to indicate that such a negative competitiveness effect could not be detected since

---

[15]   Toxic intensity is measured in emissions per unit of GDP.

[16]   Hettige/Lucas/Wheeler 1992; see also Lucas/Wheeler/Hettige 1992.

costs are simply too low.[17] The observed shift in the high growth rates of toxic intensity away from industrialized countries towards the developing countries can but need not be attributable to increased environmental regulation. Hence, the impact of environmental taxes on comparative advantage seems to be either not measurable given todays statistical information or — if it were measurable — negligible so far. That still comparatively low levels of environmental regulations are likely to be responsible for these findings can be seen from simulation studies which investigate much higher levels of intervention and come to quite different conlusions.

3.2   Simulation Studies

Larger trade effects of environmental taxes can only be investigated in simulations studies which try to project the incidence of environmental policy instruments at levels which are widely believed to be efficient or at levels which governments have agreed to pursue in international conventions, declarations and treaties, but which are not implemented at all or at less than the declared and aimed at levels. The in many cases inefficient rates of environmental taxes, subsidies, or other regulations which are to a large extent responsible for the overall negative results of the econometric studies mentioned in chapter 3.1 should become amended by the "correct" interventions and then their impact on the international division of labor should be assessed. This approach needs to rely on scenarios of counterfactual experiments. Unfortunately such simulations studies seem to be done only for climate policies, in particular CO_2 policies. In addition, these climate studies are mostly concerned with the implications of tradable or non-tradable permit systems or with predetermined reduction quotas.

One can, however, derive some conclusions for environmental taxes from these studies because they usually employ models with perfectly competitive markets such that there is no difference between quantative restrictions and price regulated policies; in fact, some studies on emission quotas work with the shadow prices of these quotas which can be interpreted as the dual taxes achieving the same objective. This advantage of competitive models comes with the cost of being unrealistic for many especially polluting industries which often do not

---

[17]   It should be added that Chapman (1991) claims that the conventional way of measuring environmental abatement costs underestimates drastically because some costs can not be separated from general production costs, because joint costs of monitoring, planning etc, costs of health regulation, and others are not included in these calculations.

There exists a number of different multi-country applied general equilibrium models which assess the impact of different CO_2 reduction strategies and offer some insight into the adjustments of sectoral production as well as changes in the volume and structure of international trade. They include comparative-static models comparing 1990 with 2100 in present value terms (e.g. Whalley/Wigle 1991, or Perroni/Rutherford 1993), recursive dynamic general equilibrium models (Rutherford 1992, the GREEN-Model of the OECD, or Felder/Rutherford 1993). All these models have in common a detailed structure of the energy sector coupled with highly aggregated non-energy sectors. They will therefore average out some of the sectoral changes within these sectoral aggregates. The regional structure is generally highly aggregated. These models do not report specifically the impact of their simulation experiments on world trade but focus on specific questions of instrument choice such as coordinated vs. uncoordinated strategies, the distribution of tax revenues, the sectoral cost structures, etc. Some of these issues are discussed in the following sections.

An indication of the relative price changes which would determine the trade effects of a CO_2 tax in different countries is given by Pezzey (1991). He has computed the increase in production costs by sector of a \$100/tC carbon tax from which the tax revenues are redistributed to industry per unit value of production. His results are reproduced in Table 3.2 and can be interpreted as the change in the relative prices of the different commodities if the industries were perfectly competitive. Mainly the basic energy intensive industries experience cost increases, in particular the iron & steel industries in the USA, Germany, and Japan.

Table 3.2:   *Impact Cost of a \$100/tC Carbon Tax with Redistribution of Tax Revenues (a)*

	Iron & Steel	Chemicals	N-F Metal	N-M Mineral	Transp. Equipm.	Machinery	Food etc.	Paper etc.	Wood etc.	Cloth. etc.
USA	10.5	4.5	4.9	5.4	−1.8	−1.9	−1.1	0.2	−1.1	−0.8
Japan	6.8	2.0	0.5	1.7	−1.1	−1.2	−1.0	−0.3	−1.3	−0.5
Germany	6.6	3.7	3.3	3.5	−1.5	−1.8	−1.3	0.1	−1.4	−1.2
France	4.7	2.0	1.9	2.5	−1.0	−0.9	−0.8	−0.5	−1.0	−0.8
UK	2.4	2.1	2.9	2.8	−0.7	−1.0	−0.8	−0.7	−1.4	−0.7
Italy	3.0	1.9	0.3	4.1	−1.3	−1.0	−1.0	−0.5	−1.1	−1.0
Spain	4.1	1.8	2.3	2.4	−1.1	−1.2	−1.1	−0.3	−1.1	−0.9

(a) Cost of tax minus rebate as a percentage of the value of production of the sector.

Source: Pezzey (1991) Table 6.9.

These additional costs translate into losses of international competitiveness only in so far as these industries are subject to international competition. Pezzey assumes that the trade volume can be used as a proxy for the dependence of an industry on international markets and finds that the previously high losses of sectoral competitiveness of the American energy intensive industries are much lower than those of more outward oriented economies like Germany and Japan. But at the same time the gains in international competitiveness of the other manufacturing industries are lower in the USA and quite high in Germany.[18] Measuring the competitiveness with sectoral trade volumes, i.e. the sum of exports plus imports, is a crude indicator, however. It has been shown in chapter 2.1 that the net trade position — and not the trade volume — is important in determining the impact of an environmental tax on the international competitiveness of a sector.

The numbers computed by Pezzey (1991) show again as other studies like that by Low (1992a) that the impact of an environmental tax such as a carbon tax on costs is quite low. They still indicate that a reallocation of production towards sectors which use the untaxed factors of production intensively is likely to take place although to a limited extent. The repercussions of this reallocation on sectoral trade balances are not reported in the models mentioned above. These trade effects can hardly be predicted in general. The discussion in chapter 2.1 has already shown that the trade effect depends even in the very simple context on the net trade position of the sector and on the impact of the tax. In the carbon tax models repercussions of a multi-sector structure, of the multi-country framework, of differing emission coefficients and input coefficients, and the exact design of the tax — unilateral or global, with or without international redistribution of tax revenues — all interact to determine a specific outcome. In any case, the changes in trade flows may not be negligible when high and important environmental taxes are introduced. Whalley and Wigle (1991) report that their simulations of CO_2 taxes produce frequent cases were the direction of trade changes but they do not provide exact numbers for these trade flows.

4.   POLICY ISSUES

4.1   Leakages

Imposing an environmental tax unilaterally or only regionally will necessarily improve the comparative advantage of the other countries in the taxed commodity thus having the tendency to increase its production abroad. Through this channel at least a part of the emissions which have been reduced in the taxing countries will then become emitted in the unregulated countries. Such a leakage of emissions is not important from the viewpoint of the regulating

---

[18]   See Pezzey (1991), Table 6.11.

country if by imposing a tax it is not concerned about foreign pollution because it sees such pollution as a local phenomenon and if the taxing country follows only domestic interests. In the case of transfrontier pollution this is different. In the most extreme case of climate policies it is irrelevant where the emissions of carbondioxid, methane, CFC's, and other gases take place as their impact remains the same for all parties involved. Consequently, there have been concerns that "carbon leakages" may be so strong that unilateral policies may be self-defeating since they only lead to the relocation of production but not to global reductions of emissions of greenhouse gases.

A number of studies have investigated the extent of carbon leakage of a CO_2 tax imposed in one or all OECD countries unilaterally (Oliveira-Martins et al. 1992; Pezzey 1993; Felder/Rutherford 1993, Perroni/Ritherford 1993). Simulations of the OECD's GREEN-Model (Burniaux et al. 1992, 1992a, 1992b; Oliveira-Martins et al. 1992a) had computed the carbon leakage for unilateral action of the USA, Japan, the EC, Other OECD, and the whole OECD (Oliveira-Martins et al. 1992) and found that the overall leakage is "less serious than some observers have argued" (ibd. pg. 124). Table 4.2 summarizes the leakage rates for these countries and country groups. The leakage rate is defined as the change in emissions of those countries not participating in the reduction policy relative to the emission reduction of the region imposing the policy.[19] It turns out that the carbon leakage is relatively low with at most 15.8 % of emission reductions. It is also evident that more export oriented regions are more strongly faced with carbon leakage. Consequently, the United States has low leakage rates. The coordinated policy of all OECD countries would result in leakage rates of less than 3.5 % which even become negative with the advent of backstop technologies around the year 2010.[20]

The GREEN model captures three channels of transmissions of carbon leakage. The CO_2-tax leads to:

− shifts in the comparative advantage of energy intensive industries,
− income effects through lower resource use, and
− price adjustments for the world market price of crude oil.

---

[19] Negative leakage rates then mean that the policy will reduce emissions in non-paritcipating regions as well.

[20] Such low leakage rates should not be misunderstood as successful climate policies. Even a coordinated policy of stabilizing CO_2-emissions within the OECD would only reduce global emissions by 10 % relative to the business as usual scenario in 2050 which is little compared the Toronto target of 20 % by the year 2005 (Oliveira-Marins et al. 1992).

Table 4.2:   *Leakage Rates for Unilateral Stabilization Scenarios of CO_2*
                 Emissions (in percent)

Unilateral Action by	1995	2000	2005	2010	2030	2050
United States	2.8	2.4	1.5	0.5	−0.7	−0.2
Japan	15.8	13.5	10.2	3.1	1.2	2.1
EC	11.9	11.2	8.6	5.5	2.9	2.2
Other OECD	7.7	8.4	6.2	5.8	3.2	0.6
All OECD	3.5	2.4	0.9	−0.5	0.3	1.4

Source: Oliveira-Martins et al. 1992.

The first effect is induced by the change in the relative input prices which will shift the comparative advantage in energy-intensive products towards those countries with low energy prices. However, this classical competitiveness effect is mitigated by the two other reactions. The reduction in the use of carbon fuels will reduce energy demand in the energy-importing regions and thus reduce income and growth perspectives for the energy-exporting regions. The resulting income effect will reduce the use of carbon fuels, hence a negative leakage. The negative leakage through the income effect will be accentuated by the change in oil prices. The fall in demand for crude oil lowers world market oil prices thus leading to a substitution away from coal towards oil with lower CO_2-emissions. But lower oil prices will also increase demand for energy such that the just mentioned substitution effect may compensate the price effect. The net effect remains unclear at least on the basis of a qualitative analysis.

The model of Felder and Rutherford (1993) investigates in more detail the leakage of different OECD wide targets for CO_2 reductions until the year 2100. Unlike the GREEN model, this study presents marginal leakage rates which are derived from the marginal externality of reducing carbon emissions within the OECD through a tradable certificate system such that between 1 % and 4 % of emissions are reduced yearly. The marginal leakage rate is simply the marginal emission in the rest of the world induced by the marginal emission reduction in the OECD. These marginal leakage rates — not surprisingly — are significantly higher than those of the GREEN model, going up to 45 %. The corresponding average leakage rates peak at about 35 percernt. A comparison of the low reduction target of 1 % to the higher targets reveals quite different paths of leakage rates over time. Whereas the 1 % path has low leakage rates between 1990 and 2010 — even negative in 2010 — they rise to over 40 % after 2030. In contrary, under the high reduction scenarios the leakage rates peak in the first 50 years and then fall to become negative after 2040.[21]

These studies necessarily ignore several adjustment processes because they are diffcult to model and difficult to predict. The simulation models do not allow for factor movements which might at first increase leakage rates. Later on, however, the diffusion of new abatement technology which has been developed in the regulated economies might well reduce leakage rates. The study of Wheeler and Martin (1992) suggests that such positive effects are possible if the economies do not restrict capital movements and if the abatement technologies are tied to the production technologies.

Environmental regulations generally induce the development of abatement techniques. At first they mostly consist of end-of-pipe measures to control emssions. Yet, process changes towards clean technologies have recently become more frequent, sometimes because end-of-pipe reduction possibilities are exhausted, sometimes because intergrated abatement turns out to be less costly. These new processes often do not only possess lower emission intensities but they also exhibit lower unit production costs. Klepper/Michaelis (1992) illustrate this relationship between emission control regulation for Cadmium and the improvements in dust arrester technologies and new production processes in the non-ferrous metal industry. These joint advances in technology not only mitigate the reallocation of resources away from the taxed commodities, they might even create new comparative advantage in environmentally friendly products.

Another phenomenon which is not modelled in the simulation studies comes from the non-competitive character of some of the industrial sectors. The discussion of the model of Ulph (1993) has shown that non-competitive market structures can lead to much higher leakage rates either because the location decision of firms is more sensitive to the regulation at hand such that plants are preferrably opened in less regulated countries or because the scale effects lead to a stronger reaction of firms than when they are operating under increasing marginal costs.

It is practically impossible to predict in general the likely impact of environmental taxes on leakage rates. The detailed GREEN-Model does create low leakage rates, but misses several factors which would increase leakage. Innovation oriented adjustments to environmental taxes might even support negative leakage. The overall result therefore remains inconclusive.

---

21   See Fig. 8 in Felder/Rutherford 1993.

4.2   Short-Term vs. Long-Term Effects

There is an important difference in the impact of environmental taxes on trade
structure and trade volumes whether the short-term or the long-term adjustment by producers and consumers is included in the analysis. A short-term reaction of a firm to the imposition or an increase of an environmental tax
would be a reduction in supply or a change in the input mix, for consumers it
would consist of a change in the consumption basket as well as a substitution
through imports. The long-run reaction of firms will typically involve either
changes in the technology, i.e. innovation, or a relocation of plants, i.e. capital exports, since such activities typically involve considerations with a
longer time horizon.

The ability of producers to adjust to the increased environmental tax is the
smaller the shorter the time period in which the adjustment can take place.
The opportunity for moving inputs between sectors remains rather limited
such that the reduction of production in the most affected sector will not — or
only to a very limited extent — immediately become compensated by an increase in production in the unaffected sectors. Consequently, the short-run
will be characterized by a move inside the transformation frontier with an inefficient allocation which is induced by the time the economy needs to adjust
to the new optimal allocation. Therefore, the reduction in production and real
income under an emission tax will be stronger in the short- than in the
medium- or long-run. The resulting short-run trade effects will therefore turn
out to as ambivalent as they are in the case under a more flexible response.
The same will happen in the case of a production tax, whereas the adjustment
under a consumption tax is less important since the reallocation of production
is smaller than under the other two taxes anyway.

The speed of adjustment on the demand side depends very much on the
characteristics of the products involved. The direct and cross price elasticities
elasticities are important as well as preferences and product loyalty of consumers for the taxed product. It is clear, that long-rung elasticities are larger
such that on the demand side the short-run adjustment on the new relative
prices will be slower. Only a quantitative analysis on a case by case basis can
assess by how much the short- and the long-run differ.

In the medium- and long-run the factors of production will move from the
less competitive, i.e. taxed, sector towards the untaxed sector such that the
economy moves to a new efficient production point. A reduction of the capital stock and reduced employment in the "dirty industries" will take place but
it normally will be ameliorated somewhat by introducing abatement efforts.
As far as abatement is of the end-of-pipe type, the negative employment effect
is probably relatively stronger than the reallocation of the capital stock since
the end-of-pipe technologies are usually capital-intensive.

Innovation as another long-term strategy has effects which involve not only the abatement of emissions but they often occur concurrently with new production techniques which themselves possess lower emission coefficients. In the case of innovation in pure end-of-pipe technologies, the long-term reaction will typically differ from short-run adjustments in such a way that the new abatement technology will be cheaper to operate than paying the environmental tax or than reducing output. Hence the impact of the environmental tax will in the long-run be stronger in terms of emission reduction but the reallocation of factors of production between sectors may be smaller than in the long-run. Consequently, the trade impact in terms of losses in competitiveness will be mitigated by the lower cost of the new technology.

For two reasons, the long-run adjustment of the economy will differ from the just described situation if the innovation consists of the development of new integrated technologies. First of all, these new technologies often are more efficient not only with respect to emissions but also in terms of private production costs. Consequently, the long-run effect of the environmental tax will not only result in a reduction of emissions as in the short-run, but it can — contrary to the short-run — improve the competitive situation of the firm or industry under consideration. Secondly, because of their superior efficiency such new technologies can become diffused to other countries even without environmental regulations being imposed there. The environmental tax therefore would produce positive spillovers for foreign countries in terms of an improved environment even without transfrontier pollution. Of course, this positive welfare effect will be amplified if transfrontier pollution problems are involved. Then the transport of pollutants from the foreign country will become reduced in the same way as the internal emissions.

A final long-run effect concerns international factor movements. Especially capital might move from the high taxing country to countries with weaker environmental regulations. Persistent differences in environmental taxes can lead to the shrinking of the resource base which has been described in chapter 2.3. This could increase at least the real income effects if labour is less mobile than capital, and it could amplify the loss of competitiveness of the environment-intensive sectors of the economy.

The long-run effects of environmental taxes will most likely result in larger emission reductions than in the short-run. The overall long-run effect on the allocation of resources in general and the subsequent welfare effects, however, depends on the type of innovation incentive which the environmental tax induces upon firms. Higher taxes which impose a high burden of adjustment in the short-run may have better long-run effects since the incentives to innovate are higher in terms of taxes saved. Yet, such a strategy might impose excessively high short-run costs because the short-run reaction to the introduction of environmental taxes is already more costly than the long-run adjustment. These costs may become more balanced by preannouncing environmental taxes thus giving firms time to adjust their technologies before it is actually imposed but would still contain the incentives to innovate in new technologies. Similarly, a stepwise increase of environmental taxes which is preannounced could reduce the above mentioned differences in adjustment costs to the economy.

4.3   Distributional Effects

Imposing environmental taxes which either have strong incentive effects thus changing the allocation of resources or which create large revenues for the government will result in a redistribution of incomes within a country and possibly between countries. The redistributive effects depend upon the incidence of the tax on the side of the collection as well as on the spending side. For many environmental taxes this issue may be rather irrelevant since the tax revenue as well as the reallocation of resource is small compared to other allocative effects in the economy. However, some taxes like a CO_2-tax would — if implemented — create large amounts of revenue which need to be redistributed with possibly large income effects which may have repercussions on the international division of labour. Numerous possible configurations of tax systems and tax rates within and between countries as well as mechanisms to redistribute tax revenues result in widely differing distributional impacts.

Internal distributional effects of a carbon tax have been investigated by Symons et al. (1990) for the UK. The impact of the carbon tax was evaluated by using an input-output table to calculate the price effect of direct and indirect fossil energy inputs. This is coupled with a disaggregated demand model in order to estimate the shifts in demand away from carbon intensive products. Symons et al. (1990) find that even a moderate carbon tax would increase the relative prices of foodstuffs thus making the carbon tax regressive. Yet, even the possibility of substituting carbon tax increases by lower direct taxes would not be sufficient to effectively change its regressive character because lower income groups tend to consume relatively energy-intensive commodities.

The importance of international distributional effects is illustrated by a simulation study on "The International Incidence of Carbon Taxes" by Whalley and Wigle (1991) who have found that policies which curb global greenhouse gas emissions by 50 % through taxes would yield revenues amounting to about 10 % of world GDP. Such a policy would induce a sizable reallocation of resources in the world economy through large relative price movements and through the need to distribute the tax revenues such that large income and terms of trade effects are created. Depending on the type of tax and the distribution mechanism, these changes could go hand in hand with a large international redistribution of incomes with strong political repercussions.[22] Although the study by Whalley and Wigle does not directly address the trade issues of carbon taxes it offers imteresting insights into the distributional effects of different carbon tax systems and their impact on trade volumes and trade flows.

Whalley and Wigle simulate three different scenarios of CO_2-taxes designed to curb emissions by 50 %,

- a production tax collected by national government to achieve the 50 % reduction nationally,
- a consumption tax collected by national govenrments to achieve the same reduction nationally, and
- a global tax (production or consumption) collected by an international body, with revenues distributed according to population, again to achieve a 50 % reduction of greenhouse gases.

Whereas the two national approaches result in tax rates which differ across countries, the global tax achieves an efficient solution with a uniform tax rate and at the lowest social cost. It turns out that the three scenarios yield quite different allocations with varying distributional effects. These differences are mainly the result of the different ways in which the taxes are collected and distributed.

The production tax and the consumption tax yield the same revenue, but they differ with respect to the international distribution of the revenues (Table 4.3). Whereas the user price of carbon based energy will rise by 145.4 %, the seller price will fall by 72.7 % such that not only the price difference due to the tax but also part of the scarcity rent of fossil energy will go to the respective taxing authority. Consequently, the oil exporters will experience large revenue losses under a consumption tax compared to the pro duction tax. The European Community and Japan as large importers of fossil fuels will face the just the opposite effect. The production tax will therefore work like an export tax of the oil exporters improving their terms of trade and will thus redistribute wealth from the energy importing to the energy exporting countries. The consumption tax applied in the energy importing countries, on the other hand, will work like an import tax thus raising the terms of trade of their export goods.

---

[22]   This has already become evident by the planned introduction of exemptions of carbon taxes for energy-intensive industries within the EC. See also chpt. 5 for the likely impact of such tax exemptions.

Table 4.3:   *Revenue Redistribution of Alternative CO$_2$-Taxes for a 50 %*
              Reduction of Emissions (a)

Region	National Production Tax	National Consumption Tax	Global Tax		
			Taxes Paid	Transfers Received	Net Transfer
European Community	3,324.7	6,698.2	6,492.3	3,270.1	−3,222.2
North America	11,039.1	12,362.0	11,824.6	2,765.2	−9,059.4
Japan	98.7	1,998.2	1,957.6	1,273.8	−683.8
Other OECD	1,078.5	1,144.4	1,116.4	537.3	−579.1
Oil Exporters	9,404.3	2,505.7	2,517.1	4,029.7	+1,512.6
Dev./centrally planned	21,681.2	21,950.1	22,410.8	34,442.6	+12,031.8
Global Revenue	46,626.5	46,658.6	46,318.7	46,318.7	–

(a) Taxes paid and revenues received by region under each tax option over the period 1990–2030; in billions of 1990 US$.

Source: Whalley/Wigle (1991).

The welfare calculations of Whalley and Wigle emphasize this redistributive effect. The production tax would increase welfare[23] of the oil exporting countries by 4.5 % whereas the consumption tax would lower it by 18.7 %.Conversely, Japan which looses 3.7 % under the production tax would even gain 0.5 % with a consumption tax through improved terms of trade of Japans manufacturing exports. The difference for the European Community is similar but it experiences negative welfare effects even under the consumption tax. These simulations help to explain why politico-economic aspects are so important in designing internationally coordinated environmental taxes.

5.   MITIGATING TRADE IMPACTS

Several arguments can and have been developed which could support policy initiatives intended to mitigate adverse impacts of environmental taxes on competitiveness. The introduction of substantial environmental taxes might create large short-run adjustment costs which quickly endanger the competitive position of an industry, possibly beyond the level which it would loose in the longer run. Another argument would be that industries facing strong international competition should not be forced to bear the burden of the envi-

---

[23]   Measured in Hicksian Equivalent Variation over the period 1990–2030 in percent of GDP in present-value terms.

ronmental tax alone. Hence heavily polluting industries under fierce foreign competition should be exempted from the environmental taxes as it has been planned in the energy tax proposal of the European Union or as it has been already introduced through the Danish energy tax.[24] Finally, unilaterally introducing an environmental tax in a world with inefficiently low taxes will itself create distortions which impose efficiency costs on the country with the efficient tax level. These could only be completely avoided in a situation where all countries impose taxes which equate marginal damage avoided with marginal abatement costs.

Regardless whether these arguments are considered to be valid or not. Any relief from an environmental tax for specific groups of firms, industries, or consumers through exemptions, compensations, or rebates will distort the incentive effect of the environmental tax. Any tax with some form of exemption will therefore necessarily fail to achieve its environmental objective in the most efficient way. If the same environmental quality is to be preserved with exemptions, it needs to be met by larger reductions in emissions from other sources such that the costs of any environmental tax relief will be paid by other emittors with higher abatement costs than those emittors which are exempted from the tax.

The basic allocation effect can be described in the simple framework of chapter 2. Exempting the sector which uses the environment most intensively from say an emission tax would first of all not reduce the demand of this sector for the environment as a factor of production, hence the emission of this sector will not fall. In addition, the exemption would force the reduction upon the non-polluting sector such that it would need to shrink by more than the polluting sector since it has lower emission coefficients. Yet, this reduction in the low-polluting sector would also free some other resources — capital or labour — which could now move in the polluting sector. In a general equilibrium framework an emission tax with tax exemptions would therefore reduce the factor demand for the environment in the controlled sector but this reduction would be counteracted by the tendency for increased production in the high emission sector. If the polluting sector produces intermediate goods which are used in the low-polluting industry this positive factor supply effect can become offset by a negative demand effect through the reduced production in the down-stream sector.

These effects have been studied within the Green-Model. Oliveira-Martins et al. (1992) present a simulation of the change in the sectoral impacts and the carbon leakage of a unilateral CO_2-tax for the EC with tax exemption for

---

[24]   This tax is effectively levied on private households only, but not on firms. See Sørensen (1993).

energy-intensive industries[25] and compare this to the same emission target without the tax exemption. The tax exemption requires higher taxes for the other sectors in order to compensate for the higher emissions in the energy-intensive sector such that the intial CO_2-tax will be $35 per ton carbon in 1995 instead of $26 and it will rise to $79 instead of $50. Consequently the adjustment costs to the economy will be higher overall. More interestingly, the carbon leakage which was 11.9 % without the tax exemption (see Table 1) would only fall by 0.2 percentage points to 11.7 %. Moreover, the output loss — averaged over the period 1990 to 2050 and relative to the business as usual scenario — will be practically identical for the energy-intensive industries with (2.5 %) and without tax exemptions (2.4 %); it will be somewhat lower for the coal industry — 34 % vs. 35.5 % — presumably because less energy substitution takes place in the energy-intensive sector. The slightly larger output loss of the energy-intensive sector may be due to the increased distortion of the CO_2 policy targeted exclusively against the rest of the economy. The secondary effects of exemptions would therefore hurt the exempted sectors more than they can gain from the tax exemption itself. Tax exemptions could therefore help to alleviate the trade impacts of foreign competition, but they will have costs in terms of domestic demand distortions which could be as damaging as those of foreign competition.

These simulations of the EC's tax exemption plan are likely to represent a rather crude bound for the carbon leakage since a more precisely targeted policy towards minimizing leakage would produce less distorting scenarios if done in a more disaggregated sectoral model. The reason for such a little effect of tax exemptions is partly due to the already small leakage of unilateral action without corrective measures and it is partly due to a number of specific aspects of that industry. The CO_2-tax mostly affects coal prices, yet the energy-intensive industry has a relatively small share of coal in its intermediate consumption such that the tax exemption will not be as powerful as it were if the industry would depend more on coal (Nicoletti/Oliveira-Martins 1992). In addition, under the CO_2-tax without tax exemption output of the energy-intensive industry in the EC would shrink by between 2.5 % and 3.5 % — depending on the simulation (Nicoletti/Oliveira-Martins 1992 or Oliveira-Martins et al. 1992) compared to a decrease of that industry's output in the world overall by 0.1 %. All these factors together explain that tax exemptions for energy-intensive industries will provide little relieve from carbon leakage. This may be different if the tax exemption were specifically targeted at the coal consuming production processes; this would, however, impose an even

---

[25]   Energy-intensive industries are defined as those producing pulp and paper products (ISIC 341), chemicals (ISIC 351 and 352), iron and steel (ISIC 371), and non-ferrous metals (ISIC 372).

greater burden and heavier distortion on the rest of the economy because it would need to contribute an even larger reduction effort in emissions or the environmental objectives will simply not be achieved.

If the environmental objective is partly ignored the policy with the lowest price effect on producers relative to foreign suppliers is a consumption tax since it taxes imports in the same way as domestic production and it is not levied on exports. Hence, regardless whether the economy is a net-importer or a net-exporter of the environment-intensive commodity the consumption tax creates the smallest price differences between domestic and foreign suppliers which is possible. In the case of environmental production externalities the environmental effect of such a consumption tax could well be non-existent if no terms-of-trade effects occur. In this case the production decision will be unaffected and only consumption is substituted away from the environment-intensive commodity.[26] The only environmental incentive effect can therefore come from the terms-of-trade effect which would be a grossly inefficient way of tackling environmental problems.

6. CONCLUSIONS

It is by now widely accepted that the use of economic instruments in environmental policy has many advantages over command and control measures (OECD 1989, 1991). The implementation of environmental taxes and their role in the general system of fiscal policies have been considered at the OECD (OECD 1993). The widespread introduction of environmental taxes — especially if they cover more than a small part of the economy, e.g. a CO_2-tax — will generally have economy wide repercussions for which presumably negative employment effects and the expected loss in international competitiveness belong to the politically most important ones. This paper has investigated the general equilibrium effects of different environmental taxes and has reviewed the empirical evidence concerning the relationship between trade and environmental policy.

The conceptual simple model has shown that no clear-cut prediction about the impact of environmental taxes on trade flows and trade volumes can be made. Even in a simple theoretical framework, the impact on trade depends on

- the resource endowment of the country relative to the rest of the world,
- the type of the environmental tax, i.e. a tax on emissions, on products, or on consumption, and

---

[26]   See Figures 6, 7, and the accompanying text in the appendix.

- the presence or absence of terms-of-trade effects.

If, in addition to the pure marginal effects, welfare considerations or optimal taxes are considered, it also matters whether the environmental problem is confined to the national borders or is a transborder pollution problem.

It becomes even more difficult to predict the impact of environmental taxes on trade if the simple trade model is extended to incorporate imperfect competition and mobile factors of production. Under imperfect competition, the strategic behaviour of firms in making locational choices as well as the impact of environmental taxes on the degree of competition within the industry can produce rising as well as falling prices in the industries facing environmental regulations. As the trade impact depends on these price changes anything can happen after the imposition of an environmental tax and predictions can only be made by considering the exact situation of the industry, the behaviour of firms, their technological characteristics, the degree of competition, and many more factors. Factor mobility has the tendency to increase the probability that environmental taxes lead to a relocation of production facilities into less regulated regions thus increasing the leakage of such taxes.

The historical empirical evidence on the relationship between environmental regulation and changes in trade patterns is similarly inconclusive. As far as cost figures are available, environmental regulations seem to impose only a small burden upon industries and environmental taxes make up only a small part of these costs. Although "dirty industries" are faced with regulatory costs of several percent of their turnover, it is still little compared to the variation of other exogenous factors facing the industries such as exchange rate variations. The statistical analyses consequently find little or no evidence for a loss of competitiveness through environmental policies. In those cases where some change in the factor content of trade has been observed, it is not clear whether it reflects a secular trend in the division of labour between the industrialized and developing countries or whether it is attributable to environmental regulations.

Simulations studies of proposed environmental taxes have been performed mainly for assessing the likely national and international allocation effects of a CO_2-tax. The main conclusions in terms of the changes of sectoral competitiveness is the following: The basic industries like iron&steel, chemicals, etc. of more outward oriented economies like the member countries of the EC and Japan experience a larger loss in competitiveness than e.g. the United States. On the other hand, the other manufacturing sector gains competitiveness, again symmetrically the outward-oriented economies more than the others.

Most simulation studies on CO_2-taxes have considered the much discussed leakage problem according to which the environmental tax will induce increased production of the taxed products in the rest of the world. This will lead to a substitution of domestic production by imports and at the same time to increased emissions in the rest of the world. In the case of transfrontier pollution such as CO_2, the environmental effectiveness of the tax could more or less become compensated through this substitution effect and the loss in competitiveness would need to be added to the economic cost of the tax. The GREEN model of the OECD and some other models find very little leakage. However, since they are all perfect competition models within a Heckscher-Ohlin framework they miss the high leakage potential stemming from strategic firm behaviour and from the movement of capital or labour to the less regulated economies. Factor movements between countries can also include the diffusion of technology which generally has the tendency to reduce leakage since the new technology replaces inefficient older ones and it provides new opportunities for exporting the technology itself thus creating new comparative advantage in the country with the higher environmental taxes.

Imposing environmental taxes on polluting activities is intended to induce a reallocation of resources within an economy away from the polluting towards the cleaner processes and products. This adjustment has costs and it takes time. The reallocation of resources between sectors of the economy produces effiiciency and capital stock losses if the factors of production are at least partially sector specific, and the building up of new capital in the "cleaner" sectors as well as the development of new technologies takes time. One can therefore expect that the economy will incur higher costs in the short-run than in the long-run. Yet, this should not be an argument in favour of lower taxes as these would also undermine the long-run incentive effect of the environmental policy. Preannouncing taxes and designing taxes which increase to their optimal level in preannounced steps would be more effective.

Environmental taxes on products or factors of production which create large revenues also produce differential income effects on the side of the tax collection and through the way in which the tax revenues are recycled. These distributional consequences occur within a country but also between countries when international taxes like a CO_2-tax are concerned. The distributional effect depends on the particular tax such that general predictions can not be made. Projections of the national distributional effects of a CO_2-tax suggest that such a tax is regressive because lower income groups tend to consume relative high energy-intensive goods. In order to counteract this redistributive effect, the recycling of the tax revenues should be channeled towards lower income groups.

In order to alleviate the negative impact of environmental taxes on the competitiveness of the exporting industry measures to reduce the tax burden have been called for. Tax exemptions, compensations, or tax rebates have been advocated and they all amount to effectively not levying the tax on the most polluting sectors. If the same environmental objective is to be achieved with such tax exemptions, the emission reduction must come from the low emission sectors. However, this entails efficiency losses because the abatement costs or the opportunity costs of reduced production are higher in those sectors than in the exempted industries. Moreover, such a policy could be self-defeating if the exempted sector mainly produce intermediate products for the now heavily taxed sectors as it is common in the industrial countries. Seen from the perspective of the tax exempted industry, the reduced domestic demand for intermediate products may be worse than the loss in comparative advantage of the basic industry paired with increased comparative advantage of the other manufacturing sector.

The tentative but general conclusions which can be drawn from the above can be summarized as follows:

- The general equilibrium impact of environmental taxes does not simply consist in a reduction of international trade. The trade effect rather depends on the particular circumstances in which the tax is imposed.
- The trade impacts of environmental regulation which have been measured empirically are almost negligable. Even simulation studies predict strong effects only for very few sectors of the economy.
- Since the environmental taxes are imposed in order to induce a reallocation of the economy away from the polluting towards the less polluting activities, one can not expect that the polluting industries will not need to shrink or need to introduce abatement measures. This internal reallocation will necessarily be accompanied by a restructuring of trade between economies. Hence, mitigating these trade effects is about as meaningful as lessening the internal restructuring of the economy.

REFERENCES

Anderson, Kym (1992): The Standard Welfare Economics of Policies Affecting Trade and the Envrionment, in: Kym Anderson and Richard Blackhurst (eds.) (1992): *The Greening of World Trade Issues,* Harvester Wheatsheaf, Ann Arbor.

Anderson, Kym and Richard Blackhurst (eds.) (1992): *The Greening of World Trade Issues,* Harvester Wheatsheaf, Ann Arbor.

Baldwin, Robert (1970): *Nontariff Distortions of International Trade,* The Brookings Institution, Washington D.C.

Barrett, Scott (1992): *Strategic Environmental Policy and International Trade,* CSERGE Working Paper GEC 92–19, Norwich.

Burniaux, Jean-Marc, John P. Martin, Giuseppe Nicoletti, Joaquim Oliveira Martins (1992): *GREEN — A Multi-Sector, Multi-Region General Equilibrium Model for*

Quantifying the Costs of Curbing CO₂ Emissions: A technical Manual, Economics Department Working Papers No.116, OECD, Paris.

Burniaux, Jean-Marc, John P. Martin, Giuseppe Nicoletti, Joaquim Oliveira Martins (1992a): *The Costs of Reducing CO₂ Emissions: Evidence from GREEN,* Economics Department Working Papers No.115, OECD, Paris.

Chapman, Duane (1991): Environmental Standards and International Trade in Automobiles and Copper: The case for a Social Tariff, *Natural Resources Journal,* Vol.31, No.3, pp.449–461.

Dean, Judith M. (1992): Trade and the Environment: A Survey of the Literature, in: Patrick Low (ed.): *International Trade and the Environment.* World Bank Discussion Papers, No.159, The World Bank, Washington, D.C.

Felder, Stefan and Thomas F. Rutherford (1993): Unilateral CO₂ Reductions and Carbon Leakage: The Consequences of International Trade in Oil and Basic Materials, *Journal of Environmental Economics and Management,* Vol. 25, No.2, pp.162–176.

Grossman, Gene M. and Alan B. Krueger (1991*): Environmental Impacts of a North American Free Trade Agreement,* Discussion Paper #158, Discussion Papers in Economics, Woodrow Wilson School of Public Affairs and International Affairs, Princeton University, Princeton NJ.

Helpman, Elhanan and Paul R. Krugman (1986): *Market Structure and Foreign Trade,* MIT Press, Cambridge Mass.

Hettige, Hemamala, Robert E.B. Lucas, and David Wheeler (1992): The Toxic Intensity of Industrial Production: Global Patterns, Trends, and Trade Policy, *American Economic Review,* Vol.82, No. 2, pp. 478–481.

Klepper, Gernot and Peter Michaelis (1992): *Reducing Cadmium Emissions into the Air,* Kiel Working Paper No.531, The Kiel Institute of World Economics, Kiel.

Low, Patrick (ed.) (1992): *International Trade and the Environment,* World Bank Discussion Papers, No.159, The World Bank, Washington, D.C.

Low, Patrick (1992a): Trade Measures and Environmental Quality: The Implications for Mexico's Exports, in: Patrick Low (ed.): *International Trade and the Environment,* World Bank Discussion Papers, No.159, The World Bank, Washington, D.C.

Lucas, Robert E.B., David Wheeler, Hemamala Hettige (1992): *Economic Development, Environmental Regulation and the International Migration of Toxic Industrial Pollution: 1960–1988,* Policy Research Working Papers, WPS 1062, The World Bank, Washington D.C.

Markusen, James R., Edward R Morey, and Nancy Olewiler (1991): *Environmental Policy when Market Structure and Plant Locations are Endogenous,* National Bureau of Economic Research Working Paper No.3671.

Ludema, Rodney D. and Ian Wooton (1992): *Cross-Border Externalities and Trade Liberalization,* Department of Economics, University of Western Ontario, Canada, Manuscript.

Merrifield, John D. (1988): The Impact of Selected Abatement Strategies on Transnational Pollution, the Terms of Trade, and Factor Rewards: A General Equilibrium Approach, *Journal of Environmental Economics and Management*, Vol.15

Nicoletti, Giuseppe and Joaquim Oliveira-Martins (1992): *Global Effects of the European Carbon Tax,* OECD Economics Department Working Papers No. 125, Paris.

OECD (1989): *Economic Instruments for Environmental Protection,* OECD Paris.

OECD (1991): *Environmental Policy: How to Apply Economic Instruments,* OECD Paris.

OECD (1993): *Taxation and the Environment,* OECD Paris.

OECD (1993a): *Integrating Environment and Economics: The Role of Economic Instruments*, Manuscript, Environment Directorate, OECD Paris.

Oliveira-Martins, Joaquim, Jean-Marc Burniaux, and John P. Martin (1992): Trade and the Effectiveness of Unilateral CO_2-Abatement Policies: Evidence from Green, *OECD Economic Studies*, No.19, Paris.

Oliveira-Martins, Joaquim, Jean-Marc Burniaux, John P. Martin, Giuseppe Nicoletti (1992a): *The Costs of Reducing CO_2 Emissions: A Comparison of Carbon Tax Curves with GREEN,* Economics Department Working Papers No.118, OECD, Paris.

Perroni, Carlo and Thomas F. Rutherford (1993): International Trade in Carbon Emission Rights and Basic Materials: General Equilibrium Calculations for 2020, *Scandinavian Journal of Economics*, Vol.95, No.3, pp. 257–278.

Pezzey, John (1991): *Impacts of Greenhouse Gas Control Strategies on UK Competitiveness,* Department of Trade and Industry, London.

Rauscher, Michael (1993*): Environmental Regulation and International Capital Allocation,* Nota di Lavoro 79.93, Fondazione Eni Enrico Mattei, Milano.

Robison, H. David (1988): Industrial Pollution Abatement: The Impact on Balance of Trade. *Canadian Journal of Economic*, Vol.21, No.1, pp.187–199.

Sørensen, Peter Birch (1993): Pollution Taxes and International Competitiveness: Some Selected Policy Issues. In OECD*: Environmental Policies and Industrial Competitiveness,* Paris, pp.63–68.

Symons, E.J., John L.R. Proops, P.W. Gay (1990): *Carbon Taxes, Consumer Demand and Carbon Dioxide Emission: A Simulation Analysis for the UK*, Department of Economics and Management Science, University of Keele.

Tobey, James A. (1990): The Effects of Domestic Environmental Policies on Patterns of World Trade: An Empirical Test, *Kyklos*, Vol.43, No.2.

Ulph, Alistair (1993): *Environmental Policy, Plant Location and Government Protection,* Nota di Lavoro 43.93, Fondazione Eni Enrico Mattei, Milano.

Ulph, David (1993): *Strategic Innovation and Strategic Environmental Policy,* Nota di Lavoro 42.93, Fondazione Eni Enrico Mattei, Milano.

Whalley, John and Randall Wigle (1991): The international Incidence of Carbon Taxes, in: R. Dornbusch and J. Poterba (eds.): *Economic Policy Responses to Global Warming,* MIT Press, Cambridge MA.

Wheeler, David and Paul Martin (1992): Prices, Policies, and the International Diffusion of Clean Technology: The case of Wood Pulp Production, in: Patrick Low (ed.): *International Trade and the Environment,* World Bank Discussion Papers, No.159, The World Bank, Washington, D.C.

Wießner, Elke (1991): *Umwelt und Außenhandel,* Nomos Verlagsgesellschaft, Baden-Baden.

Winter, L. Alan (1992): The Trade and Welfare Effects of Greenhouse Gas Abatement: A Survey of Empirical Estimates, in: Kym Anderson and Richard Blackhurst (eds.) (1992): *The Greening of World Trade Issues,* Harvester Wheatsheaf, Ann Arbor.

APPENDIX

Simple Mechanics of Environmental Taxes

The basic principles of the price and competitiveness effects of different forms of environmental taxes are presented in a simple 2x2x2 Heckscher-Ohlin model of international trade. It has two factors of production, the environment — or environmental services — denoted by E and a composite of other factors, e.g. land, labour, capital, denoted by K. There are two countries, the home country and the rest of the world. Finally two tradable commodoties are produced, one which uses the environment relative intensively Q_E and Q_K which uses the composite factor relative intensively.

The effects of anvironmental taxes depend on several factors. The different cases which need to be distinguished concern the existence of terms-of-trade effects, i.e. whether the taxing country is

– Small country (S) — large country (L).

The environmental and the welfare effects depend on the type of environmental externality, i.e.

– no transfrontier pollution (N) — transfrontier pollution (I).[27]

The trade structure and the trade volume are influenced by the environmental tax in different ways depending on whether the taxing country is

---

[27] This distinction is important when optimal tax rates are to be determined. In this paper it is ignored.

– relatively scarcely endowed with environment (K) — rel. well-endowed with environment (E).

And most importantly, the trade effects of environmental taxes depend on the type of tax which is imposed to mitigate the environmental externalities. Three types of environmental taxes are considered:

– tax on — domestic production (P) — on consumption (C) — on emissions (X).

All combinations of these different cases are conceivable. It is therefore clear that no clear-cut trade effect of environmental taxes can be expected. To the contrary, it is shown that the effects differ substantially. Instead of going through each combination in detail, some important cases are presented here graphically. They show that especially the decision concerning the tax base is an important determinant of the potential trade and competitiveness effects.

Emission Taxes

If emissions can be taxed directly as a first best policy the tax acts like an artificially set price for the input factor environment and thus determines the relative factor prices between the composite factor and the factor E and the absolute amount of environmental services which are demanded by domestic producers. If the home country is small such that its policy has no influence on world market prices, the tax will reduce total domestic production because of a reduced use of the factor E. In Figure 1 the transformation frontiers of the home country for the environment-intensive commodity Q_E and the composite factor-intensive commodity Q_K are shown. The home country is assumed to have a comparative advantage in the environmentally intensive commodity (case E), i.e. it is an exporter of Q_E. Commodity prices are equal to world market prices and correspond to the tangent through point A on the outside transformation frontier.

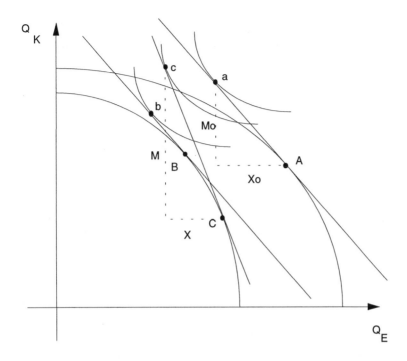

Figure 1:   *Emission Tax in a Country with a Comparative Advantage in*
              Q_E *(Cases S,N,E,X and L,N,E,X)*

Without an emission tax domestic production is located in point A, the consumption point is **a** with exports X_0 and imports M_0. If the emission tax is
imposed the transformation frontier shrinks such that the new production
point becomes B and the corresponding consumption point is **b**. The trade
volume will shrink, firstly because the country looses some of its comparative
advantage and secondly because the real income has fallen due to the smaller
factor endowment in productive use. This parallels the classical Rybczynski-
effect of a change in the resource endowment of an economy.

   If the home country is large enough to influence world market prices, the
the Rybzcynski-effect will be supplemented by a terms-of-trade effect (Case
L,N,E,X). The move from A to B changes world demand and supply of the
two commodities such that the relative price of the environmentally intensive
good Q_E rises. The production point moves from B to C because of the
favourable terms-of-trade change. In addition, consumption rises to **c** and
exports may increase or decrease to X, whereas imports will increase to M.

   To summarize, in the small country case the imposition of an emission tax
will lead to a shift away from the production of the environmentally intensive

commodity to the environmentally-extensive commodity. Due to the smaller resource base and the loss in competitiveness of the exportables sector trade volumes will decrease. In the large country case these reduced specialization effects are mitigated by the terms-of-trade effect which works in favour of the exportables sector.

The same analysis can be done for the case in which the home country has a comparative advantage in the commodity which uses the composite factor most intensively, i.e. in which it is an importer of the environmentally intensive good (Cases S,N,K,X and L,N,K,X). Figure 2 characterizes such a situation. Again, the original allocation is A (production point) and **a** (consumption point) with exports X_0 and imports M_0. The emission tax shifts the transformation frontier inwards such that in the small country case production will take place at B and consumption at point **b**. The Rybzcynski effect leads to a further specialization in commodity Q_K in which the home country has a comparative advantage. This further specialization has the tendency to increase trade volumes. However, since the real income in the home country falls at the same time, the overall effect on trade volumes remains ambiguous and depends on the degree of homogeneity of the welfare function together with the shape of the transformation surface.

If the home country is large enough to influence through its tax the relative world market prices (case L,N,K,X), the terms-of-trade effect shifts the production point from B to C and consumption from **b** to **c**. Trade volumes shrink to X and M because the terms-of-trade effect works against the comparative advantage of the home country.

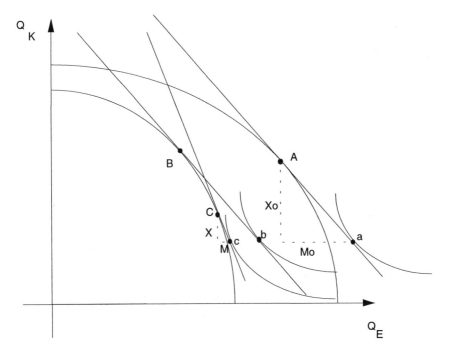

Figure 2:   *Emission Tax in a Country with a Comparative Advantage in*
               Q_K *(Cases S,N,K,X and L,N,K,X)*

If trade volumes are small before the imposition of the emission tax and if the terms-of-trade effect is sufficiently strong, then it is possible that the home country looses its comparative advantage in the commodity which uses the composite factor most intensively and becomes an exporter of the environmentally intensive good. This seemingly odd result of the emission tax leading to a specialization in the production of Q_E which uses the factor with the increased price most intensively depends on the price elasticity of world demand for the environmentally intensive good. A lower resource availability of E raises the price of Q_E. If the price elasticity is sufficiently high in the world market the home country may become an exporter of Q_E although at a lower level of production than the no-tax case.

Production Taxes

A production tax is imposed on domestic producers of an emission-intensive commodity. Consequently, imports are not subject to the tax but exports are. Such a production tax might be imposed because emissions occur during the production process and not during the consumption of the commodity and because they may not be directly measurable.

The previous model with the environment — or more precisely, the environment's assimilative capacity for emissions — as a factor of production is inappropriate for modelling production or consumption taxes as a second best policy to control emissions. Contrary to a partial equilibrium analysis which shows a reduction in the production and consumption of a taxed commodity and — in connection with this — a reduction of emissions, in a general equilibrium analysis of a perfectly competitive economy without factor market rigidities, a product tax at the producer or at the consumer level would have no influence on the full use of all available factors of production. The reallocation away from the environmentally intensive product would take place, but the factors becoming idle through this reduction would be used in the production of the other commodity using the composite factor most intensively.

One variant of a meaningful simple model for analyzing the effects of such taxes consists of emissions being the joint product of the production process. Hence, an economy produces with some factors of production two different products Q_e and Q_k which both have the same joint product, called "emission" E. Now suppose, E is a monotonic function of Q_e as well as Q_k and that the emission coefficient of product Q_e is higher than that of Q_k, i.e. $E/Q_e > E/Q_k$ for all levels of production. A second-best policy of taxing the "dirtier" product Q_e will then shift the production away from the commodity with a high emission coefficient to that with a low emission coefficient. This is illustrated in panel (a) of Figure 3 as a move along the transformation surface from C to B. The corresponding effect on total emissions is shown in panel (b) of Figure 3 which maps emissions against the composition of production between Q_e and Q_k under a full resource utilization. At the origin only the good with the low emission coefficient is produced. As more of the resources are shifted towards the production of the emission intensive good emissions increase and Q_k falls. Because of the concavity of the transformation frontier emissions will first increase and reach a maximum at the point where the increase of the emissions from the additional production of Q_e just outweighs the decrease in emissions from the fall in the production of Q_k and will fall thereafter. This maximum may be close to the maximum output of Q_e but it need not be depending on the concavity of the transformation frontier and the difference in the emission coefficients.

In the particular situation chosen total emissions increase as the economy moves from specializing in the product with a high emission coefficient to the product with the low emission coefficient. It is obviously impossible to predict the environmental effect of a tax in such a situation. If the tax would have shifted the allocation further left to point B, then emissions could fall below the original level of allocation C (panel (b) in Figure 3). However, this is a normal result if the production tax is not perfectly correlated with the emissions for which it was introduced.

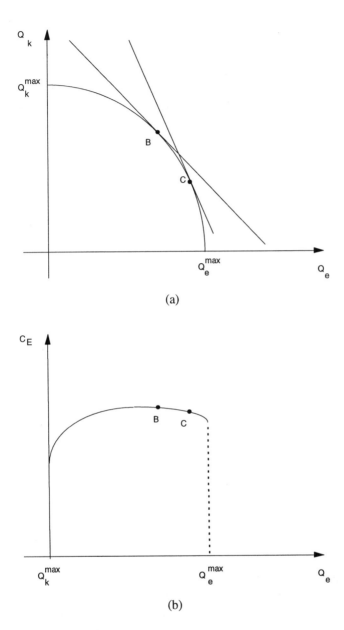

Figure 3:   *Emissions as a Joint Product*

The trade effects of a production tax in the small country case with fixed world market prices and a comparative advantage of the taxing country in the production of the relatively emission intensive commodity (case S,N,E,P) are illustrated in Figure 4. The pre-tax allocation is C (production) and c (consumption) with imports M_o and exports X_o clearing domestic markets. The tax drives a wedge between producer and consumer prices. Consumer prices are still determined by world market prices. The optimal production decision is then determined by the relative domestic producer prices, i.e. point B. Consumers choose **b** at world market prices. The product tax reduces the comparative advantage of the taxed product Q_e such that trade volumes shrink because the economy reduces its specialization away from its competitive product.

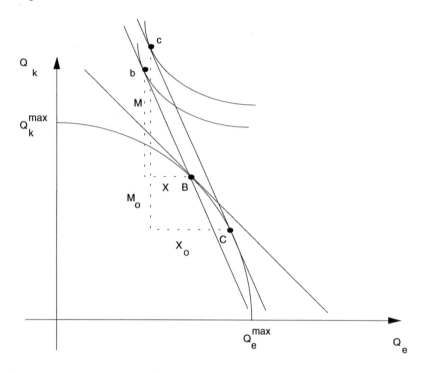

Figure 4:   *Production Tax on an Emission-Intensive Exportable (Case S,N,E,P)*

If the taxing country's comparative advantage is in the low emission commodity Q_k, i.e. Q_e is imported and Q_k is exported (case S,N,K,P) then the production tax would force producers to even further specialize in the production of the low emission commodity. Consequently trade volumes will increase since the relative price of the exportable for the domestic producer increases.

Taking account for terms-of-trade changes leads to a softening of the reallocation effects of the production tax. First consider the case of the high emission commodity being the exportable (case L,N,E,P). The imposition of a product tax on Q_e in a large country will reduce the world supply of the high emission product such that its relative price at the world market increases to p'_w in Figure 5 and the corresponding production and consumption decisions move to B' and **b'**. The tax induced production change is smaller than in the case of a small country. The consumers also gain from the increasing price of the export good and reach a higher indifference curve than under constant world market prices.

Compared to the small country case the new production point will be located between the points B and C (Figure 4). If the commodities are normal goods the new consumption point will be located in the north-east of the con-

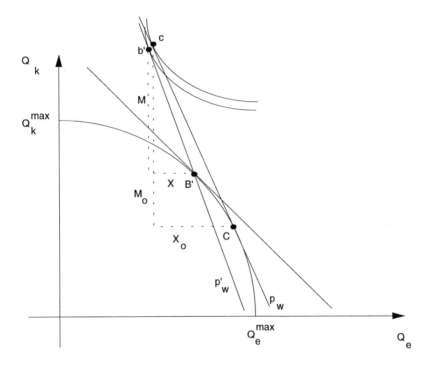

Figure 5:   *Production Tax on an Emission-Intensive Exportable (Case L,N,E,P)*

sumption point **b**. The extent of the terms-of-trade effect determines whether it will also be on an indifference curve outside the one which is tangent to c. In such a case the production tax for environmental reasons has increased the welfare of goods consumption because in addition to the environmental objective it also works like a trade policy instrument.

In the case where the taxing country has a comparative advantage in the low emission product (case L,N,K,P) the terms-of-trade works against the country's welfare because the world supply of Q_k increases thus inducing a fall in its relative price. Again the production decision will be located somewhere between the no-tax allocation C and the cum-tax allocation without the terms-of-trade effect B, e.g. at B'. The consumption decision will be on a lower indifference curve than that corresponding to the no-tax consumption point and even possibly below that of the cum-tax small country allocation.

Consumption Tax

Instead of taxing a product at the domestic producer level it can be taxed at the retail level. This implies that not only domestic production is taxed but imports as well whereas exports are not taxed. The price wedge between consumer and producer prices also exists, but relative producer prices are now identical to world market prices whereas relative consumer prices deviate from world market prices.

The analysis for a small country with a comparative advantage in the high emission product (case S,N,E,C) is depicted in Figure 6. The original allocation is C (production) and c (consumption) with the difference between the two being supplied by the world market at the relative price p_w. The consumption tax on Q_e will not change the producer decision since the price net of taxes, i.e. the world market price will not be affected by the tax. Consumers face a higher relative price for Q_e, i.e. p_d, such that they choose the consumption point **b**. Hence, exports of Q_e and imports of Q_k will rise. In this case there will be merely a reallocation of consumption which will increase trade volumes.

If the country has a comparative advantage in the low emission commodity, i.e. it imports the high emission product, but still can not influence world market prices (case S,N,K,C), then production will again not change. Consumers facing higher prices for the import good will substitute the import by the export good such that the trade volume, i.e. exports and imports, contract. If the reaction on the demand side is strong enough — through preferences or sufficiently high taxes — the direction of trade could become reversed. Such a situation is illustrated in Figure 7. The original trade pattern consisted of exports X of Q_k and imports M of Q_e with consumption c and production C. After the imposition of the tax consumers choose such that imports M' of Q_k and exports X' of Q_e are necessary to meet demand.

If the tax is lower trade flows may not become reversed and the consumption point will be located between C and c on the international price line but the trade volume shrinks relatively fast since there is no reaction on the producer side.

Including the terms-of-trade effects in the analysis of a consumption tax extends the reaction to the imposition of the tax to the producers as well. Figure 8 illustrates the case where the country is exporting the taxed high

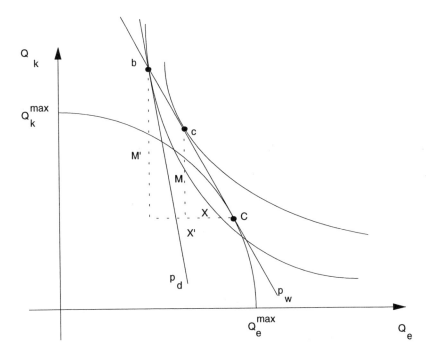

Figure 6:   *Consumption Tax on an Emission-Intensive Exportable (Case S,N,E,C)*

emission product Q_e (case L,N,E,C). Similar to Figure 6, the original production and consumption decisions are C and c. The tax increases the world demand for Q_k and lowers that for Q_e such that the relative world market price changes from pw to p'_w. The domestic retail price becomes p_d. Producer react to this terms-of-trade change by moving to B thus loosing competitiveness of their export product. In this case consumption as well as production of the high emission product falls and that of the low emission product increases.

If the exportable before taxation was the low emission commodity Q_k and the consumption tax changes the terms-of-trade of the country (case L,N,K,C), the producers will react to this relative price change by moving production from C to B in Figure 9. A reversal of the direction of trade is still possible as in case S,N,K,C but it becomes less likely since production as well as consumption decisions move in the same direction, i.e. to a haigher Q_k and a lower Q_e.

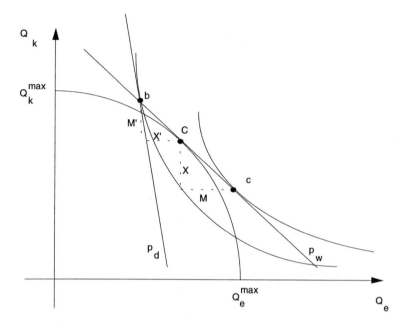

Figure 7: *Consumption Tax on an Emission-Intensive Importable (Case S,N,K,C)*

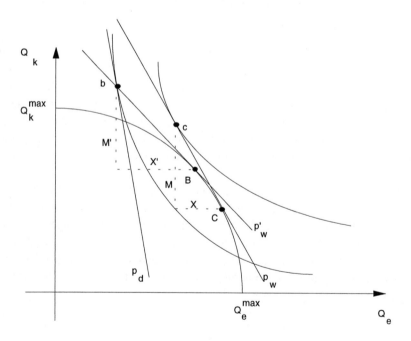

Figure 8: *Consumption Tax on an Emission-Intensive Exportable (Case L,N,E,C)*

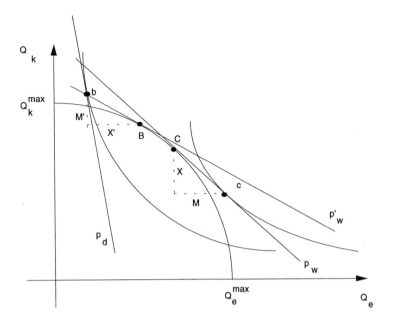

Figure 9:   *Consumption Tax on an Emission-Intensive Importable*
                (Case L,N,K,C)

6. The International Dimension of Sustainability Policies

Gernot Klepper and Frank Stähler

1. INTRODUCTION

At least since the Earth Summit in Rio, global environmental problems are on the international policy agenda. The main problems which obviously require international policy coordination are the risks of global warming, the loss of biological diversity and the destruction of the ozone shelter. Although all these problems call for different actions to cope with, they are closely inter-connected. For example, the burning or clearing of tropical forests does not only add to greenhouse gas accumulation which is responsible for the risks of global warming. Additionally, tropical forests host an unknown reserve of genetic codes the size of which is assumed to depend on the diversity of species.

As an answer to all the challenges associated with managing global environmental problems, ecologists have demanded that any resource use should be sustainable. The concept of sustainability has, therefore, become a keyword in international and national environmental policies. It seems that this keyword has entered almost every environmental policy objective by now. However, concrete definitions as to which resource use is sustainable and which one is not are hard to find. Hence, one may suspect that sustainability is often used as a catchword without any concrete definition in mind, hence old wine in a new bottle.

In this paper, we will discuss some of the rather rare concrete definitions of sustainability which have entered at least the academic discussion. We will focus on the international aspects of sustainability policies because we feel that the repercussions of international trade have not yet received enough attention. Neglecting international repercussions may be appropriate for problems which are local in the sense that they affect only local markets and local environmental problems. In a lot of cases, however, markets as well as environmental resource uses are embedded in an international setting which makes international repercussions likely.

This paper is organised as follows. Section 2 gives a classification for environmental problems which may call for a sustainability concept. Section 3 introduces into the relevant parts of standard international trade theory in order to be able to evaluate the impact of international trade repercussions. Section 4 discusses the role of resource mobility for sustainability policies. Section 5 evaluates the need for and the problems with international policy coordination. Section 6 concludes this paper by some policy implications.

2.   A CLASSIFICATION OF POTENTIAL ENVIRONMENTAL PROBLEMS

Before going into some details of international trade issues, it is worthwhile to structure the potential problems under consideration. Table 1 gives a classification of possible factors which shape the environmental problems.

Table 1:   A classification of possible factors

Concept of Sustainability	resource-based
	capital- and resource-based
Type of exhaustible resource	non-renewable
	renewable
Resource Use	solely as a production factor
	solely as a consumption good
	both as a production factor and a consumption good
Type of Country	small country
	large country
Factor Mobility	only intersectorally mobile
	intersectorally and internationally mobile
Factor Endowment	given for all periods
	determined by investments
Market structure	perfect competition
	imperfect competition
International coordination	unilateral introduction
	international introduction

The first entry of Table 1 classifies two different *concepts of sustainability*. A resource-based concept of sustainability considers only a single resource by requiring that its stock should remain constant, or at least, that its reproductive capacity should not be destroyed by harvesting so much of the resource that it can not reproduce itself. Therefore, this concept does not allow to balance resource extractions through other beneficial economic activities which are not strictly connected with the resource under consideration. For example, a resource-based concept for a sustainable forest management in a region does not allow to compensate forest clearing by improving regional water quality. A resource-based concept is also called a concept of *strong sustainability*. A capital- and resource-based concept allows these compensations in general and employs a certain rule which specifies which kind and which degree of investment may compensate for resource extractions. Two rules of this concept will be discussed in detail below. A capital and resource-based concept is also called a concept of *weak sustainability*.

The selection of the concept is not only a matter of taste or an indicator for the stringency of environmental policies but depends also on the *type of the resource*. Typically, environmental resources are in principle exhaustible because they cannot be reproduced after extinction. Exhaustible resources may either renew themselves (if they are not extincted completely) or regeneration is impossible. Capital and resource-based concepts may be applied to both renewable and non-renewable resources. When resource use is essential, however, resource-based concepts make sense only for renewable resources. An essential use is given if the economy cannot produce or consume without strictly positive resource extractions. If the resource is not renewable, fixing the stock means prohibiting resource use, and prohibiting resource use meant prohibiting production in general. The exploitation of fossil fuels is an example. Hence, we find that resource-based concepts may apply in the relevant cases only to renewable resources.

In order to determine the environmental problem, one must determine the *resource use* in detail. Resources may be used as production factors and/or consumption goods. Environmental problems arise if at least one resource use exists which is not marketable because this resource use defines a public good or a public bad. In this case, private resource use implies a positive or negative externality which is not taken into account by the decisions over the marketable resource use. Hence, resource uses differ from a private and a global perspective and make policy intervention necessary. For example, clearing a forest is beneficial for timber producers and timber consumers but may not take into account the benefits of biological diversity which are supposed to be substantial when forests are not cleared.

We are now able to give an example for a resource-based sustainability policy for a renewable resource. Suppose that a resource (e.g. a forest) is a private good and serves for production of a resource (e.g. timber). The regeneration of the stock depends on the stock size, and resource producers do not take a positive externality of holding a large stock into account. A stylised example is given in Figure 1.

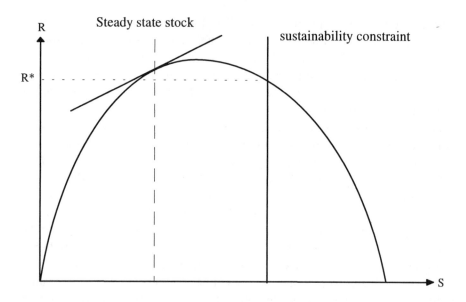

Figure 1:   *Steady state stock and sustainability constraint for a renewable resource*

Figure 1 mirrors a simple regeneration function which has an interior maximum yield. When the stock of the resource is completely exploited, no regeneration is possible such that this resource is exhaustible as well. From the economic theory of renewable resource uses, it is well-known that unregulated resource exploitation leads to a steady state stock which equalises the marginal regeneration rate (see the depicted slope) and the interest rate. When there are positive externalities the size of which depends on the stock, the steady-state stock is too low from a social perspective. Hence, resource-based sustainability policies may set a sustainability constraint which regulates resource use such that the stock does never fall short of this limit. In Figure 1, this constraint specifies a limit which lies in the range of a negative marginal regeneration, a stock which would never be hold by private users voluntarily. Figure 1 shows that regulated resource users are still able to exploit the resource as they may extract R* in every period.

Capital- and resource-based rules must be applied on essential, non-renewable resources. They require that resource extractions should be compensated by investment. There are two rules which specify different investment levels:

Table 2:   Two different rules for weak sustainability

Rule (a) Hartwick Rule	**Invest your resource rent.** net investment = resource price $\times$ resource use
Rule (b) Rule of constant wealth	**Keep the value of the sum of all stocks constant.** capital price $\times$ net investment = resource price $\times$ resource use

The first rule is called the Hartwick Rule (Hartwick, 1977, 1978). The second rule ensures that the value of all stocks is not decreasing. It should be emphasized that these rules have different motivations. Hartwick's Rule originates from searching for the necessary investment level in a closed economy which would guarantee constant consumption for all future generations in an economy with a non-renewable resource. The second rule which we call a rule of constant wealth essentially consists of an intergenerational welfare judgement demanding that every generation should be endowed with the same total stock of natural and man-made resources. As there are in principle many stocks which determine the total stock, they must be weighted by their respective prices. We will take these rules as they stand and will not discuss their appropriateness. These rules are - to our knowledge - the only rules for weak sustainability which can be identified and formulated in a formal economic model.

When turning to the international dimension of sustainability policies, additional aspects need to be taken into consideration. The *type of a country* which engages in international trade determines the country's influence on the world market. According to the usual terminology, a country is called small if any change in this country can not influence world market prices. A country is called large if her policies affect world market prices. These effects may then no longer be neglected because environmental policies in one country will have repercussions on the use of resources in the rest of the world.

When the resource serves as a production factor, different assumption can be made with respect to *factor mobility*. In standard models, factors are assumed to be intersectorally but not internationally mobile. This feature holds for some resources as well. For example, water use is almost exclusively concentrated on domestic industries since water is almost never exported. However, international immobility may be no longer an appropriate assumption for other resources such as fossil fuels. A large share of fossil fuels like crude oil is not used in their country of production. In this case, one should treat resources as an internationally mobile factor.

One of the important factors in determining the pattern of international trade consists of the different relative *factor endowments* of countries. The notion of factor endowments includes not only land, labour, and capital, but natural and environmental resources as well since they also serve as inputs in production processes. It is therefore clear that sustainability policies will have an impact on resource endowments and these endowments will in turn influence the international division of labour. Two forces are at work in this case. First, sustainability usually requires a reduction in the use of resources, and secondly, it requires substitution of natural resources by man-made resources such as physical or human capital. These issues are discussed in the next two sections.

The world oil market as well as other markets for natural resources make evident how important *market structure* is for the allocation of resources. Substantial differences in the pricing of resources exist depending on the degree of competition in such markets. Consequently, policy interventions in such markets may produce quite different reactions of the participants.

Finally, the question whether sustainability policies should be subject to *international coordination* plays an important role in formulating the policy objectives within the political process. Unilateral policies in an open economy result in two different effects. First, a sustainability policy will change the price and cost structure within that economy and thus will affect the competitiveness of particular sectors. In our case, it is likely that industries which use environmentally intensive technologies will tend to loose competitiveness. This will change trade patterns and it will lower the income of industry-specific factors with obvious political repercussions. The second impact concerns environmental and natural resources which are inherently international such as the ozone layer, some water resources, fish stocks, and specific issues in biodiversity. In these cases, unilateral action is in general inefficient such that only international coordination can lead to an optimal pattern of policy intervention.

3.   INTERNATIONAL TRADE AND SUSTAINABILITY

The international division of labour constitutes an integral part of today's economic activities. The flow of goods between countries is influenced by factors such as comparative cost advantages e.g. due to different technologies or different factor endowments or due to different tastes. One of the fundamental differences between countries consists of the different composition of factors of production. Whereas traditionally attention was mainly paid to the endowment with land, labour, and capital as the determinants of the wealth of a nation, it is now clear that the environment, both as a source of raw materials and as a receptor of wastes generated in the course of economic activities, needs to be considered as an indispensable factor of production as well. The notion of sustainability takes account of this fact in an intertemporal setting by stressing the need for an economical use of the resource "environment". Of course, sustainability policies will then also have repercussions on international trade.

One of the basic results of the theory of international trade says that a country specializes in the production of those goods which use that factor of production most intensively with which the country is relatively well endowed. An extreme example can be found in Arabian countries being endowed with huge oil reserves compared to other factors such as labour, land, or capital. Sustainability policies aim at restricting the exploitation of the environment either for maintaining a constant stock of a renewable resource or for saving non-renewable resources for future generations. Therefore, such policies will restrict the availability of one factor of production, namely the environment, and thus changes the factor endowment of the country. This will then influence the comparative advantage of certain sectors of the economy with the result that the export and import structure of the economy changes.

Even in a simple trade model things become complicated quite quickly. The environment in its different forms can be either used as a factor of production inside the country endowed with that resource or it can be moved across borders and be used as a factor of production abroad. Both possibilities have different results as long as sustainability policies are not coordinated across countries.[1] We first discuss the case of environmental resources which are not tradable between countries, i.e. only goods which contain environmental resources as factors of production can be traded.

Sustainability policies commonly amount to a reduction in the availability and use of environmental resources over time. This is often supplemented - especially in the case of non-renewable resources - by a deliberate increase in the stock on man-made capital in order to compensate future generations for the irreversible loss in that resource stock and in order to maintain a desirable stream of consumption over time. The reduction in the supply of environmental resources as a factor of production will reduce the total amount of goods which can be produced - this loss is of course compensated by an increase in environmental quality - and it will change the trade structure of that country.

A typical industrial country being well-endowed with man-made and human capital but comparatively poor in environmental and natural resources which moves towards a sustainable resource use will tend to produce less of those

---

[1]   At least for local environmental resources which impose no transfrontier pollution problems there is no need to coordinate sustainability policies.

goods which use the environment most intensively. Since demand has not changed, this reduction in domestic output of the environment-intensive commodity will be compensated by increased imports of that commodity. In turn, it will produce more of the capital-intensive commodity, mainly for financing the increased imports through exports. As a consequence, the sustainability policy will reduce the domestic use of the environment but this is partly or fully compensated by the import of goods which contain foreign environmental resources as factors of production. Thus, the unilateral sustainability policy leads to an indirect import of sustainability.

If the country is large enough to influence world market prices through its policies the price of the environment-intensive good will rise. This is equivalent to a terms-of-trade loss of this typical industrial country. Therefore, the sustainability policy will be accompanied by welfare losses from the international division of labour. The opposite, of course, happens in the foreign countries which possess a comparative advantage in the production of the environment-intensive commodities. They will experience terms-of-trade gains through higher world market prices of their export good (Klepper 1998). But this comes at the danger of a deterioration of environmental quality within these countries.

The weak sustainability version is mainly concerned with environmental resources which are nonrenewable or which exhibit regeneration rates so low that the resource use at a constant stock is not possible. In such cases it is advocated that the decrease in the environmental stock should be compensated by increases in other stocks, namely the physical and human capital stock (Pearce, Atkinson 1993). Such a policy of weak sustainability presupposes that capital and the environment can be substituted in the production of commodities. This policy of capital accumulation has repercussions on the international division of labour as well.

Sustainability induced investment in the man-made capital stock beyond the investment which is determined by the autonomous decisions of investors will also change the relative endowment of the country relative to its trading partners abroad. Again taking a capital-intensive industrial country, this investment will increase that country's comparative advantage in the production and export of commodities which are produced capital-intensively even more than before. As a result, exports of the capital-intensive good increase and imports of the environment-intensive good increase as well. In addition, the industrial country experiences a terms-of-trade gain. In summary, the unilateral sustainability induced investment will also be partially financed by increased imports of environmentally intensive commodities and welfare gains due to the improved comparative advantage. Hence, unilateral sustainability policies by a country which is already less endowed with the environment will further improve its comparative advantage in the capital/labour-intensive goods.

Of course, the opposite will happen if a country well-endowed with - or currently strongly overusing - the environment will change course. It will lose some of its comparative advantage in environment-intensive goods. Since this comparative advantage was based on an unsustainable resource use this policy change will increase welfare in terms of environmental amenities and in terms of intergenerational welfare but not in terms of income. The loss in the terms of trade will impose some additional costs on the relatively resource-rich country which the capital-rich country can avoid.

Since in the long-run weak sustainability rules increase capital-accumulation and resource extraction, sustainability policies if performed unilaterally will make the country's capital stock ever larger and will enable it to eventually finance some of its costs of sustainability through trade. Especially, if its sustainability rule is only defined over domestic resource extraction, it will make the rest of the world less sustainable.

These results are derived under the assumption that environmental resources can only be traded indirectly when they are enclosed in produced commodities. In the next section, the impact of unilateral sustainability policies is investigated for the case in which environmental resources can be traded directly.

4. THE EFFECT OF SUSTAINABLE DOMESTIC RESOURCE USE ON INTERNATIONAL RESOURCE TRADE

Conventional trade models do not assume that any production factor like labor, capital or resources is tradable but is only mobile between sectors within an economy. When only commodities are tradable, commodity trade is a substitute for factor trade because it tends to equalize factor prices as well. This is a fundamental result of trade theory which was developed in times in which factor immobility was a quite reasonable assumption. From the perspective of today's environmental policies, however, it makes a substantial difference whether resources are tradable or not. When resources are tradable, sustainability policies are likely to influence trade in resources. Of course, the impact on resource trade is different when sustainability policies are introduced unilaterally compared to an international policy coordination. Hence, resource mobility deserves special attention when designing environmental policies for a sustainable resource management.

When environmental resources are internationally mobile, national resource markets become interdependent. Integration of resource markets means that the supply and demand for resources are cleared on a world market and not on separated domestic markets. Unless some countries erect trade barriers, integration implies that the same market forces operate in all countries. This effect may restrict the policy options of a single country significantly. If a country is small, its policy does not vary the world market prices for resources. Hence, a country has significantly less influence on supply and demand conditions in an open trading system than in a closed economy.

Another feature of integrated resource markets is that reduced domestic extraction policies can be substituted by resource imports. This feature raises the question whether domestic resource use or domestic resource extraction should define the objective of sustainability policies. The difference between resource use and resource extraction are resource imports. When domestic resource extraction should be lowered to a sustainable level, one may expect that the decrease in resource extraction is at least partially compensated by an increase in resource imports. When domestic resource use is lowered, domestic resource extraction may by and large remain unaffected. Hence, it is a basic question whether sustainability policies intend to tackle a local resource problem or a resource problem which can only be solved on a global scale.

As long as a resource possesses a purely local nature in that the jurisdiction of a country can completely control that resource, there are no direct repercussions through trade on the sustainability in another country. Of course, the reduction in the availability of that resource or other investments in order to achieve sustainability may indirectly change trade flows because the relative resource endowments have changed. This change in comparative advantage may have a negative impact on other environmental resources in a foreign country because the demand for those substitutes of the protected resource may increase.

The more complex case is that in which the stock of an (environmental) resource is distributed over several countries. A unilateral sustainability policy will then directly affect trade flows of that resource, resource extraction, and resource use in those countries not pursuing sustainability policies. This raises the question what the appropriate sustainability rule should be. Should domestic resource extraction or domestic resource consumption be the reference to which the weak sustainability rule is applied? As this is a normative question, both approaches will be discussed.

In order to illustrate the basic relationship between different sustainability policies and trade in natural resources the results of a dynamic general equilibrium trade model with a non-renewable resource will be presented (Klepper, Stähler 1998). The basic intertemporal aspects of sustainability rules in an open economy come from the intertemporal resource extraction decisions of resource owners and the investment decisions based on the sustainability rules. Both will change the size and structure of the economies which are engaged in trade of resources and commodities. In addition, it will turn out that both decisions are interdependent.

The calculus of a resource owner for determining the amount of resources which he supplies depends on the price of the resource at a point in time and the expected price change in the future. In an open economy these prices are not any more determined domestically but by the world market. For an individual resource owner who feels unable to influence world market prices his extraction decision can be derived from the resource price path over time. If he expects resource price to increase at a rate faster than the rate of interest he will reduce extraction — in the most simple but also unrealistic case to zero. The reason is that the resource is worth more if extracted in the future than the return from extraction today, even when the returns are invested and pay interest. Conversely, if the resource price increase at less than the interest rate — or even decreases — it is profitable to increase extraction since the revenues from extraction will yield a higher interest than the alternative option of leaving the resource in the ground. Finally, a resource owner will be just indifferent between extracting and waiting if the resource price is expected to increase at a rate which is just equal to the interest rate. This is the famous Hotelling-rule for resource extraction. Although resource prices in reality do not exactly follow such a price path, it is still the most plausible theory so far.

We are now able to discuss sustainability policies for a tradable, non-renewable resource. Suppose that public action is necessary in order to restrict an excessive resource use. An excessive use may result from significant externalities which are not taken into account by resource users. For example, fossil fuels cause environmental damages which make restriction of their use necessary. Another example would be the extraction of resource stocks below some critical level at which they can not reproduce themselves. When non-renewable resources are subject to sustainability policies, it depends also on the type of production technology whether weak or strong sustainability concepts should be applied.

An example for the possible application of both concepts are endangered species which are protected by CITES. If strong sustainability policies are introduced for a certain species which is in danger of becoming extincted, any economic use of this species needs to be prohibited. However, prohibition does not imply that commodity production breaks down. These species are not essential for maintaining human consumption or production activities. The contrary holds for so-called necessary resources like energy resources. Energy resources are necessary because a certain input level is necessary to sustain any production. A strong sustainability would imply zero production levels. Therefore, only weak sustainability can make any economic sense.

Suppose now that a small country restricts the extraction of a resource on grounds of sustainability. In an open economy input and output prices are determined by the world market. Consequently, demand for the natural resource will not change and the reduced domestic supply will be substituted by resource imports. In order to finance these resource imports the country needs to export manufactured goods and thus experience a loss in real income. Hence, a restriction in domestic resource extraction will lead to resource imports and to a loss in real income.

Another strategy would be not to restrict the extraction of the resource but the consumption of the resource. This would require higher resource prices which could be achieved through a tax on resource consumption. This strategy would raise production costs for consumer goods and would in turn make commodity imports more competitive. At the same time, the balancing of trade would lead to a possible export of the natural resource. In summary, a restriction in the consumption of the natural resource would not lead to an equivalent reduction in extraction since some resources may now be exported.

If this small country follows a weak sustainability rule and induces investment in the capital stock in order to substitute for the reduction in the resource stock an additional effect on the use of natural resources is induced. The larger capital stock will, other things such as prices being equal, increase the demand for other factors of production notably natural resources. This increased demand will have no price effects and thus will not change the domestic extraction decision of resource owners. Hence, the additional input of natural resources in production will be met by imports. A policy of reducing resource extraction and increasing capital accumulation will thus lead to a combined increase in resource imports, hence an import of sustainability.

Now suppose that the country which imposes a sustainability rule is large enough to influence world market prices. A restriction in domestic resource extraction will then raise the world market price for the resource thus leading to a reduction in world demand and in the country following the sustainability policy. Therefore, the increase in import demand for the natural resource will be less pronounced. The price policy of lowering demand domestically will lead to an excess supply of resources and a fall in the world market price such that the world demand for resources increases. As a consequence, exports of the natural resource may increase as well.

If that large country follows a policy of weak sustainability it will need to increase its capital stock if voluntary investment in the country is insufficient to compensate for the decrease in the resource stock. This increase in investment triggers two effects. Firstly, the increase in the capital stock will over time change the factor endowment of the country relative to the rest of the world. The consequences of this effect have been described in the previous section. An already capital-intensive industrial country would increase its comparative advantage in the production of capital-intensive goods and thus will experience a terms-of-trade again.

The second effect is induced by the changes in world market prices. The increased investment will increase the world capital stock which in turn changes the relative prices of the factors of production. I.e., the rate of return on capital will fall since a larger capital stock will have lower productivity. In addition, the world market for natural resources will react because the price path of resource prices depends on the interest rate on capital.

Irrespectively of the particular weak sustainability rule chosen the interplay of a unilateral sustainability policy on resource extraction, investment, trade flows and sustainability are as follows. The country which introduces a sustainability policy through investing in the man-made capital stock will increase the imports of natural resources. However, these imports do not grow without limits; in most cases the import ratios attain relatively low bounds, at least within a relatively simple dynamic model of international trade with mobile resources. The time profiles of output and consumption depend on the particular sustainability rule chosen. Whereas resource extraction remains equal within the country and abroad since world market prices determine the supply behavior, the resource use increases in the country trying to achieve sustainability when compared to a situation without such a policy.

The rest of the world reacts by specializing in the export of natural resource and importing consumer goods. This specialization leads to an increase in income when compared to a situation without the unilateral sustainability policy. Parallel to this foreign consumption is also higher. The impact on the sustainability of the rest of the world ambiguously depends on the particular sustainability rule chosen in the country mentioned above.

In section 2, two different rules for weak sustainability have been presented, the Hartwick-Rule — demanding to invest the resource rent in each period — and the rule of constant wealth — demanding to keep the value of all capital and resource stocks constant over time. These two rules become ambiguous in an open economy since resources extracted and resources consumed are not identical any more if trade in resources is possible. It is therefore necessary to decide whether the weak sustainability rule is defined over the resources extracted within a country or over the resources consumed.

There is no a-priori reason to prefer one rule over the other. An extraction based rule assigns the responsibility of maintaining sustainability to the country in which the resource stock is located, the consumption based rule assigns it to the consumer of the resource although the resource rent is appropriated in the country which extracts the resource. Since this is essentially a normative issue, Klepper and Stähler (1998) have investigated all four possible configurations, i.e. the Hartwick-Rule, extraction and consumption based, as well as the rule of constant wealth, extraction and consumption based.

The best weak sustainability rule when used unilaterally by one country in terms of sustainability for the rest of the world is the Hartwick-Rule compared to the rule of constant wealth irrespective of whether the consumption or the extraction based variant is used. Only the extraction based rule of constant wealth leads to a strongly deteriorating sustainability in the rest of the world. Under the other rules, the rest of the world remains unsustainable but this situation does not deteriorate. It may even improve slightly.

In terms of consumption, i.e. the utility of consumers, the consumption based sustainability rule is particularly bad for the country pursuing the sustainability policy and particularly advantageous for the rest of the world. This rule requires large investments which, firstly, reduce the amount of output available for consumption and, later on, they deteriorate the terms of trade of that country. Consequently, the rest of the world can increase its consumption which is mainly financed through the export of resources.

These illustrations show that even in a rather simple model of an open economy with trade in natural resources quite complex interactions can take place and the definition of a sustainability rule is not obvious anymore. However, the interactions described and the sustainability rules used so far belong to only one set of model assumptions, the most important being the requirement to invest in the physical capital stock. Since such a policy reduces the productivity of the capital stock and thus the interest rate, it also accelerates resource extraction although at a sustainable pace. An alternative would be to invest in other man-made capital stock such as human capital which would increase interest rates and over time increase the rate of price increase of the natural resource.

There are quite a few examples which demonstrate the relevance of this distinction. Take again energy resources: If the use of energy resources is merely compensated by physical capital accumulation, one must expect that this additional capital will need energy resources to be employed. Instead, qualitative growth would substitute energy-intensive technologies by less intensive technologies like solar technologies or by energy saving programs. This measures may be able to increase the productivity of the existing capital stock, and they may be able to decrease the necessary energy input. Other measures include investment into human capital and promotion of research and development, especially for resource conservation.

5.   INTERNATIONAL POLICY COORDINATION

The last two sections have demonstrated that national sustainability policies imply international repercussions which should be taken into account carefully when designing national policies. The need for international policy coordination depends primarily on the type of the environmental resource in question. An environmental resource may predominantly provide local services, for example local ecosystems. Any policy which intends to make their use more sustainable does not need international policy coordination. The reason is that all environmental services associated with a local resource are under the complete control of the host country. If policies for preserving a local resource change trade patterns, changed trade patterns are the consequence of changed relative environmental scarcities. A country which restricts excessive exploitation of local resources thereby corrects its relative endowment with environmental resources into the right direction.

A lot of environmental resources, however, predominantly provide global services. These resources may be of benefit not only to one country but to other countries as well. If all other countries benefit from this resource, the resource is called a global resource. The crucial point is that the other countries cannot be excluded from the benefits of global resource conservation. In this case, every country benefits from the resource as a whole, and any action taken affects all countries. Examples include tropical forests, large-scale ecosystems like rivers and seas and the ozone shelter.

Suppose that a certain country considers to take actions which yield environmental benefits for all countries. For example, a single country may consider to promote the introduction of energy-efficient technologies or restrict energy consumption by introducing energy taxes in order to curb carbon dioxide emissions. Then, this country has to carry the costs of this program whereas its benefits are little compared to the benefits across all countries. If one country takes a certain action in order to make the use of a global resource more sustainable, all other countries will benefit from this policy. Without any policy coordination, we must expect that a single country has only minor incentives to pursue unilateral policies because it has to carry all costs but benefits only little. This incentive may even disappear if the national efforts are expected to be completely offset by other countries which react on national policies by increasing their resource use. Hence, it is evident that global environmental resource policy needs coordination in order to make sustainability on a global scale profitable for all countries.

International policy coordination, however, carries its own problems. These problems originate from the sovereignty status of all countries involved in international policy coordination. Sovereignty means that every country may in principle decide autonomously about its policy. Coordination requires that all involved countries agree upon a certain joint policy. Hence, sovereignty and policy coordination conflict with each other unless countries only agree upon what is also in their purely national interest.

However, only policy coordination leads to an efficient solution in the case of joint environmental policies for global resources and global commons. Although all countries are better off by coordinated actions, each country is even better off if all other countries coordinate their actions but itself does not. This incentive may lead into a dilemma because each country refrains from cooperation and hopes that all other countries will cooperate. This dilemma could be avoided if all countries could sign a binding contract which specifies coordinated actions. But the sovereignty status of every country makes any commitment to behave according to coordinated actions incredible if defection benefits this country.

In fact, there are two restrictions which are due to the sovereignty status. The first restriction is that no country can be forced into cooperation. Every country may opt for an outsider position because it hopes that other countries cooperate. This incentive explains why countries are so reluctant to sign environmental treaties which specify concrete obligations. Instead, such treaties often contain only imprecise declarations of intent. The declaration of countries to look for policy options to freeze carbon dioxide emissions is an example.

The second restriction originates from the non-enforceability of a signed treaty. If a country does not meet its obligations whereas the other countries do, it is obviously better off than meeting its obligations. As no supranational authority is able to enforce the treaty, other mechanisms must substitute for legal enforcement. The threat that a country breaches an agreement is not hypothetical. The debt crisis has impressingly revealed that sovereign countries are in fact able to deviate from an international agreement. In this case, debts were repudiated by indebted countries, and in subsequent negotiations creditors accept to write off a part of debt services although they were laid down in a contract.

Hence, global sustainability policies may not be as effective as other policies because they need to cope with the significant problem of international policy stabilisation. The lack of a supranational authority and the sovereignty of countries are likely to make international policy coordination more complicated than national policies. Therefore, international policy stabilization requires that every country participating in coordinated actions has no long-run incentive to quit joint sustainability policies. Heister et al. (1995/6) demonstrate that institutional arrangements which guarantee compliance must build on repetition and use utility transfers, economic sanctions and treaty adjustments.

6.   POLICY IMPLICATIONS

This paper has given a discussion of some of the problems which arise with sustainability policies in an international setting. It turned out that international repercussions may threaten the success of national sustainability policies. This threat is twofold: First, unilateral sustainability policies will change the international allocation of resources. In particular, the import of natural resources may make the rest of the world even more unsustainable. Secondly, in the case of transfrontier externalities of resource conservation there is also an incentive to free-ride on environmental preservation.

It is therefore more promising to coordinate national sustainability policies. The last section has demonstrated that international coordination is much more difficult to achieve than national environmental policies. However, for environmental problems which cross national borders, there is no alternative because uncoordinated actions will not guarantee sustainability in this case.

From all these considerations, we draw the following conclusions:

− Any sustainability policy which intends to compensate resource extractions through other beneficial economic activities should not accumulate physical capital. Physical capital accumulation may lead to increased resource exploitation in the long run, and this effect is the substantially stronger when resources are traded. Instead, such a policy should take actions which increase the productivity of the existing capital stock, like investment into human capital and research and development which enhances resource conservation.

− Even for environmental resources which do not create transfrontier externalities, the question is open as to whether sustainability rules should be defined with respect to the consumption of an environmental or natural resource or with respect to its extraction.

− In the case of transfrontier externalities policy coordination is essential for reaching sustainability.

ACKNOWLEDGEMENT

This paper is a part of a research project on „The Measurement and Achievement of Sustainable Development". We gratefully acknowledge financial support by the European Union.

REFERENCES

Hartwick, J.M. (1977), Intergenerational Equity and the Investing of Rents from Exhaustible Resources, *American Economic Review,* 67:972-974.

Hartwick, J.M. (1978), Substitution Among Exhaustible Resources and Intergenerational Equity, *Review of Economic Studies,* 45:347-354.

Heister, J., Mohr, E., Stähler, F., Stoll, P., Wolfrum, R. (1996), Strategies to Enforce
    Compliance with an International CO_2-Treaty, *International Environmental
    Affairs*, 9:22-53.

Klepper, G. (1998), Trade Implications of Environmental Taxes, Chapter 5 of this
    volume.

Klepper, G., Stähler, F. (1998), Sustainability in Closed and Open Economies,
    forthcoming in *Review of International Economics*.

Pearce, D.W., Atkinson, G.D. (1993), Capital Theory and the Measurement of
    Sustainable Development: An Indicator of „Weak" Sustainability, *Ecological
    Economics,* 8: 103-108.

7. Who Will Win the Ozone Game?

On Building and Sustaining Cooperation in the Montreal Protocol on Substances that Deplete the Ozone Layer

Johannes Heister

---

1. INTRODUCTION[1]

The history of Chlorofluorocarbons (CFCs) is a remarkable story. It tells about successful research, high-rising industrial production of CFCs for numerous purposes and the emergence of a pressing global environmental problem — the destruction of the earth's ozone layer — which can only be solved by international cooperation.

Thomas Midgley Jr. discovered the CFCs in 1930 [Shea (1988:18)]. In 1974, worldwide production of CFC-11 and CFC-12 had reached 800,000 tonnes annually.[2] In the same year, Molina and Rowland presented the theory that CFCs destroy the stratospheric ozone layer. Although the use of CFCs in aerosols (spray cans) were banned in the United States of America in 1978,[3] in 1986, world consumption of CFCs and halons had risen to 1,140,000 tonnes annually with a total ozone depletion potential of 1,232,000 tonnes.[4]

---

1   The paper was written in 1993 as a contribution to a project on the stability of international environmental agreements supported by the Volkswagen Foundation. I wish to thank Gernot Klepper, Andreas Kopp, Peter Michaelis, Ernst Mohr and Frank Stähler for valuable comments on an earlier draft. The usual disclaimer applies.

2   Production data for the countries reporting to the Chemical Manufacturers Association. EPA (1987), here adopted from Morrisette (1989:795).

3   On the long discussion in the USA about possible damage to the ozone layer see Morrisette (1989).

4   CFC-11 and CFC-12 have an ozone depletion potential of 1.

North America produced 29 percent, Western Europe 37, Eastern Europe 12, and Asia, the Pacific countries and Latin America 22. In 1984/85, per capita consumption of CFC-11/12 was around 0.85 kg in the USA and in the European Community, whereas in China, per capita consumption was 0.02 kg.[5]

The main virtue of the CFCs is their chemical stability. CFCs are not toxic, since they do not react with other chemicals, and they are not inflammable. Moreover, CFCs are cheap to produce. CFCs are ideal as a coolant in refrigeration (Freon), as a foam blowing agent (Styrofoam), as aerosol propellants in spray cans and as a solvent in the electronic industry and in dry-cleaning. Halons, a similar chemical, are mainly used in fire fighting.[6] But CFCs and halons are by no means harmless, when released into the environment.

Life on earth is protected against dangerous solar radiation by a layer of relatively ozone rich air in the stratosphere (12-25 km above ground level). The ozone layer hinders the passage of ultraviolet radiation to the earth's surface. Particularly the powerful short-wave UV-B radiation is destructive to biological systems. UV-B radiation causes or promotes skin cancer, cataracts, allergic reactions, immune insufficiency and other diseases. It reduces the growth of plants and has adverse effects on crop yields and possibly on entire (aquatic) food-chain systems. It even damages some materials (plastic products) and increases smog [UNEP (1989), chapter 5].

Ozone, the three-atom form of oxygen (O_3), is built up by a chemical reaction triggered by sunlight above the tropics, from where global air circulation transports some of it to the poles [Shea (1988:7)]. The delicate ozone equilibrium in the stratosphere is tipped off by the release of CFCs and halons (and some other less used trace gases). The characteristic ozone destroying element is chlorine in CFCs and bromine in halons. During their long life-time, which for some compounds lasts up to 100 years, CFCs and halons emitted into the troposphere migrate slowly to the stratosphere. There, the compounds are broken up by powerful solar radiation and release their chlorine or bromine parts. Each chlorine or bromine atom then catalyses the destruction of a myriad of ozone molecules. This chain reaction depletes the ozone layer, which then lets dangerous UV-B radiation penetrate to the earth's surface.[7]

---

[5]   The data show a weak relationship between CFC consumption and GNP of roughly 60 tonnes per billion dollars of GNP. All data UNEP (1989), chapter 2, and OTA (1989).

[6]   Besides CFCs and halons, which were first controlled by the MP, there are some other ozone depleting substances. Some of them were added to the list of controlled substances by the London and Copenhagen Amendments to the MP. In this paper, CFC represents all ozone depleting substances.

[7]   The exact chemical process is much more complicated. See UBA (1989). Apart from depleting the ozone layer, CFCs and related compounds are very potent greenhouse gases, which significantly contribute to global warming.

2. IMPACT OF OZONE DEPLETION ACROSS WORLD REGIONS

Although every part of the world is affected by ozone depletion, there appear to be some systematic regional differences concerning the impact level and its (political) perception and valuation. The latitudinal distribution of ozone depletion is not even. Less depletion occurs around the equator. Depletion levels are considerably higher towards the poles with a particularly heavy loss of stratospheric ozone after the extremely cold Antarctic winter (ozone hole). Figure 1 illustrates this pattern for the southern hemisphere.

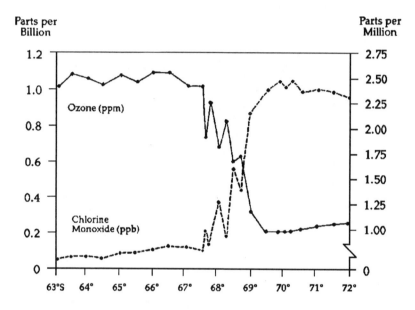

Figure 1:   *Atmospheric concentration of chlorine monoxide and ozone by latitude, southern hemisphere, 1987* [Shea (1988:10)].

The ozone hole over Antarctica sometimes reaches the southernmost part of South America, New Zealand and southern Australia. In some regions in Australia and New Zealand, the current level of UV-B radiation and the "burn time" is regularly broadcast to warn people to protect themselves when outdoors.[8] Inhabitants of Chile's far south were reported to suffer from eye irri-

---

8   "Ripa mahnt Vorreiterrolle der Gemeinschaft an", Handelsblatt, 5 March 1992. "Tödliche Sonnenflecken: Die Angst vor dem Ozonloch über der südlichen Erdhälfte hat den Lebensstil der Neuseeländer nachhaltig verändert", Süddeutsche Zeitung, 19 March 1993.

tations, allergies and severe skin burns; farmers and fishermen have reported that sheep, wild rabbits and salmon are going blind.[9]

A similar ozone hole has not yet opened up over the North Pole. However, depressed ozone levels and a serious increase in chlorine concentration has been detected in the northern hemisphere, too. [10] In the winter of 1992, scientists voiced warnings that the exceptionally high level of chlorine in the stratosphere of the northern latitudes could, under unfavourable weather conditions, develop an ozone hole by spring. In spring 1993, ozone concentration over Europe was down by more than 20 per cent.[11] Figure 2 shows a remarkable (estimated) decline in total ozone concentration for different northern latitudes between 1960 and 2030.

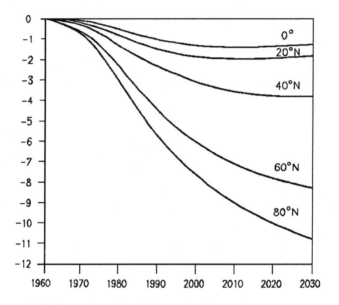

Figure 2:   *Loss of total ozone for different northern latitudes between 1960 and 2030 (spring, in per cent of total ozone concentration)* [UBA (1989:23)].

9   L. Crawford, "Russian scientists to assist Chile in study of ozone layer depletion", The Financial Times, Frankfurt and London, 18 February 1992.

10   To some extent, ozone depletion is set off by the screening effect of air pollution in industrial countries.

11   J. Wille, "Das Ozonloch ist – noch – nicht über uns", Frankfurter Rundschau, 8 February 1992. B. James, "Ozone Hole Widens, Populated Regions Face Radiation Risk", International Herald Tribune, 5 February 1992. "Wir haben noch kein Ozonloch, aber genug Grund zur Sorge", Frankfurter Rundschau, 23 March 1993.

Ozone layer erosion near the equator has not yet been detected. Obviously, the countries of the northern and southern high latitudes face higher ozone depletion rates and are therefore probably more severely affected than countries located more closely to the equator.

The impact of UV-B radiation shows a similar latitudinal bias. The biosphere in equatorial regions is adapted to the naturally higher solar radiation levels in these regions. Therefore, higher UV-B levels may be less damaging to the vegetation in equatorial regions and the impact on crop yields may be less severe. Similarly, dark-skinned people are generally less susceptible to UV-caused skin cancer than light-skinned people. Therefore, without adaptive measures being taken, fewer lives may be lost due to ozone depletion among the dark skinned population in countries closer to the equator than in more distant regions [UNEP (1989:37)].

In addition, the valuation of UV-B-caused damage is likely to differ between regions and countries of different level of economic development and different political systems [UNEP (1989:37f)]. The political valuation of diseases and lost lives is probably lower in developing countries (DCs) than in developed industrial countries (ICs). The social discount rate in DCs tends to be higher due to a relatively higher weight of today's needs. Global causes for local environmental disasters are probably not easily recognised by the majority of people in DCs. Moreover, the political system in many DCs offers not much opportunity for democratic participation and public pressure. Therefore, a less pronounced reflection of peoples' needs and preferences in the political valuation and decision making process in DCs as compared to ICs is likely. The danger of ozone depletion may thus be undervalued by DCs.

The above observations indicate that there probably is an important difference in the perceived costs of ozone depletion in DCs as compared to ICs. This difference exists, because the distribution of damages is biased against ICs, which are generally located closer to the poles than the great majority of DCs, and because richer countries have a higher valuation of such damages. This view is supported by the observation that rich northern and southernmost countries, particularly Canada, Norway, Finland, Australia and New Zealand, have fought vigorously for a strong ozone treaty [Benedick (1991:7)].[12]

3. THE MONTREAL PROTOCOL

In March 1985, the Vienna Convention for the Protection of the Ozone Layer was signed; later in spring of the same year, the ozone hole over Antarctica

---

[12]   The noted imbalance may be set off to some extent by the global warming effect of most ozone depleting substances, since global warming may affect DCs more severely than most ICs. However, some recent research indicates that ozone depletion may reduce warming. The regional costs of global warming are still uncertain and ignored in this paper.

was discovered [Farman et al. (1985)]. In the Vienna Convention, which is in force since August 1988, a great number of nations agreed on the principle objective to "protect human health and the environment against adverse effects resulting from modifications of the ozone layer".[13] In particular, Parties agreed to cooperate as is relevant for reaching the purpose of the Convention. Cooperation covers research, the formulation and implementation of measures, particularly the development of a protocol to the Convention, and exchange of information and the development and transfer of technologies and knowledge.

Based on the Vienna Convention, and after growing scientific evidence that a serious threat to the ozone layer and the earth exists, the Montreal Protocol (MP) was adopted in September 1987 and came into force in January 1989.[14] The Protocol imposed a time table for the phase-down of consumption of CFCs (50% by the year 2000) and a freeze of halons. Already in June 1990, in London, the Parties to the MP agreed on adjustments and amendments to the MP. Existing controls were tightened and more ozone depleting substances were included. Provisions for a complete phase-out of CFCs (by the year 2000), halons and some other ozone depleting substances were introduced. In November 1992, in Copenhagen, the Parties decided to phase out the production of CFCs already by the end of 1995 (as had earlier been announced by the USA and the EC) and to stop the production of halons by the end of 1993.[15] The Parties also adopted new or stricter phase-down provisions for other compounds. In reaction to the Copenhagen decision, the EC moved its own CFC-phase-out deadline forward to the end of 1994.[16]

Apart from the principle obligations to reduce CFCs and related substances, the MP shows two important features. First, it contains a great number of concessions for DCs including a grace period and financial transfers. Second, it provides for trade restrictions against non-members. Both features are designed to induce newly industrialised countries and DCs to accept the MP, and to defend the Protocol against free-riding. Of some importance for strengthening and adjusting the MP is the regular revision process concerning controlled substances. Here, decisions by a two-third majority vote are possible. Weakly developed are monitoring procedures. Monitoring relies entirely

---

[13]   The Vienna Convention and the Montreal Protocol with its amendments and adjustments are reprinted in Rummel-Bulska and Osafo (1991).

[14]   The story of negotiating the MP is told in a remarkable way by US diplomat Richard Benedick (1991).

[15]   "Bush verfügt Produktionsverbot für FCKW bis 1995", Frankfurter Allgemeine Zeitung, 13 February 1992. M. Simons, "Ozone Peril is Shocking Europeans into Action", International Harald Tribune, 4 March 1992. "Schon ab 1996 Verzicht auf schädliche FCKW", Nachrichten für Außenhandel, Eschborn, 2 December 1992.

[16]   "Umweltminister beschließen schärfere Abgaswerte ...", Handelsblatt, 17 December 1992.

on national control and self-reporting.[17] Non-compliance procedures were introduced at the Copenhagen meeting in November 1992. They mainly consist of procedural rules. But non-compliance reports shall be made available to any person upon request. And, apart from rendering appropriate assistance, Parties may decide upon and call for steps to bring about full compliance.

For the purpose of this paper, it is of particular interest to note how the MP treats DCs that operate under its Article 5.[18] As was pointed out above, DCs are probably less affected by ozone depletion and hence may be less interested in an agreement on CFC control than ICs. DCs may therefore behave opportunistically, and, in order to win their permanent cooperation, ICs must advance the MP and entice DCs to participate. This is possible, in principle, by side payments and other concessions and by calling for sanctions against non-Parties and non-compliant Parties (carrot and stick approach) [Somerset (1989)].

3.1   Trade restrictions

Trade restrictions in the MP ban imports of CFCs and other controlled substances from non-Parties (beginning January 1990) and exports to non-Parties (beginning January 1993). They also comprise im- and export restrictions for products that contain, or are produced with, controlled substances and include technologies, products, equipment etc. for producing controlled substances.

Newly industrialised export-oriented countries and DCs that are unable to produce CFCs themselves would be hit particularly hard by the MP's trade restrictions. The Republic of Korea is an example: Korea acceded to the Vienna Convention and the MP only in reaction to the threat of trade restrictions.[19] A similar example is Taiwan, which is reported to suffer an estimated loss in exports of between 100 and 200 New Taiwan \$ (ca. 6.5 - 13 million DM) if the trade restrictions of the MP came into effect.[20]

The MP does not explicitly extend those trade restrictions to Parties found in non-compliance. However, the Copenhagen meeting of the Parties has produced an indicative list of possible measures against countries found in non-

---

[17]   For difficulties with reporting and monitoring see Benedick (1991:179f).

[18]   Article-5-countries are developing countries (UN definition) with a calculated consumption of controlled substances of less than 0.3 kilograms per capita. Only very few newly industrialised or oil exporting countries do not fall under Article 5. For the sake of brevity, Article-5-countries are collectively referred to as DCs in this paper.

[19]   "Korea schließt sich Ozonschutz an", Nachrichten für Außenhandel, Eschborn, 6 March 1992.

[20]   "Ozonloch schafft auch in Taiwan Bewegung", Nachrichten für Außenhandel, Eschborn, 3 March 1992. Taiwan has not signed the MP for diplomatic reasons, but countries that fulfil the MP's obligations are treated like Parties.

compliance. These measures include the suspension of specific rights and privileges under the MP, which permits to use the trade restrictions of the MP against a defector.[21]

3.2 · Concessions concerning DCs

The following special concessions for DCs are contained in the MP.

- *Grace period*: DCs that consume less than 0.3 kg of CFCs and halons (Annex-A-substances) per capita enjoy a grace period of 10 years. They may delay reductions until after 1 July 1999, and then obligations are based on the 1995-97 average consumption level or 0.3 kg per capita if lower.[22] The figure of 0.3 kg may seem small compared with a per capita consumption of 0.85 kg in the USA (1984/85). It is, however, very large when measured against the actual consumption level in many DCs (e.g., China: 0.02 kg in 1984/85) and when considering the large population of some of these countries. Even within the bounds of the MP, DCs have theoretically the potential to offset the reduction efforts of all ICs. The MP may induce DCs to step up their production in order to reach the highest possible base year level and to build up a stock of CFCs for recycling after controls have become obligatory.[23]
- *Technology transfer*: Parties agreed to take every practical step to "ensure that the best available, environmentally safe substitutes and related technologies are expeditiously transferred" to DCs "under fair and most favourable conditions" (London revision). ICs did not accept an outright obligation to transfer technologies for reasons of intellectual property rights policy.
- *Multilateral Fund*: Parties agreed to establish a financial mechanism, including a Multilateral Fund, for the implementation of the MP in DCs.[24] The Fund is financed by contributions from ICs and managed by the Parties jointly.[25] The financial mechanism shall meet all agreed incremental

---

21   On the possible application of trade restrictions against non-Parties to Parties found in non-compliance see also Sorensen (1988).

22   For Annex-B-substances (London amendment) the level is 0.2 kg per capita.

23   Recycling is not covered by the MP. It does not add to production neither to consumption figures and is in fact encouraged.

24   An Interim Multilateral Fund was established as part of the London Revisions (London Revisions of the MP, Annex IV, Appendix IV, cf. Benedick 1991:259f). The Fund was re-affirmed and permanently established as the Multilateral Fund by the Copenhagen meeting.

25   Some 50 per cent of the Fund's revenues is covered by contributions from only three countries: Germany (10,66%), Japan (14,87%) and the USA (25%), see: Forth Meeting of the Parties to the MP, Draft Decisions, Annex XIV, Nov.92, UNEP/OzL.Pro.4/L.1/Rev.2. The Fund is operated by the World

costs in DCs.[26] For the first three years, the Fund was set to US $160 million plus 80 million if more countries (notably India and China) joined.[27]

- *Non-compliance*: DCs may notify the secretariat that, having taken all practical steps themselves, assistance remains inadequate to fulfil the obligation to control ozone depleting substances. The Parties then consider the case and decide on appropriate remedial actions. Until a decision, no non-compliance procedure shall be invoked on the notifying Party.
- *Revision*: No later than 1995, the situation of DCs, including the effective implementation of financial and technological assistance, shall be reviewed by the Parties and any necessary adjustments concerning the time schedule of control measures applicable to DCs shall be adopted.

3.3   Compliance in the long-run

The MP has achieved nearly worldwide cooperation and has successfully imposed strict environmental obligations in a prisoners-dilemma-like situation characterised by free-riding incentives and important differences in the Parties' national interests. One may therefore wonder how it was possible to induce so many countries (including China and India) to sign the MP.

The prospects for side payments and the promise of ICs to pay the incremental costs of DCs may have played a role. Incremental cost funding leaves DCs at least not worse off than without the MP. But DCs have a relatively strong bargaining position. Since ozone depletion is felt more in industrial countries, DCs could have demanded higher side payments. But ICs were able to restrict payments to incremental costs. Hence, it seems that DCs were unable to exploit their bargaining power. The threat of trade restrictions may have helped to limit payments to DCs. Another explanation may be found in the concessions, especially the ten-year grace period, which render the implementation of the MP in DCs more flexible.

The particular design of the MP gives rise to questioning its long-run stability. It is not clear whether all Parties will comply with and adhere to the MP or whether a breach is likely to occur in the future. Permanent compliance with the MP by an opportunistic country can only be expected if, for each and all future periods, the discounted gains from compliance exceed those from

---

Bank. It pays for country studies, capacity building and CFC reduction project undertaken by DCs voluntarily.

[26] Incremental costs are those costs of a project that exceed the costs of an alternative project that a country would implement in its self-interest.

[27] India, for instance, has claimed substantial compensation before joining. See, "Wider die Öko-Kolonialisten: Wie man in Indien über den Erd-Gipfel denkt", Frankfurter Rundschau, 13 February 1992.

breaching the MP. Compliance by DCs is likely as long as the grace period is in effect, since for that period control obligations are weak and do not seriously conflict with growth expectations in DCs. In the grace period the incremental costs in DCs for merely complying will the MP are relatively low so that large transfers to DCs are not required.

This, however, may be different when ICs have irreversibly stopped their CFC consumption and phasing-out in DCs, who may have stepped up CFC production by that time, is to begin. Reciprocity in CFC reductions, which is already weak due to the smaller ozone depletion and radiation effect in most DCs, can no longer be employed to strengthen compliance. Rising incremental costs may be difficult to cover by the Multilateral Fund and disputes between Parties over funding may arise.[28] In this situation, DCs may have an incentive to disregard the MP. They may simply fail to fulfil their reduction obligations, tacitly or openly. Moreover, it is conceivable that with further ozone depletion over ICs' territory DCs discover their bargaining power and, in return for compliance, demand transfers from ICs substantially higher than incremental costs.[29]

It therefore seems that the concessions to DCs have burdened the MP with a serious time inconsistency. Moreover, the gains from saving the ozone layer seem to be unevenly distributed between ICs and DCs, which may not be acceptable in the long-run. These observations cast some doubt on the eventual stability and effectiveness of the MP. Whether trade sanctions will be used in cases of non-compliance and whether this would be sufficient to guarantee long-run compliance, particularly by countries with a large internal market, remains an open question.[30]

The remainder of this paper is a stylised analysis of the MP, which investigates some features of the MP in a formal framework. The analysis treats non-Parties and non-compliant Parties alike. It assumes that the ozone game is played by two homogeneous groups of countries, namely ICs who advance the MP and opportunistic DCs. Section 4 analyses the MP as a one-shot game with two players. It shows that the threat of sanctions is not suitable for achieving agreement and compliance. This Section compares the outcome of the non-cooperative ozone game with the solution of a hypothetical cooperative Nash bargaining game of identical structure. Section 5 extends the analysis to a game with many DC-players who face a coalition of ICs indi-

---

[28] Already during the Copenhagen meeting, DCs criticised ICs for hesitating to make agreed upon funds available to the Multilateral Fund (UNEP/OzL. Pro4/L.2, 24 Nov. 92). See also "Sehr hohe Beitragsrückstände: Sieben EG-Staaten schulden Ozonschicht-Fond Geld", Nachrichten für Außenhandel, Eschborn, 16 December 1992.

[29] In this context, it is interesting to note that the Multilateral Fund was only established at the London Meeting of the Parties upon pressure from DCs who were already members of the MP. See Markandya (1991:7).

[30] On the question of compliance see also Enders and Porges (1992).

vidually. This Section studies the willingness of DCs to accede to and comply with the MP in a multi-player setting when non-Parties and defecting Parties face the threat of trade sanctions. Section 6 models the MP as a two-period ozone game with two players. It derives strict conditionality between transfer payments and irreversible CFC reductions as an important condition for the stability of the MP. Section 7 concludes the paper by discussing whether the MP can be expected to be stable in the long-run.

4.   THE TWO-PLAYERS ONE-SHOT OZONE GAME

I assume that binding commitments are not possible in the ozone game as described in the Sections 4.1, 5 and 6. Hence, I apply non-cooperative game theory and the subgame perfect Nash equilibrium as the relevant solution concept. The leading question in those Sections is under which conditions cooperation will emerge and will be stable. If the stabilisation of cooperation proves feasible, it seems possible that the non-cooperative ozone game mutates into a cooperative game, in which the distribution of the gains from cooperation between the partners is the relevant issue. This question will briefly be dealt with in Sections 4.2 by applying the cooperative Nash bargaining concept.

The following model is simplistic. It assumes that the direct gains from CFC reductions (U) can only be realised in full cooperation between ICs (player A) and DCs (player B). The notion behind this assumption is that, in the long-run, the ozone layer can be destroyed by either group's emissions, since either group is individually capable of pushing the accumulated quantity of ozone depleting substances in the atmosphere beyond the relevant threshold. Moreover, the model assumes that all direct gains from cooperation accrue only to ICs ($U = U_A$), which reflects the much smaller expected damage in DCs. The assumption allows to isolate the effects of side payments and sanctions and study them more conveniently. The model is completed by the costs of reducing CFCs for both players (C_A, C_B), by side payments, T, to DCs, and by A's costs of imposing sanctions (S_A) and their impact on B (S_B).

4.1   Conditions of cooperation

The scenario described above is captured by the game *Ozone I*. The payoff matrix in Table 1 shows the gains from stopping CFC emissions and the relevant costs for both players and for each strategy combination.

Table 1:   *Ozone I: Payoff matrix, base case*

		Strategies Player B	
		phase-out	*emit*
Strategies *phase-out*		$(U_A - C_A ; -C_B)$	$(-C_A ; 0)$
Player A *emit*		$(0 ; -C_B)$	$(0 ; 0)$

The payoffs in *Ozone I* are calibrated against the status-quo situation (no MP) in which each player maximises his/her own utility function without respect to the other player's utility. Hence, phase-out costs C_A and C_B are incremental costs in the language of the MP. In the non-cooperative outcome (*emit*; *emit*) both players have utility zero. If both players A and B choose *phase-out*, they have to face costs C_A or C_B respectively, and player A gains utility U_A ($U_A > C_A$) whereas B gains nothing but is left with her costs C_B.[31] Hence, cooperation is not a feasible solution. To continue emissions is always the dominant strategy for B, even if A could commit himself to playing *phase-out*. Since the strategy combination (*phase-out*; *emit*) would leave A with a real loss, A plays *emit* as well. The outcome of *Ozone I* is the non-cooperative (*emit*; *emit*).

The cooperative solution can only be reached if player A is able, and willing, to alter the payoff matrix. He can do so by raising the costs of continued emissions for B through imposing sanctions with impact S_B on B and costs S_A for himself, and/or by making side-payments T to B that give B a positive payoff from cooperation. The adjusted payoff matrix for the game *Ozone II* is shown in Table 2.

Table 2:   *Ozone II: Payoff matrix with side payments and sanction*

		Strategies Player B	
		phase-out	*emit*
Strategies *phase-out*		$(U_A - C_A - T ; T - C_B)$	$(-C_A - S_A ; -S_B)$
Player A *emit*		$(0 ; -C_B)$	$(0 ; 0)$

Ozone II assumes that sanctions will only be imposed if A phases out and B emits and that transfers are only paid if both players phase out. Depending on

---

31   To assume a cooperative utility gain U_B for B, too, would not alter the results qualitatively as long as $U_B < C_B$.

the severity of sanctions and/or on the amount of transfers, *Ozone II* may have a cooperative outcome. On first sight, this is the case if the following conditions hold:[32]

A:
$$U_A - C_A - T \geq 0 \qquad\qquad (1)$$

B:
$$T - C_B \geq -S_B \qquad\qquad (2)$$

Inequality (2) is the participation condition for B, who will only cooperate if the impact of sanctions S_B is not more costly than her costs of phasing out minus received transfers. Since sanctions will only be imposed by A if A plays *phase-out*, B's decision is subject to A's rationality constraint in (1), namely that A's total gains are not negative.

If A could commit himself to imposing sanctions on B despite his potential loss, *Ozone II* would have two Nash equilibria: (*phase-out*; *phase-out*) and (*emit*; *emit*). But being sovereign, A cannot credibly commit himself to punishing B, because executing sanctions would hurt A more than simply playing *emit* as well. The threat of sanctions is therefore not credible. Since both players know that sanctions are an ineffective threat, the non-cooperative outcome (*emit*; *emit*) remains the only Nash equilibrium. A different outcome is only possible if (2) is replaced by (3).

B:
$$T - C_B \geq 0 \quad \text{or} \quad T \geq -C_B \qquad\qquad (3)$$

In this case, in which A pays at least B's costs, B's payoff from cooperation is non-negative and the cooperative Nash equilibrium is at least as good for both players as the non-cooperative one. Hence, A can safely play *phase-out*, since (3) ensures that B will play *phase-out*, too. Condition (3) reflects the fact that in *Ozone II* sanctions are not credible and thus have no effect.[33] Therefore, to achieve cooperation, A must adopt a transfer scheme that satisfies (3) and (1). Hence, only for those transfers for which $U_A - C_A \geq T \geq C_B$ holds will the cooperative Nash equilibrium result.

The result of this Section can be summarised as follows: In a one-shot ozone game with two sovereign players, sanctions are not credible and ineffective. The transfers necessary to lure a coalition of opportunistic countries into cooperation are independent of announcing sanctions to be imposed in case of non-cooperation. Transfers must in any case be selected in such a way that both players receive a non-negative payoff from cooperation.

---

[32] I assume that players behave sympathetically: if a player is indifferent between two alternatives, he chooses the cooperative alternative.

[33] Sanctions may, however, have an effect in a repeated game with alternating moves. See Eaton and Engers (1992).

4.2   The cooperative Nash bargaining solution

The above result describes the lower bound for transfers that guarantee a cooperative solution. This lower bound is, however, not necessarily the outcome of a bargaining game between A and B over the amount of transfers that are acceptable for both players in a situation of cooperation. If cooperation can be made certain by paying transfers, cooperative bargaining theory may provide the relevant solution concept for predicting the distribution of the total gains from cooperation.

Strategic bargaining between A and B over sharing net gains can be modelled by Rubinstein's (1982) strategic bargaining approach of alternating offers over infinite time, in which players' shares depend on the difference in their time preferences (or other bargaining costs). If players' time preferences are equal, Rubinstein's model yields a symmetric equal-split outcome (safe of a small first mover advantage). An equal-split outcome can be reproduced by the axiomatic Nash bargaining solution, which I employ here as a benchmark. The simple Nash bargaining solution distributes the gains from cooperation minus the conflict payoffs to both players in equal shares.[34] Formally, the Nash bargaining solution is a joint maximisation problem of the form $(u_1{}^* - c_1)(u_2{}^* - c_2) = \max (u_1 - c_1)(u_2 - c_2)$, in which u_i is the utility of cooperation and c_i the utility of non-cooperation (conflict payoff) for both players $i = 1,2$ and Σu_i is constant. $u_i{}^*$ is the redistributed utility.

In our case, $c_i = 0$ for A and B, since sanctions are not a credible threat against B and therefore the non-cooperative strategy combination (*emit*; *emit*) yields 0 for both players. Maximising (4) with respect to T produces the Nash-transfers T^* in (5).

$$\max_{T}: \left(U_A - C_A - T\right)\left(T - C_B\right) \tag{4}$$

$$T^* = \frac{1}{2}\left(U_A - C_A + C_B\right) = C_B + \frac{1}{2}\left[U_A - \left(C_A + C_B\right)\right] \tag{5}$$

The result (5) shows that A pays B's costs of phasing out CFCs and transfers half of his total net gains from saving the ozone layer to B: the net gains from cooperation are shared equally between both players.

---

[34] The Nash bargaining solution applied here assumes that the bargaining power of both players is equal. Asymmetries in preferences, disagreement points, the bargaining procedure and in players' beliefs about their environment can be captured in the construction of the relevant threat points. Asymmetries in players' time preferences can be captured when using the asymmetric generalised Nash solution of the form $(u_1 - c_1)^{\varepsilon} (u_2 - c_2)^{(1-\varepsilon)}$, $0 \leq \varepsilon \leq 1$. See Binmore et al. (1986:186).

4.3   Plausibility of the Nash bargaining result

The above Nash bargaining result seems to contradict the limitation of transfers in the MP to incremental costs (C_B), which, in the model world of *Ozone II*, denies DCs any profit from cooperation. However, most DCs have signed the MP and have agreed to its adjustments and amendments. If the assumption is correct that DCs have considerable bargaining power in the ozone game there must be other explanations for this outcome. Such explanations may include: (a) The direct returns from cooperation for ICs (U_A) may be very small. (b) There may be large returns from reducing CFCs cooperatively in DCs as well ($U_B > 0$). (c) There may be tacit side payments. (d) The above result that sanctions are irrelevant may not apply. (e) The approach of a one-shot game with two players may be too simplistic to describe the problem adequately. The following paragraphs examine those explanation.

It seems that prospective gains from cooperation can become very large. Several countries have conducted extensive studies on the costs and benefits of phasing out CFCs. Such studies are subject to great ecological and economic uncertainties. In particular, the valuation of health effects and the applied social discount rate heavily affect the results [UNEP (1989), chapter 5.4]. Nevertheless, they are intuitive with respect to the magnitude of net benefits. A US EPA (1988) study suggests that, under a wide range of alternative assumptions, the benefits of phasing out CFCs worldwide outweigh the possible costs by far. A typical example is given in Table 3. A similar result is presented by Smith and Vodden (1989), who assess the costs and benefits of the MP for Canada (Table 4). The reported total gains are impressive. However, the data do not permit to derive the value of cooperation between ICs and DCs, which is the incremental benefit of adding DCs to the ozone coalition.

Table 3:   *Costs and benefits of CFC reductions through 2075 by scenario, United States only, in billions of 1985 dollars* [US EPA
(1988) Segment of Exhibits 10-9. Reproduced from UNEP
(1989:41)]

Scenario[a]	Health and envi- ronmental benefits	Costs	Net benefits	Net incremental benefits[b]
CFC Freeze	3314	7	3307	3307
CFC 20% Cut	3396	12	3384	77
CFC 50% Cut	3488	13	3475	91
CFC 80% Cut	3553	22	3531	56

[a]See Regulatory Impact Analysis (US EPA 1988) for assumptions and definitions of scenarios. Estimates assume a 2 % discount rate and $3 million per unit mortality risk reduction. All dollar values in the Table reflect the difference between the No Controls scenario and the specified alternative scenario. Valuation of health and environmental benefits applies only to people born before 2075; costs are estimated through 2075. [b]Changes in net incremental benefits represent movement to the indicated scenario from the scenario listed above it.

Table 4:   *Net present value (NPV) of implementing the Montreal
Protocol under various assumptions, Canada only, in
million dollars* [Smith and Vodden (1989:420)]

Scenario	Benefits	Costs	NPV
Base case[a]	3237	194	3043
High social discount rate[b]	995	196	799
Low value of life[c]	939	194	745
Low social discount, low value of life[d]	28766	1415	27361
Low value of life, slow industry response[e]	939	292	647

[a]Assumes 7.5% social discount rate, 8.0% private discount rate, and value of life of $10 million. [b]Assumes 10% social discount rate, 10% private discount rate, and value of life of $10 million. [c]Assumes 7.5% social discount rate, 8.0% private discount rate, and value of life of $2.8 million. [d]Assumes 2.0% social discount rate, 6.0% private discount rate, and value of life of $2.8 million. [e]Assumes 7.5% social discount rate, 8.0% private discount rate, and value of life of $2.8 million and slow response by all industries other than the aerosol industry.

Barrett (1989, 1991) suggests that the benefits of cooperation between all countries are relatively small. He argues that the signatories have not committed themselves to making more reductions than is in their national interest, i.e. U_A is small. Hence, according to Barrett, the MP was easy to sign. This assessment appears to hold even more in the case of cooperation between the coalitions of ICs and DCs, since DCs presently have a small share of worldwide production capacity for, and consumption of, ozone depleting substances. However, what is relevant for our analysis is the potential future production capacity of DCs under conditions of economic development unimpeded by any ozone treaty. Lack of technology is no hurdle. CFCs are relatively easy to produce [Benedick (1991:4)]. The U.S. Office of Technology Assessment (1989:295) estimates that the consumption of CFC-11 and CFC-12 in DCs could, by 2009, reach the 1986 level of 660 metric tonnes in ICs.[35] Mintzer (1989:20) estimates that, if only China, India, Indonesia, and Brazil increased their domestic consumption of CFCs to the level of 0.3 kilograms per capita by 1995, which would be allowed by the MP, global production and use of controlled substances would approximately double from the 1986 level. Hence, the impression seems justified that cooperation with DCs is needed, since the gains from cooperation (U_A) can become large in the future relative to a situation without any ozone treaty.

Another question is whether DCs will have returns from cooperation other than side payments, i.e. $U_B > 0$. I have argued above that the damage in DCs caused by ozone depletion is substantially smaller than in ICs and that large benefits for DCs would not exist or would not be reflected in the political process. Gains from cooperation may nevertheless exist in DCs. However, the difference between the perceived benefits U_A and U_B prompts the magnitude of side payments. If this difference is large, high Nash-transfers are an inevitable result of the cooperative Nash bargaining game. The ecological uncertainty of ozone depletion is substantial, which may in fact have led many DCs to cooperate without demanding more than coverage of incremental costs.

The Parties may have linked the ozone treaty to other issues of international relations. This increases the complexity of the game and permits side payments that can pass undiscovered by the public. Such out-of-treaty side payments are often non-monetary, which is an important advantage in diplomatic negotiations and international relations. They may even come as tacit agreements on completely different issues.[36] However, the larger the number of participants in a multilateral treaty is the less likely are out-of-treaty side payments between the parties. A reason for this is that an equal and clearly observable treatment of all parties to a treaty is an important prerequisite for

---

35   OTA's estimates seem particularly plausible with a view to the huge need for refrigeration in most of these countries. According to press reports, new CFC production facilities were under construction in China and India. See "Ozonkiller FCKW noch bis Ende 1994", Süddeutsche Zeitung, 15/16 February 1992. Compare also "Wider die Öko-Kolonialisten: Wie man in Indien über den Erd-Gipfel denkt", Frankfurter Rundschau, 13 February 1992, and Simonis and von Weizsäcker (1990:4,6).

36   Examples are the International Columbia River Treaty between Canada and the U.S. [Krutilla (1966)] and the Colorado River Treaty between Mexico and the U.S.

broad agreement. In the ozone case, DCs may hope for more development aid or may believe that the technology transfers agreed in the MP will pave the way to additional export earnings and beneficial cooperation in other fields. However, these motivations must remain largely speculative. It seems that the information at hand on benefits and tacit side payments does not provide sufficient evidence for a different result.

Section 4.1 concluded that transfer payments are independent of the threat of sanctions. Intuition and evidence do not support this result.[37] The *Ozone II* game may not be correctly specified. *Ozone II* is a one-shot game with two players. It reflects a bilateral monopoly with ICs, who demand ozone protection, on the one side and DCs, who supply this service against payment, on the other side. A bilateral monopoly model is, however, unlikely to reflect the reality of the ozone world correctly. It may be justified to treat ICs as a cartel for issues that affect them jointly vis à vis DCs. But it is probably misleading to assume that DCs act as a cartel, too. Instead, it is more plausible that they face the block of ICs one by one. Hence, the situation could rather be characterised as a monopsony. In a monopsony situation, the bargaining power of DCs is much reduced. They may be more susceptible to pressure and to the threat of sanctions, because isolation, i.e. the non-existence of a DC-coalition, enhances the impact of sanctions on the isolated country and reduces the cost of imposing sanctions. Section 5 investigates this approach.

Another complication arises from the fact that the ozone game is not a one-shot game as was assumed above. As a one-shot game, *Ozone II* describes a long-run result, not a development. Contrary to the ineffectiveness of sanctions as noted above, the trade restrictions in the MP may indeed have a short-run effect. ICs are probably not capable of building up their own CFC production rapidly. Therefore, CFC trade restrictions may, at least temporarily, reduce DCs' consumption of CFCs. Since reduced CFC consumption in DCs benefits the ozone layer and thereby ICs, trade restrictions may not necessarily imply net costs for ICs. Hence, the trade restrictions in the MP may be a credible threat initially. In the long-run, however, their stabilising effect may wear out with the installation of large-scale CFC production capacities in DCs to supply their domestic market. In addition, these capacities can be used strategically as an instrument of pressure in future negotiations over the MP and over ICs' side payments.[38] The ozone game, represented by the Vienna Convention and the MP, is a repeated game with quite a number of provisions for renegotiations. But the players' set of strategies is even larger. It comprises numerous out-of-treaty options over time reaching from hidden violations to an open breach of the ozone treaty. These strategic options are discussed in Section 6.

---

[37]   Compare the behaviour of some newly industrialised countries (Korea, Taiwan) reported in Section 3.1.

[38]   Compare, e.g., "Die Ozon-Locher kommen bald aus Indien", Frankfurter Rundschau, 23 February 1993.

5. THE MULTI-PLAYERS ONE-SHOT OZONE GAME

This Section models an ozone game in which a cartel of ICs (player A) faces each DC (player b) individually. Player A is determined to ensure full cooperation at minimum costs. A's strategic parameters are transfers T and sanctions $S(\Gamma)$, with Γ denoting the intensity of sanctions.

5.1 The model

Player A must be prepared to deal with a group of non-cooperative players, B^-, and a group of cooperative players, B^+, which together form the group B. The absolute size of each group A, B, B^-, B^+ is measured in terms of each group's GDP, i.e. Y_A, Y_B, Y_B^-, Y_B^+.[39] k denotes the degree of cooperation: $k = Y_B^+/Y_B$ ($0 \leq k \leq 1$) measures the relative size of B^+, $(1 - k) = Y_B^-/Y_B$ measures the relative size of B^-.[40] B consists of arbitrarily many identical members b_i of size Y_{bi} ($\Sigma Y_{bi} = Y_B$). Player b of size Y_b is one representative, arbitrarily small member of B. b plays the game against A and decides whether to cooperate or not.[41] Table 5 shows the payoffs in the game *Ozone III*.

A's *phase-out* payoff function is $kU_A - C_A - kT - S_A^+$ no matter whether b plays cooperatively or not. It reflects A's costs of possible sanctions (S_A^+) against the non-cooperative players in B^-. Moreover, the existence of B^--players leads to a decline in A's utility from cooperation, hence kU_A,-but it also reduces A's transfer bill, hence kT instead of T under full cooperation ($k = 1$). A's strategy and payoff function is independent of the particular strategy of any particular b_i, but it depends on the number of cooperative versus non-cooperative members in B, i.e. on k.

Table 5:   *Ozone III: Payoff matrix in the multi-players game*

Strategies Player A	Strategies Player b	
	phase-out	*emit*
phase-out	$\left(kU_A - C_A - kT - S_A^+ ; (t_b - c_b)Y_b - s_b^+\right)$ $\left(kU_A - C_A - kT - S_A^+ ; - s_b^-\right)$	
emit	$(0 ; -c_b Y_b)$	$(0 ; 0)$

---

[39]   GDP is used as a proxy for a country's reliance on CFCs. Compare Section 1.

[40]   For a different approach that involves fixing a minimum participation level k in order to build large cooperating coalitions and counter free riding see Black, Levi and de Meza (1993).

[41]   The assumption that all players in B are identical entails that b's participation decision coincides with the participation decision of all other players in B. The assumption is relaxed later.

Player b's cooperative payoff is $(t_b - c_b)Y_b - s_b^+$, her non-cooperative payoff is $-s_b^-$.[42] If b plays cooperatively, she faces costs c_b ($= C_B/Y_B$) and receives transfers t_b ($= T/Y_B$) both weighted with b's size Y_b. But in addition, b must take into account that she has to share the costs of sanctions against (possible) B^--members (s_b^+) if she signs the phase-out treaty. If b does not sign, she must face the impact of sanctions imposed on herself (s_b^-).

Hence, there are two conditions for a stable cooperative solution. A's payoff must be positive (6) and b's payoff from cooperation must be larger or equal to his payoff from non-cooperation (7). If only one of both conditions is not met, cooperation is impossible.

A: $\qquad kU_A - C_A - kT - S_A^+ \geq 0$ $\hfill$ (6)

b: $\qquad (t_b - c_b)Y_b - s_b^+ \geq -s_b^-$ $\hfill$ (7)

The model is completed by specifying the costs and the impact of sanctions for each type of player. The specification is simplified, but it captures the basic notion pursued in this paper.

A: $\qquad S_A^+ = \Gamma\gamma(1-k)Y_A$ $\hfill$ (8)

b^+: $\qquad S_b^+ = \Gamma\alpha(1-k)Y_b \qquad\qquad$ for $k > 0$ $\hfill$ (9)

$\qquad\qquad = 0 \qquad\qquad\qquad\qquad$ for $k = 0$

b^-: $\qquad S_b^- = \Gamma\left[\delta + \beta\left(k - \dfrac{Y_b}{Y_B}\right)\right]Y_b \qquad k > 0$ $\hfill$ (10)

$\qquad\qquad = \Gamma\delta Y_b \qquad\qquad\qquad$ for $k = 0$

(8) - (10) reflect that the cost and impact of sanctions for all types of players depend on the intensity of sanctions Γ, on the share of cooperative versus non-cooperative b-players k, on the players' size Y_A and Y_b and on the cost or impact parameters characteristic for each type of player. γ and α measure the basic costs for A and for the cooperative b^+-player of imposing sanctions, and δ and β measure the basic impact of A's and b^+'s sanctions on the non-cooperative b^--player. ($0 \leq \Gamma, \gamma, \alpha, \delta + \beta \leq 1$)

The costs of sanctions S_A^+ and s_b^+ are zero in the case of full cooperation ($k = 1$). They increase with falling cooperation ($k \to 0$) up to a maximum that depends on Γ and on γ or α respectively. s_b^+ jumps to zero again in the case of zero cooperation ($k = 0$), since in this case B^+ is an empty set. The impact of sanctions s_b^- is $\Gamma\delta Y_b$ in the case if zero cooperation, since this share of the

---

[42]   Player b's payoff may be supplemented by a utility gain if A plus a number of b-players phase out. But this would hardly affect our results, since most of the effect cancels out in (7) and is zero for a marginal b-player.

burden can be inflicted on b^- by A alone. In the case of partial cooperation ($k > 0$), b^- suffers an additional impact that the cooperative b^+-players inflict on her. But k decreases when b defects. Therefore, in comparing cooperation with defection in (7), the relevant degree of cooperation for specifying s_b^- in (10) is $k' = (Y_B^+ - Y_b)/Y_B = k - Y_b/Y_B$. When full cooperation is reached ($k = 1$), sanctions imposed on a defecting marginal b-player ($Y_b \to 0$) have maximum impact. (See figure 3 for s_b^+ and s_b^-.)

5.2   Minimum participation

For both players A and b, the value of k is critical in choosing a strategy: cooperation must be large enough to render the proposed scheme profitable for A and to induce b to participate in it. I deal with b's participation constraint first. Inserting (9) and (10) into (7) yields (11), which can be solved for k to derive the critical value k_b^* (12).

$$b: \qquad (t_b - c_b)Y_b - \Gamma\alpha(1-k)Y_b + \Gamma\left[\delta + \beta\left(k - \frac{Y_b}{Y_B}\right)Y_b\right] \geq 0 \qquad (11)$$

$$k_b^* = \frac{c_b - t_b + (\alpha - \delta)\Gamma + \beta\Gamma\dfrac{Y_b}{Y_B}}{(\alpha + \beta)\Gamma} \qquad\qquad \big|\ \Gamma \neq 0 \qquad (12)$$

$$= \frac{c_b - t_b}{(\alpha + \beta)\Gamma} + \frac{\alpha - \delta}{\alpha + \beta} + \frac{\beta}{\alpha + \beta}\frac{Y_b}{Y_B}$$

k_b^* is the minimum level of participation for any player b. Effective participation at or beyond k_b^* guarantees that b cooperates. The last term of (12) reflects the fact that defection reduces cooperation and thus the impact of sanctions on the defector. k_b^* increases in player's size, but the term's influence is normally very small and disappears for marginal b-players ($Y_b \to 0$). Assuming that A has fixed his transfers to incremental costs ($t_b = c_b$), (12) simplifies further to $k_b^* = (\alpha - \delta)/(\alpha + \beta)$ and the minimum participation level depends solely on b's cost and impact parameters, since the intensity of sanctions cancels out. Hence, in this case, the intensity of sanctions does not influence b's decision. If A is able to threaten b with credible sanctions such that $\delta \geq \alpha$, then k_b^* is set to zero and b always cooperates. But if $\delta < \alpha$, it is only rational for b to cooperate if a sufficiently large number of b-players does likewise so that at least k_b^* is reached (Figure 3). If incremental costs are not covered by A, it is obvious from (12) that reducing transfers below incremental costs increases the minimum participation level and vice versa.

Moreover, in this case, the intensity of sanctions comes into play in that the less severe sanctions are (Γ small) the more $k_b{}^*$ increases (for $t_b < c_b$) or decreases (for $t_b > c_b$).

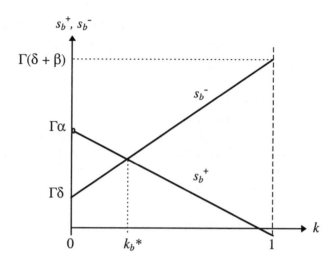

Figure 3:   *Minimum participation level for b ($t_b = c_b$, $Y_b \rightarrow 0$).*

Successful cooperation between A and b requires that A's rationality condition (6) holds, too, because otherwise A's threat of sanctions against outsiders is not credible. Inserting (8) into (6) and solving for k yields A's minimum participation level $k_A{}^*$.

$$A: \qquad k_A^* = \frac{C_A + \Gamma\gamma Y_A}{U_A - T + \Gamma\gamma Y_A} \qquad (13)$$

$\Gamma\gamma Y_A$ reflects the influence of the costs of sanctions on $k_A{}^*$. If sanctions are not used ($\Gamma = 0$) or are costless for A ($\gamma = 0$), then $k_A{}^*$ depends solely on U_A and on the associated costs C_A and T. $k_A{}^*$ is necessarily larger than zero, even without costs of sanctions, since only a minimum level of cooperation gives A sufficient utility (kU_A) to cover his costs C_A and the associated transfers kT. With increasing costs of sanctions, $k_A{}^*$ increases quickly, surpasses $k_b{}^*$, and becomes the overall binding participation constraint.

To convince b that A will stick to his sanction scheme when minimum cooperation at $k_b{}^*$ is realised requires $k_A{}^* \leq k_b{}^*$. Hence, (14) must hold. (To keep things simple I assume incremental cost transfers, $c_b = t_b$ or $C_B = T$, and a marginal b-player, $Y_b \rightarrow 0$.) Solving (14) for Γ yields the maximum intensity of sanctions (Γ^*) that A can impose without overriding b's minimum participation level $k_b{}^*$.

$$k_A^* = \frac{C_A + \Gamma \gamma Y_A}{U_A - C_B + \Gamma \gamma Y_A} \leq \frac{\alpha - \delta}{\alpha + \beta} = k_b^* \qquad \Big| c_b = t_b, \quad Y_b \to 0$$

$$\tag{14}$$

$$\Gamma^* \leq \frac{\alpha(U_A - C_A - C_B) - \beta C_A - \delta(U_A - C_B)}{\gamma(\delta + \beta)Y_A} \tag{15}$$

A numerical example illustrates that Γ must indeed be small to satisfy (14): assuming $\alpha = 0.05$, $\beta = 0.1$, $\gamma = 0.05$, $\delta = 0.02$, $U_A = 100$, $C_A = 10$, $C_B = 10$, $Y_A = 100{,}000$ produces $k_A^* = k_b^* = 0.2$ and $\Gamma^* \leq 0.002$.

Above, I have established minimum conditions for cooperation which, if satisfied, guarantee that cooperation between A and b-players is stable. Furthermore, assuming that all players in B are identical, partial cooperation at or beyond the minimum participation level k_b^* ($\geq k_A^*$) immediately leads to full cooperation ($k = 1$). In the event of full cooperation, sanctions are not executed, but they remain a credible and effective threat against isolated players who consider reneging. Cooperation, once achieved and then supported by sanctions, is self-enforcing if coalition-forming by players who are inclined to renege is unlikely or can be prevented, since for an isolated marginal b-player it is better to participate in punishing a defector instead of suffering sanctions herself. Additionally, the threat of sanctions against non-cooperative or reneging players can be reinforced by raising the intensity of sanctions *after* cooperation has emerged and by creating suitable institutions.[43]

5.3 Cooperation and transfers

We have not yet addressed the question of why cooperation should emerge at all and how A can initiate it. An isolated player b_i has no reason to believe a priori that cooperation will emerge and reach a level at or beyond the critical values k_b^* and k_A^*.[44] Hence, the threat of sanctions by other b-players and by

---

[43]   For instance, side payments can be paid into a fund that is shared out to the intended recipients in the following period. If a party violates the treaty, it forfeits its share, which can then be used to compensate complying parties for their cost of imposing sanctions on the violator.

[44]   In international legal practice, the risk for each Party that signs an agreement as to whether a minimum participation level will be reached is contained by making the agreement's coming into force conditional on a certain minimum number of ratifications. Contractual obligations to sanction non-Parties is additional justification for this practice. The MP requires the deposition of at least 11 instruments of ratification, acceptance, approval or accession representing at least two-thirds of 1986 estimated global consumption of the controlled substances.

A may not be credible. This impasse is not easy to break, particularly in the framework of a one-shot game and under the assumption that all b-players are identical. Promoting cooperation and reducing transfers are competing goals. More interesting in terms of A's strategy, and perhaps more realistic, is the case of a dynamic game with non-identical players in B with which A negotiates individually and in sequence. In this case, underpaying incremental costs and inducing cooperation is theoretically feasible. In the following paragraphs, I discuss some conceivable strategies under both assumptions.

First, players may hold certain a priory beliefs regarding other players intentions. Some player b_j may have a distinct expectation k_{bj}^e regarding the emerging level of cooperation.[45] In a world of uncertainty and imperfect information, A may be able to promote such expectations to jump-start cooperation and b_j may have to rely on them for choosing her strategy.[46] If b_j's expectations for cooperation exceed k_b^* ($k_{bj}^e \geq k_b^*$), she will cooperate — and so will every other identical player b_i so that the level of cooperation will immediately jump to full cooperation ($k = 1$). In this case, expectations are a self-fulfilling prophecy. Obviously, A can exploit possible high expectations for cooperation. If k_b^e is much larger than k_b^*, A can reduce his transfers somewhat below incremental costs in a trade-off for a higher k_b^*.

Sequential negotiations with non-identical players in B allow A to exploit possible differences in expectations ($k_{bi}^e \neq k_{bj}^e$) or minimum participation levels ($k_{bi}^* \neq k_{bj}^*$) for reducing the transfer bill and/or promoting cooperation.[47] If players in B are different, A can select his negotiation partners strategically. He can first deal with those players b_j who have a high willingness to sign an agreement, because their expectation for cooperation k_{bj}^e is higher and/or their minimum participation level k_{bj}^* is lower than those of b_i, since, for instance, b_j may be more susceptible to sanctions. If the number of b_j-players is large enough so that their signing the agreement lifts cooperation above the minimum participation level k_{bi}^* of the yet abstaining players b_i, the latter will follow suit. If b_j's cooperation lowers the participation expectation of the ab-

---

45   Distinct expectations are possible, if b_i does not know that all b-players are identical, which I assume here.

46   A different approach would be to specify b_i's willingness to cooperate as a random variable that would be updated upon observing k_b^* and the behaviour of all other members in B. A low k_b^* would raise the level of cooperation and the probability of full cooperation, but full cooperation need not emerge instantaneously. On the contrary, if cooperation remains below k_b^* in a first round, the individual willingness to cooperate may collapse, which makes it much more difficult to reach an agreement in a second round.

47   Differences in minimum participation levels are possible if players in B differ with respect to the relevant parameters (c_b, α, β, δ) or in size (Y_b). Compare (12) above.

staining b_i-players, it will be easier and less costly for A to induce the latter to sign the agreement in a second or third round of negotiations.

Second, with identical players, A can try to reduce $k_b{}^*$ (and $k_A{}^*$) as much as possible (to zero or below $k_b{}^e$) to induce the start of cooperation. As can be seen from (12), A can reduce $k_b{}^*$ by selecting a sanction scheme with large parameters δ and β. If $\delta \geq \alpha$, $k_b{}^*$ is set to zero (under incremental cost transfers). Alternatively, A may reduce $k_b{}^*$ by overpaying incremental costs, possibly coupled with a weak intensity of sanctions (Γ small). But increasing transfers raises $k_A{}^*$, which, as can be seen from (13), cannot be reduced below a minimum level larger zero by weakening the intensity of sanctions ($\Gamma \rightarrow 0$) or by introducing an appropriate institutional commitment to pay transfers and/ or to impose sanctions. Hence, A's strategy to drive down $k_b{}^*$ may not be credible in the eyes of a b-player, whose participation expectation is too low. Even sanctions that benefit A and can reduce $k_A{}^*$ to zero may not allow to reduce transfers, since reducing transfers always increases $k_b{}^*$.

In the case of sequential negotiations with non-identical players, A may use his transfer payments strategically to reduce the minimum participation requirement $k_{bj}{}^*$ of those players b_j who move first. By promising early movers payments above incremental costs ($t_{bj} > c_{bj}$), A can induce them to cooperate. This either raises participation immediately above the minimum participation level or it reduces the participation expectation of yet abstaining players or both. In both cases, abstaining players become increasingly willing to cooperate. A can than gradually lower his transfer offer to late-comers — even below their incremental costs. Thus, the strategy of sequential negotiations can lead to competition between players in B for being served first.[48]

A third option for promoting cooperation is available to A if A happens to earn a benefit from imposing sanctions on b-players ($\gamma < 0$, in contrast to our previous assumption). In this case, A can reduce $k_b{}^*$ as described above *and* relax his own participation constraint $k_A{}^*$ simultaneously, so that his strategy, including the sanction scheme, becomes a credible threat for b-players, for whom cooperation is then imperative. Under such particular conditions, sanctions can be an instrument to start cooperation and sustain it after the agreement has come into force.

It seems that this third option was used by ICs for designing the MP and promoting cooperation. First, at least initially, the impact of ICs' CFC-trade restrictions on CFC importing DCs (δ) is probably severe whereas the costs of participating in such trade restrictions against outsiders (α) is probably very small for most DCs. Hence, ($\alpha - \delta$) is presumably smaller than zero and, un-

---

48   Whether A can use this strategy to reduce his total transfer payments T below overall incremental costs C_B must be left open here. It also needs to be investigated how the strategy of sequential negotiations is affected by A's rationality constraint.

der incremental cost transfers, $k_b{}^*$ can be set to zero. Second, sanctions in the form of trade restrictions on CFCs are likely to reduce world wide CFC consumption and emissions at least temporarily, which is good for the ozone layer and benefits ICs. Additionally, selling CFC substitutes to DCs may be more profitable than selling ordinary CFCs.[49] Hence, with beneficial trade restrictions, $k_A{}^*$ may well be zero, which renders A's threat of trade restrictions credible. Therefore, signing the MP may have been the dominant strategy for most DCs whereas complying with its terms later on may be a different matter.

The above results can be summarised as follows. The role of sanctions in international environmental agreements is ambiguous. A sanction scheme is a powerful tool for stabilising existing international cooperation if parties do not collude in breaching the agreement. But proposing a sanction scheme against outsiders and defectors before cooperation has started can make the initiation of cooperation much more difficult. Special cases that facilitate the start of cooperation are: high a priori expectations for the emergence of cooperation, positive returns from sanctions and the dynamics of sequential negotiations with non-identical players. In these cases, which may have played a role in designing and negotiating the MP, sanctions can be compatible with initiating cooperation. But in any case, chances to reduce transfer payments below incremental costs seem to be very limited.

6.   THE MONTREAL PROTOCOL AS A GAME IN TWO PERIODS

Repeated games are different as compared to one-shot games in that the time dimension opens the possibility to retaliate for non-cooperative moves Above, I have analysed a situation in which the state of the world was fixed after the signing of the treaty. Renegotiations were excluded and the treaty had to be kept no matter what. However, in analysing the role of sanctions, I have already pointed to their contract stabilising effect. In this Section, I introduce a distinct time structure and investigate the strategies that players then have. I use the bilateral situation of player A against player B as in Section 4 and make the same assumptions concerning payoffs and costs. But I assume a rather simplistic time path as in Figure 4 and model the game as a two-period game, period 1 ($_1t$) from year 1-10 and period 2 ($_2t$) starting with year 11. In period $_1t$ the agreement is signed, A phases out CFCs and makes transfers to B. In period $_2t$, B phases out or breaches the agreement. This pattern is motivated by the MP; it is meant to reflects the grace period for DCs.

---

49   This effect is probably temporary, since suppliers in DCs may take over. But the transitional period may have been enough to induce DCs to sign the MP.

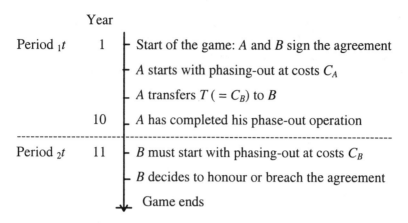

Figure 4:   Time path in the two-period ozone game

The payoffs for A and B in each single period are given by *Ozone IV* in Table 6. If A and B sign the agreement in period $_1t$, player A invests in CFC substitutes and in transfers to B. If B does not sign the agreement in $_1t$, A can invest in substitutes and impose sanctions on B or he can continue emissions. In period $_2t$, A harvests the gains from phasing out CFCs if B complies, or he continues sanctions against B.[50]

Table 6:   Ozone IV: Payoffs in period 1 and 2

		Strategies Player B	
Strategies Player A		*phase-out*	*emit*
Period $_1t$	*phase-out*	$(-_1C_A-_1T\;;\;_1T)$	$(-_1C_A-_1S_A\;;-_1S_B)$
	emit	$(_10\;;\;_10)$	$(_10\;;\;_10)$
Period $_2t$	*phase-out*	$(_2U_A\;;-_2C_B)$	$(-_2S_A\;;-_2S_B)$
	emit	$(_20\;;-_2C_B)$	$(_20\;;\;_20)$

In both periods, considered separately, cooperation is impossible. This is obvious in $_1t$; in $_2t$ the threat of sanctions is not credible, since A cannot commit himself to sanctions that would make him worse off than continuing emissions. However, in non-cooperative repeated games, players are confronted in each period with a payoff matrix that reflects not only their current but also their expected future payoffs. But they do not take past payoffs into account, which are sunk costs or bygone profits. Since the players' strategies in $_2t$ are anticipated by both players when entering the game in $_1t$, their strategy set is

---

50   Possible phasing-out costs for A in $_2t$ have been neglected here for simplicity.

larger in the two-period game. It combines the possible actions for both play-ers in both periods. This yields a new game, *Ozone V*, that can be represented by a four-by-four matrix that shows the payoffs for each two-period strategy combination. In *Ozone V* (Table 7) *po* stands for *phase out* and *e* for *emit* strategies.

Table 7: *Ozone V: Combined two-period payoff matrix (po = phase-out, e = emit)*

$A \backslash B$	po/po	po/e	e/e
po/po	$\begin{pmatrix} {}_2U_A - {}_1C_A - {}_1T\,; \\ -{}_1T - {}_2C_B \end{pmatrix}$	$\begin{pmatrix} -{}_1C_A - {}_1T - {}_2S_A\,; \\ -{}_1T - {}_2S_B \end{pmatrix}$	$\begin{pmatrix} -{}_1C_A - {}_1S_A - {}_2S_A\,; \\ -{}_1S_B - {}_2S_B \end{pmatrix}$
po/e	$\left(-{}_1C_A - {}_1T\,;\, {}_1T - {}_2C_B \right)$	$\left(-{}_1C_A - {}_1T\,;\, {}_1T \right)$	$\left(-{}_1C_A - {}_1S_A\,;\, -{}_1S_B \right)$
e/e	$\left(0\,;\, -{}_2C_B \right)$	$(0\,;\,0)$	$(0\,;\,0)$

Table 7 ignores the strategy combinations (*e/po* ; •/•) and (•/• ; *e/po*), since I am mainly interested in those combinations in which both players agree to cooperate in ${}_1t$ and choose their actions freely in ${}_2t$.[51] However, I have added the combination (*e/e* ; *e/e*) as the ultimate conflict situation.

Can the fully cooperative strategy combination (*po/po* ; *po/po*) can be reached? The game *Ozone V* has two trivial Nash equilibria (*e/e* ; *po/e*) and (*e/e* ; *e/e*). Additionally, the cooperative outcome (*po/po* ; *po/po*) is a Nash equilibrium if the strategy *po/po* yields a larger pay-off for each player than each player's second best alternative. Hence, for cooperation to emerge (16) and (17) are necessary conditions.

A:
$$ {}_2U_A - {}_1C_A - {}_1T \geq 0 \tag{16} $$

B:
$$ {}_1T - {}_2C_B \geq {}_1T - {}_2S_B \tag{17} $$

But the cooperative outcome may not yet be subgame perfect. Although (16) may hold, (17) is not a sufficient condition for cooperation, since sanc-tions ${}_2S_B$ are not credible: If *B* signs in ${}_1t$ and breaches the agreement in ${}_2t$, i.e. *B* plays *po/e*, *A* is caught in a very bad situation, since then *A* has not only borne his costs of total phase-out but has also paid transfers to *B* in ${}_1t$ without getting any return from doing so in ${}_2t$. Hence, *B* can be sure that *A* will play *po/e* to minimise his loss by avoiding the cost ${}_2S_A$ of imposing sanctions on *B*.

---

[51] The first combination omitted here would amount to starting the same game in period ${}_2t$, since *B* will not respond with *phase-out* if *A* does not play *phase-out* in ${}_1t$. The second omitted combination is similar to the one-shot game except for sanctions being imposed on *B* in ${}_1t$ for not signing.

However, since A will anticipate B's defection, he will select e/e right in the beginning, which means that the treaty will never be signed. Hence, full cooperation is not a subgame perfect equilibrium and the combinations (e/e; po/e) and (e/e; e/e) are the only feasible outcomes of *Ozone V*.

Taking the non-credibility of sanctions in $_2t$ into account, cooperation in *Ozone V* is only sustainable if holding on to the agreement in $_2t$ is more profitable for B than to renege. This means that A must pay transfers in $_2t$ that satisfy (18).

$$B: \qquad _1T - {}_2C_B + {}_2T \geq {}_1T \qquad \text{or} \qquad {}_2T \geq {}_2C_B \qquad (18)$$

(18) supersedes (17). Hence, transfers must match B's incremental costs in each period and there is no room to prepay B for investments to be undertaken later. Furthermore, transfers in $_1t$ are redundant as an instrument to sustain cooperation. But if they are paid to get cooperation started, overall transfers will exceed incremental costs.

Applying these arguments to the MP, stability of the MP requires that the Multilateral Fund pays DCs' incremental costs and that it does so on the grounds of strict conditionality. Moreover, if the costs of using ozone friendly substances remain permanently higher than the corresponding costs of using CFCs, then paying transfers to opportunistic countries becomes a permanent engagement.

7.   WHO WILL WIN THE OZONE GAME?

The grace period for DCs is a critical feature the MP. On the one hand, the grace period has helped ICs to keep down their transfer payments to DCs and to render the trade restrictions against outsiders more credible. This has helped to stabilise the MP for the following reasons:

1.   The compliance costs of DCs after the grace period will be lower than those in ICs a decade earlier, since by that time substitutes will have become available at decreasing costs. This reduces the need for transfers.
2.   The grace period has reduced the present value of DCs' compliance costs, since DCs tend to have a relatively high rate of time preference. Therefore, the introduction of the grace period has probably curtailed DCs' bargaining power, which has probably helped to keep the transfers to DCs down.
3.   The grace period permitted to conclude an early treaty at a time when DCs had not yet developed their production capacities for CFCs and other ozone depleting substances. Hence, the threat value of future CFC-emissions by DCs was lower at the time of negotiations compared to a possible later situation with substantial CFC production capacities and related sunk costs in DCs.

4. Supplying DCs with CFCs or cheap (subsidised) substitutes during the
    grace period and possibly thereafter reduces the risk that DCs build up an
    irreversible domestic CFC production, which would render trade restric-
    tions ineffective and which would have to be bought out by higher trans-
    fers.
5. The early phase-out in ICs renders the envisioned sanctions more credi-
    ble, since the costs of a ban on trade in CFCs fall for ICs with the devel-
    opment and immediate introduction of substitutes and the replacement of
    the related equipment in ICs.
6. Moreover, selling substitutes is probably more profitable than selling
    CFCs, which are easier to imitate by DCs. A conversion and phase-down
    programme for CFCs in DC that is supported by a successful worldwide
    ban on CFC exports, which de facto excludes competition from DCs se-
    cures a big export market for ICs' chemical companies. Thus, trade re-
    strictions against outsiders may prove to be even profitable instead of
    costly for ICs.[52]

On the other hand, the grace period has created a problem of time inconsistency. In combination with ICs' transfer payments and trade restrictions
against outsiders, the grace period has enticed DCs to accede to the MP. But
as sovereign states, DCs have not been able to commit themselves credibly to
their phase-out obligations after the grace period. It remains an open question
whether incremental cost transfers and the MP's trade restrictions will be sufficient to keep DCs from eventually reneging. Hence, ICs have accepted a
certain risk, which must be countered in the course of implementing the MP.

The regular meeting of the Parties to the MP and public pressure, which
can be supported by the publication of the official reports, is likely to make
any attempt of serious non-compliance an unpleasant adventure for governments. Reputation plays an important role in international relations. Since the
ozone game is embedded in a much broader supergame between sovereign
states, reneging on the MP can have negative side effects in other areas of
(potential) cooperation. Moreover, elaborate non-compliance procedures, including the imposition of trade restrictions, have been established to rectify
individual cases. If DCs do not collude in breaking the MP and if the Parties
to the MP can deal with non-compliant DCs separately, which is likely given
the provisions for assistance and the non-compliance procedures, then sanc-

---

52   The development and expected availability of substitutes was a major reason
     for achieving a breakthrough in the negotiations over reducing CFCs. Fur-
     thermore, some leading chemical companies, particularly DuPont in the USA,
     had eventually realised that a profitable market for CFC substitutes lies ahead.
     Hence, the true reason for trade restrictions may well be commercial rather
     than environmental — and enforcing the MP may be but a welcome side ef-
     fect. See Markandya (1991), who emphasises the benefits from technology of
     CFC substitution, and Oberthür (1992), who gives an account of the role of
     industry in deciding to abandon CFCs.

tions can be credible. In addition, a widening of the game by resorting to general principles and enforcement mechanisms of international treaty law remains always possible.

The stability of the MP is further enhanced by applying the Multilateral Fund strategically. First, the Fund should be administered on the basis of strict conditionality. It should pay for real reduction investments, if possible ex post. Second, the Fund should invest extensively in CFC reductions in DCs as early as possible already during the grace period in order to forestall the installation of new CFC production capacities in DCs. Third, the Fund should give priority to irreversible investments that build up a stock of ozone-friendly capital in DCs, which would become obsolete if a country decided to renege. For instance, investment in new refrigeration equipment that cannot run on CFCs are sunk costs, which reduces the incentive to breach the MP.[53] The Word Bank as the Fund's manager is well positioned to employ those principles. And finally, the Fund should be available to pay compensation to loyal Parties for costs that these incur if sanctions against a non-compliant Party become inevitable. This renders sanctions more credible.

The MP can be handled very flexibly. The regular revision process allows for an early adaptation of the MP's provisions to new developments and to looming violations of treaty obligations. Flexibility has the advantage that unavoidable violations can be accommodated, which gives the impression that the MP is very stable. But flexibility is an ambiguous stabilisation instrument. It also invites opportunistic parties to force renegotiations by threatening not to comply. Thus, the eventual outcome need not necessarily coincide with the provisions of the treaty that were originally agreed upon and signed. In particular, it is possible that much higher transfers will become necessary to avoid violations. In the end, it will be difficult to tell whether simply a country's incapacity to comply or an attempt to exploit its (possibly growing) bargaining power as a sovereign state was at the origin of an (imminent) violation and thus may have become the reason for a relaxation and adaptation of the MP's obligations and provision or for additional transfers. When compared with non-sovereign contractual relations, the latter behaviour would, of course, be a breach of the original treaty, although it is not observable as such.

To conclude, the ozone game is characterised by an unevenly distributed bargaining power to the advantage of DCs. If DCs built up their production capacity and extended their consumption of CFCs and other ozone depleting substances only moderately, they could easily offset all reduction efforts by ICs. Moreover, DCs could perhaps do this at relatively small environmental costs to themselves but with inflicting potentially large damage on ICs. The ozone layer problem can thus be used for putting pressure on ICs.

---

53   Compare Stähler (1992).

It seems that DCs have so far abstained form using this power. If they had formed a cartel in negotiations, they might have been able to exploit their favourable position in order to obtain higher side payments, perhaps in the form of development aid. In the long-run, the cooperative Nash bargaining outcome may reflect the distribution of the bargaining power more correctly and may thus be closer to a sustainable distribution of the gains from protecting the ozone layer than the financial provisions in the MP. Hence, it seems that ICs have outfoxed the Developing World over the ozone issue. This outcome can be attributed in particularly to two new elements in the MP: the provision for trade restrictions (sanctions) against non-Parties an non-compliant Parties in combination with the grace period for DCs. The monopsonist cartel of ICs vis à vis the many DCs may have done the rest.[54]

The question must remain open whether the MP can eventually be called a success story. We will have to wait and see which position DCs will take at the turn of the century. There are many loopholes and weak provisions in the MP. It remains to be seen in how far DCs will want, and are able to, use these opportunities for creeping out of their phase-out obligations and how high incremental costs and monetary and non-monetary transfers will finally be. Nevertheless, it seems that the MP stands a good chance of being honoured eventually — and at a moderate price for the industrial half of the world.

REFERENCES

Barrett, Scott (1989), On the Nature and Significance of International Environmental Agreements, mimeo, London Business School.

Barrett, Scott (1991), Economic Analysis of International Environmental Agreements: Lessons for a Global Warming Treaty, OECD, *Responding to Climate Change: Selected Economic Issues*, Paris, 1991.

Benedick, Richard Elliot (1991), Ozone Diplomacy: New Directions in Safeguarding the Planet, Harvard University Press, Cambridge, Mass.

Binmore, Ken; Ariel Rubinstein and Asher Wolinsky (1986), The Nash Bargaining Solution in Economic Modelling, *Rand Journal of Economics* 17(2):176-188.

---

54   A similar strategy is unlikely to be successful again in other negotiations over global environmental issues, e.g., climate change, the rain forests, biodiversity. In preparing for the UNCED in Rio in June 1992, DCs joined forces and faced pressure from ICs jointly. See: "Keine Entwicklung ohne Ausbeutung natürlicher Reichtümer", Frankfurter Allgemeine Zeitung, 28 April 1992; "Rio ist ein Schimpfwort — Malaysia: Der Süden steht geschlossen gegen den Norden", Frankfurter Rundschau, 13 February 1992; "Wider die Öko-Kolonialisten: Wie man in Indien über den Erd-Gipfel denkt", Frankfurter Rundschau, 13 February 1992. Compare also Heister, Klepper, Stähler (1992).

Black, Jane; Maurice D. Levi, David de Meza (1993), Creating a Good Atmosphere: Minimum Participation for Tackling the "Greenhouse Effect", *Economica* 60 (August): 281-293.

Eaton, Jonathan; Maxim Engers (1992), Sanctions, *Journal of Political Economy* 100(5):899-928.

Enders, Alice; Amelia Porges (1992), Successful Conventions and Conventional Success: Saving the Ozone Layer. In Kim Anderson and Richard Blackhurst (eds.), *The Greening of World Trade Issues*, New York, Harvester Wheatsheaf: 130-144.

Farman, J. C. et al. (1985), Large Losses of Total Ozone in Antarctica Reveal CLOx/NOx Interaction, *Nature* 315 (16 May 1985): 207-210.

Heister, Johannes; Gernot Klepper, Frank Stähler (1992), Strategien globaler Umweltpolitik: Die UNCED-Konferenz aus ökonomischer Sicht, *Zeitschrift für angewandte Umweltforschung* 5(4):455-465.

Krutilla, J. V. (1966), The International Columbia River Treaty: An Economic Evaluation. In A.V. Kneese and Stephen C. Smith (eds.), *Water Research*, The Johns Hopkins Press, Baltimore.

Markandya, Anil (1991), International Agreements for Global Environmental Problems: The Case of the Montreal Protocol, mimeo, University College London.

Mintzer, Irving (1989), Cooling Down a Warming World. Chlorofluorocarbons, the Greenhouse Effect, and the Montreal Protocol, *International Environmental Affairs* 4(1):12-25.

Molina, Mario J.; F. Sherwood Rowland (1974), Stratospheric Sink for Chlorofluoromethanes: Chlorine Atom-catalyzed Destruction of Ozone, *Nature* 249 (28 June 1974): 810-12.

Morrisette, Peter M. (1989), The Evolution of Policy Responses to Stratospheric Ozone Depletion, *National Resources Journal* 29(3):791-820.

Oberthür, Sebastian (1992), Die Zerstörung der stratosphärischen Ozonschicht als internationales Problem: Interessenkonstellationen und internationaler politischer Prozeß, *Zeitschrift für Umweltpolitik & Umweltrecht* 15(2):155-185.

Office of Technology Assessment (OTA) (1989), An Analysis of the Montreal Protocol on Substances that Deplete the Ozone Layer. In Dean Edwin Abrahamson (ed.), *The Challenge of Global Warming*, Island Press, Washington D.C.: 291-304.

Rubinstein, Ariel (1982), Perfect Equilibrium in a Bargaining Model, *Econometrica* 50(1):97-109.

Rummel-Bulska, Iwona; Seth Osafo (1991), Selected Multilateral Treaties in the Field of the Environment: Volume Two, United Nations Environment Programme (UNEP), Grotius Publications Ltd, Cambridge.

Shea, Cynthia Pollock (1988), Protecting Live on Earth: Steps to Save the Ozone Layer, *Worldwatch Paper 87*, Worldwatch Institute.

Simonis, Udo Ernst; Ernst Ulrich von Weizsäcker (1990), Globale Umweltprobleme: Neun Thesen, *Europa Archiv*, Folge 1: 1-12.

Smith, Douglas A.; Keith Vodden (1989), Global Environmental Policy: The Case of Ozone Depletion, *Canadian Public Policy* XV(4):413-423.

Somerset, Margaret E. (1989), An Attempt to Stop the Sky from Falling: The Montreal Protocol to Protect against Atmospheric Ozone Reductions, *Syracus Journal of International Law and Commerce* 15:391-429.

Sorensen, H. Christian (1988), International Agreements — Montreal Protocol on Substances that Deplete the Ozone Layer, *Harvard International Law Journal* 29:185-191.

Stähler, Frank (1992), Pareto Improvements by In-Kind-Transfers, *Kiel Working Paper* No. 541, Kiel Institute of World Economics, Kiel.

UBA (1989), Verzicht aus Verantwortung: Maßnahmen zur Rettung der Ozonschicht, Umweltbundesamt, Bericht 7/89, Berlin.

UNEP (1989), Economic Panel Report: Montreal Protocol on Substances that Deplete the Ozone Layer - Final Report on the Economic Assessment Panel.

US EPA (1988), Regulatory Impact Analysis: Protection of Stratospheric Ozone, Volume I: Regulatory Impact Analysis Document, United States Environmental Protection Agency, Washington D.C.

8. On the Economics of International Environmental Agreements

Frank Stähler

1. INTRODUCTION[1]

International and global environmental policy issues have been subject to increasing public attention. This increasing attention is due to two reasons. First, global environmental problems like the potential destruction of the ozone layer, global warming and biodiversity loss are at the heart of the current debate on most urgent environmental problems. Second, solving these problems requires international policy coordination. The need for international policy coordination, however, raises several problems which do not exist for domestic environmental problems. Every international policy coordination must be grounded on the voluntary participation of those countries which use the environmental resource. The sovereignty of countries, however, allows countries to change their policies whenever they want to. Hence, international environmental agreements must guarantee that every national participant is at least not worse off by holding the agreement than by breaking it.

Serious problems arise for international environmental agreements because restricting international pollution is a public good. The literature on international environmental agreements has mainly concentrated on the possibility of stable coalitions as a set or subset of all countries which are

[1] A predecessor of this paper was a contribution to a research project on the stability of international environmental agreements supported by the Volkswagen Foundation. I am indebted to Wolfgang Buchholz, Johannes Heister and Gernot Klepper for very useful discussion. The usual disclaimer applies.

subject to a global environmental problem (see Barrett, 1991, 1992, Bauer, 1992, Carraro, Siniscalco, 1993, Heal, 1992). Stability requires that every sovereign member-country is always better off by remaining in the coalition than by leaving it and every outsider is always worse off by joining the coalition. Partial cooperation can emerge if the stable coalition contains more than one member.

However, these papers deal with the notion of sovereignty only in terms of voluntary participation. When countries have decided to sign an environmental treaty, they are supposed to behave compliantly and to be able to commit themselves credibly to the agreed-upon reduction efforts. This paper addresses the problem that countries need not to behave compliantly. Accordingly, this paper assumes that the agreed-upon reduction plans must be self-enforcing and that all countries decide simultaneously whether they pursue the agreed-upon policy. It assumes that two countries go ahead with environmental cooperation whereas the third country enters the stage after cooperation between the other two countries may have already been agreed upon.[2] The paper is organized as follows. The following two sections discuss cooperation between two countries. Section 2 discusses self-enforcing cooperation when the reduction technology is reversible, i.e. when each country is able to return to the non-cooperative Nash reduction levels when another country has shown non-compliant behavior. Section 3 discusses self-enforcing cooperation when reduction efforts are irreversible which implies that introducing a certain degree of reduction measures means to carry the corresponding costs forever. It compares also both technology options. Section 4 considers how the cooperating countries can succeed in compensating a third country for reductions which surmount its non-cooperative level. Section 5 summarizes this paper and concludes.

Two results are striking when discussing international environmental problems in terms of this tighter sovereignty constraint. On the one hand, it will be shown that restricting cooperation to two countries does not mean that all other parties remain at their non-cooperative levels. Instead, the two countries may be able to compensate outsiders for additional reductions although these compensations have to meet certain compliance constraints as well. The paper demonstrates that partial cooperation among three countries is possible. It shows that multilateral agreements can be self-enforcing even in the presence of contract breach options because the coalition of two members is able to initiate additional reduction efforts of a third party through compensations. On the other hand, it will be shown that choosing an irreversible technology can be a dominant strategy for compensating an

---

2   For a model which determines the countries cooperating and those staying outside endogenously, see Stähler (1996).

outsider. Even if this technology carries the same costs as the reversible one, it can serve for commitment, and hence it can be profitable to introduce this technology in the third country by the support of the paying countries. This potential superiority contrasts the strict inferiority in the case of self-enforcing cooperation between these two countries.

2.   SELF-ENFORCING COOPERATION IN THE CASE OF A REVERSIBLE TECHNOLOGY

Throughout the paper, it is assumed that three countries use a global environmental resource, say, the atmosphere for releasing harmful emissions into this atmosphere. For the sake of simplicity, the paper assumes that all three countries i, j and k face identical benefits B of total reduction efforts R and identical costs C of individual (reversible) reduction efforts which are given by

$$\forall l \in \{i, j, k\}: \quad B_l = \alpha R, \; C_l = \frac{\beta}{2} R_l^2, \; U_l = B_l - C_l, \; R = \sum_l R_l. \quad (1)$$

Additionally, it is assumed that the intertemporal preference of i and j can be given by the same discount factor. Country k, however, is assumed to have an intertemporal preference which implies a "significantly lower" discount factor:

$$\delta = \delta_i = \delta_j > \delta_k, 0 < \delta, \delta_k < 1.$$

The discount factor measures how strongly the current policies of a country take into account the long-run effects. This paper assumes that countries i and j start with cooperation. Assume for the moment that every contract between them were enforceable. The optimal reduction level for both countries is given by

$$\forall l \in \{i, j\}: \quad R_l^* = \frac{2\alpha}{\beta}. \quad (2)$$

In order to simplify the modelling of the bargaining procedure, the paper assumes that the maximum bargaining gains will be divided equally. If compliance can be guaranteed, both countries realize (2) and bargaining gains according to

$$\forall l \in \{i,j\}: \qquad U_l^* - U_l' = \frac{\alpha^2}{2\beta}. \qquad (3)$$

The non-cooperative reduction levels are α/β which give the non-cooperative utilities U_l'. The utility reservation curves and all iso-utility curves have the slope

$$l \neq m \in \{i,j\}: \qquad \frac{dR_l}{dR_m} = \frac{\beta R_m - \alpha}{\alpha}. \qquad (4)$$

When non-compliance is an option for one country, the other country is able to punish the non-compliant country by choosing the non-cooperative reduction level after defection has occurred. The paper assumes that both countries face an infinite repetition of the reduction game and restricts their threat options to infinite punishments.[3] The non-compliance option restricts the set of credible policies. Consider e.g. country j which knows that only contracts which satisfy

$$\frac{1}{1-\delta}\left[\alpha\left(R_i + R_j\right) - \frac{\beta}{2}R_i^2\right] - \left[\frac{\alpha^2}{2\beta} + \alpha R_j\right] - \frac{\delta}{1-\delta}\frac{3\alpha^2}{2\beta} \geq 0 \qquad (5)$$

will not be broken by country i. The first term gives the sum of discounted infinite cooperation, the second term gives the instantaneous gain from breaking the contract while the other country fulfils it, and the third term gives the sum of the discounted disagreement outcome starting one period later. Comparing (5) and (2) indicates that compliance problems do arise if δ does not reach at least 0.5.[4] If $\delta < 0.5$, (5) and a corresponding condition for j give i and j respective minimum reduction efforts which they should exceed in order to guarantee compliance of the opponent:

---

[3]   However, a weakly renegotiation-proof strategy (see Farrell, Maskin (1989) and van Damme (1989)) would produce the same constraints when punishment is restricted to one period. This result holds for the reversible and the irreversible technology option and is due to the orthogonality of the reaction functions. The proof for the reversible technology option is shown in Stähler (1998), the proof for the irreversible technology option is available upon request.

[4]   This case is not a too unrealistic one because several years can elapse between repetitions.

$$\hat{R}_i = \frac{\alpha}{\beta} + \frac{1}{\delta}\left\{\frac{\alpha}{2\beta} + \frac{\beta}{2\alpha}R_j^2 - R_j\right\} = \frac{\alpha}{\beta} + \frac{1}{\delta}\frac{\beta}{2\alpha}\left[R_j - \frac{\alpha}{\beta}\right]^2 \quad (6a)$$

$$\hat{R}_j = \frac{\alpha}{\beta} + \frac{1}{\delta}\left\{\frac{\alpha}{2\beta} + \frac{\beta}{2\alpha}R_i^2 - R_i\right\} = \frac{\alpha}{\beta} + \frac{1}{\delta}\frac{\beta}{2\alpha}\left[R_i - \frac{\alpha}{\beta}\right]^2$$

with $\quad \dfrac{d\hat{R}_i}{dR_j} = \dfrac{1}{\delta}\dfrac{\beta R_j - \alpha}{\alpha}, \qquad \dfrac{d\hat{R}_j}{dR_i} = \dfrac{1}{\delta}\dfrac{\beta R_i - \alpha}{\alpha}.$

(6a) observes that the compliance constraint curves are steeper than the utility reservation curve.[5] The reduction efforts of any contract which should qualify as self-enforcing should not fall short of the minimum reduction efforts which fulfil (6a). If δ falls short of 0.5, the compliance constraints do not allow to realize the cooperative outcome.

The symmetry with respect to costs and benefits and the identical discount factors imply that the minimum reduction efforts which fulfil (6a) are the solution because same costs and benefits imply the same efforts when gains have to be split equally. Then, symmetry ensures that both countries agree upon the highest reduction efforts which just fulfil the compliance constraints when these constraints are binding. Thus, the reduction levels are

$$\forall l \in \{i,j\}: \qquad R_l = \begin{cases} \dfrac{2\alpha}{\beta} & \text{if } \delta > 0.5 \\[2mm] [1+2\delta]\dfrac{\alpha}{\beta} & \text{if } \delta \leq 0.5 \end{cases} \qquad (6b)$$

From (6b), it is clear that neither i nor j would gain when cooperating with k instead of j or i, respectively. This result may justify the assumption that i and j start to cooperate because they are able to realize the highest symmetric bargaining gains. The assumption is that two countries which take future responses to current actions stronger into account than other countries do start with cooperation.

---

[5]   For $\delta \rightarrow 1$, the compliance constraint curves and the utility reservation curves coincide.

3. SELF-ENFORCING COOPERATION IN THE CASE OF AN IRREVERSIBLE TECHNOLOGY

This section addresses self-enforcing cooperation when the introduction of the reduction technology is irreversible: when a country has introduced specific reduction efforts which are based on an irreversible technology, it cannot go back and has to carry the corresponding costs in every following period. The comparison of both technologies will give a surprising result for the potential superiority of technologies when contracts which compensate a third country must be self-enforcing. The irreversible technology substitutes for the cost function in (1) by

$$\forall l \in \{i, j, k\}, \forall t \geq 0: \quad D_l(t) = \frac{\gamma}{2} R_l(t)^2, \; R_l(t+1) \geq R_l(t). \quad (7)$$

Due to irreversibility, cost function (7) depends on time. Some preliminaries are helpful for preparing the computations which will follow. First, non-compliance means that one country does not follow a specific dynamic plan and remains at the reduction level of the previous period whereas the other country has moved a step further. Consequently, punishment means that the other country remains at this level and will never introduce additional reduction measures. Thus, irreversibility constrains both the non-compliance and the punishment options. Second, if a self-enforcing reduction plan exists, this plan can never reach the optimal outcome because both countries' reductions should never exceed the cooperative level. Reaching the optimal outcome (or any other final stage) would change the infinitely dynamic game into a finitely dynamic one. This finitely dynamic game can be solved in the usual backward induction fashion and makes only the non-compliance option a subgame-perfect strategy for both countries because no punishment is possible after the last period has been reached. When the non-compliance option is a dominant strategy in the last period, it is also a dominant one in the next-to-last period, and so on. Hence, a self-enforcing plan can maximally approach the cooperative outcome but never reach it. Two additional comments may be useful to pronounce the logic of the technology choice in an agreement. First, irreversibility implies no specific problem in terms of an option value which can only arise if the future costs and benefits are uncertain. Second, the switch to an irreversible technology does not create a credibility problem now because it is assumed that the reversible technology is not available as an alternative option in a first step.

One may now turn to the question whether such a self-enforcing reduction plan exists which meets the condition that every country expects at least the same utility from further reductions than from remaining at a level when the other country has gone one step further. This condition must hold for all periods. (8) gives the dynamic contract and specifies the piecemeal approach.

$$R(t) = \frac{2\alpha}{\gamma} - f(t)\frac{\alpha}{\gamma}, f(0) = 1, f' < 0, \lim_{\tau \to \infty} f(\tau) = \theta \geq 0 \tag{8}$$

The cooperative efforts are $2\alpha/\gamma$ for each country. Starting from the non-cooperative level, the contract increases the reduction efforts step by step and approaches $(2-\theta)\alpha/\gamma$ in the course of time. The function $f(t)$ describes the dynamics of the contract which must meet the compliance constraint. Let $V(\tau,I)$ and $V(\tau,O)$ denote the discounted value of the inside option and the outside option, respectively, when t has reached τ.[6] The benefits of the inside option are the discounted sum of utilities to be realized in all following periods whereas the benefits of the outside option are determined by the contract breach. Hence, $V(\tau,I)$ and $V(\tau,O)$ are given by

$$V(\tau,I) = \sum_{t=\tau}^{\infty} \delta^t \left\{ \frac{4\alpha^2}{\gamma} - f(t)\frac{2\alpha^2}{\gamma} - \frac{\gamma}{2}\left[\frac{2\alpha}{\gamma} - f(t)\frac{\alpha}{\gamma}\right]^2 \right\} =$$

$$\sum_{t=\tau}^{\infty} \delta^t \left\{ \frac{2\alpha^2}{\gamma} - f(t)^2 \frac{\alpha^2}{2\gamma} \right\},$$

$$V(\tau,O) = \sum_{t=\tau}^{\infty} \delta^t \left\{ \frac{4\alpha^2}{\gamma} - f(\tau-1)\frac{\alpha^2}{\gamma} - f(\tau)\frac{\alpha^2}{\gamma} - \frac{\gamma}{2}\left[\frac{2\alpha}{\gamma} - f(\tau-1)\frac{\alpha}{\gamma}\right]^2 \right\} =$$

$$\sum_{t=\tau}^{\infty} \delta^t \left\{ \frac{2\alpha^2}{\gamma} - \frac{\alpha^2}{\gamma}[f(\tau) - f(\tau-1)] - f(\tau-1)^2 \frac{\alpha^2}{2\gamma} \right\}.$$

$$\tag{9}$$

$V(\tau,O)$ takes into account that the other country goes one step further but remains at this level in order to punish non-compliance. The compliance constraint is much more complex compared to the case of reversible investments because $V(\tau,I)$ should not fall short of $V(\tau,O)$ for every positive integer value of τ:

---

6   The symmetry of countries i and j allows to omit the subscript.

$$\forall \tau \geq 1 : V(\tau, I) - V(\tau, O) \geq 0 \Leftrightarrow$$

$$\sum_{t=\tau}^{\infty} \delta^t \left\{ f(\tau-1)^2 \frac{\alpha^2}{2\gamma} - f(t)^2 \frac{\alpha^2}{2\gamma} - \left[f(\tau-1) - f(\tau) \right] \frac{\alpha^2}{\gamma} \right\} \geq 0 \qquad (10)$$

The appendix proves that a self-enforcing contract can at best induce a $\theta = 1 - \delta$ when $\tau \to \infty$. Hence, the upper limit of cooperation is given by

$$R^{\infty} = (1+\delta) \frac{\alpha}{\gamma}. \qquad (11)$$

No self-enforcing contract exists which is able to approach the cooperative level but the upper limit depends crucially on the discount factors of both cooperating countries. For instance, both countries could agree upon the timing of reductions according to a dynamic function g^t:

$$R(t) = \frac{2\alpha}{\gamma} - (1-\delta)\frac{\alpha}{\gamma} - g^t \delta \frac{\alpha}{\gamma} = \frac{\alpha}{\gamma} \left[1 + \delta - \delta g^t \right]. \qquad (8')$$

Contract (8') is no optimal contract because it satisfies (10) only for $t \to \infty$. But this specification allows to compute the discounted benefits of the inside and outside option explicitly:

$$V(\tau, I) = \sum_{t=\tau}^{\infty} \delta^t \left\{ \frac{2\alpha^2}{\gamma} \left[1 + \delta - \delta g^t \right] - \frac{\alpha^2}{2\gamma} \left[1 + \delta - \delta g^t \right]^2 \right\} \qquad (9')$$

$$V(\tau, O) = \sum_{t=\tau}^{\infty} \delta^t \left\{ \frac{\alpha^2}{\gamma} \left[1 + \delta - \delta g^\tau \right] + \frac{\alpha^2}{\gamma} \left[1 + \delta - \delta g^{\tau-1} \right] - \frac{\alpha^2}{2\gamma} \left[1 + \delta - \delta g^{\tau-1} \right]^2 \right\}$$

Applying (10) and substituting for the benefit and cost parameters gives the compliance constraint

$$\frac{\delta - 1}{1 - \delta g} + \frac{1}{1 - \delta} - \frac{\delta}{g(1-\delta)} \geq 0. \qquad (10')$$

Hence, a g satisfying

$$g = 1 + \frac{\delta}{2} - \sqrt{\delta - \frac{\delta^2}{4}} \qquad (12)$$

defines a self-enforcing dynamic contract. E.g.,

$$R(t) = \frac{\alpha}{\gamma}\left[1 + 0.5 - 0.5*0.5^t\right] \qquad (13)$$

describes this contract for $\delta = 0.5$.

Until now, the paper has addressed reversible and irreversible technologies as non-competing options. The constant-growth-model helps to explain the choice of technologies when both technologies are available and differ in costs. The availability of both technologies is only given as an option if the country has not yet decided for the irreversible technology. It will have done so if the irreversible technology implies lower costs, and since lower cost will be shown as necessary, one may ignore the role of switching costs. For obvious reasons, one may also restrict the analysis of cost comparisons on discount factors which fall short of 0.5. For a δ surmounting 0.5, the cost advantage of the irreversible technology must be very large to compensate for the benefits from choosing the reversible one because the reversible technology reaches the full cooperation level already in the first period. Additionally, it is assumed that dynamic contracts are restricted to functions according to (8'). $W(\beta)$ and $W(\gamma)$ denote the sum of discounted future utilities from compliance-constrained cooperation by choosing a reversible and irreversible technology, respectively, for $\delta < 0.5$:

$$W(\beta) = \sum_{t=0}^{\infty} \delta^t \left\{ \frac{2\alpha^2}{\beta}(1+2\delta) - \frac{\alpha^2}{2\beta}(1+2\delta)^2 \right\} = \frac{1+2\delta}{1-\delta} \frac{3-2\delta}{2} \frac{\alpha^2}{\beta} \qquad (14)$$

$$W(\gamma) = \sum_{t=0}^{\infty} \delta^t \left\{ \frac{2\alpha^2}{\gamma}\left[1+\delta-\delta g^t\right] - \frac{\alpha^2}{2\gamma}\left[1+\delta-\delta g^t\right]^2 \right\} =$$
$$\left\{ \frac{3+2\delta-\delta^2}{1-\delta} - \frac{2\delta-2\delta^2}{1-\delta g} - \frac{\delta^2}{1-\delta g^2} \right\} \frac{\alpha^2}{2\gamma}$$

Equalizing $W(\beta)$ and $W(\gamma)$ gives the relationship between the cost parameters β and γ which makes both countries indifferent between both technology options:

$$\frac{\gamma}{\beta} = \frac{1-\delta}{1+2\delta} \frac{1}{3-2\delta} \left\{ \frac{3+2\delta-\delta^2}{1-\delta} - \frac{2\delta-2\delta^2}{1-\delta g} - \frac{\delta^2}{1-\delta g^2} \right\} \qquad (15)$$

In order to shed some light on the numerical implications of equalizing both technology options, one may observe that this ratio is always below 1 but increases with a decrease of δ:

$$\frac{\gamma}{\beta}(\delta = 0.4) = 0.7992, \frac{\gamma}{\beta}(\delta = 0.3) = 0.8497, \frac{\gamma}{\beta}(\delta = 0.1) = 0.8945.$$

Thus, an irreversible technology must always show a cost advantage to be chosen by both cooperating countries. This cost advantage must be the lower the lower the discount factor is. In the case of identical costs, i.e. $\gamma = \beta$, both countries will never consider irreversible reduction efforts. There is no scope for the introduction of irreversible reduction technologies in the cooperating countries unless they compensate for the piecemeal approach by significantly lower costs. But significantly lower costs would have already induced a voluntary switch to the irreversible technology. Common piecemeal reduction policies can never initiate a switch to an irreversible reduction technology.

4. TRANSFERS TO A THIRD COUNTRY

This section will demonstrate that significantly lower costs are not necessary to make the irreversible technology subject of joint transfer policy of the two cooperating countries and that a technology switch can be profitable for the paying countries. It will show that compensating k for reductions may leave comparably more scope for employing the irreversible technology. The plan of this section is to compare an arbitrary compensation pricing rule for the case of policies which aim at irreversible reduction measures with a pricing rule which aims at reversible reduction measures and lets the donors skim the maximum bargaining gains. The section shows that the latter compensation rule is not unambiguously superior for identical costs of both technology options.

The joint compensation policies of i and j do not depend on their joint reduction efforts. Both countries are able to agree upon a specific amount of compensations which they transfer to country k. This transfer, however, raises a compliance problem. This compliance problem is solved by the assumption that the donors pay for extra reductions in the subsequent period. Then, a contract which specifies that the recipient has to introduce reduction measures only when both countries have paid can guarantee that both countries meet their agreed-upon monetary obligations. Under this assumption, i and j face no mutual compliance problem with respect to compensation policies. Additionally, the delay between payment and intended reductions is more realistic since funds have to be created and transfers have to be organized. If country k behaves non-compliantly, it will never receive any transfers in the future.

Both countries can try to initiate either irreversible extra reductions or reversible extra reductions. Their benefits from transfers which induce extra reductions must be discounted by δ because a transfer given now implies a reduction one period later. Hence, the Lindahlian marginal utility which arises from extra reductions is $2\delta\alpha$ per unit. When both countries agree upon compensating for extra reductions which are based on an irreversible reduction technology, a mutual compliance problem arises between the donors and the recipient country. On the one hand, the sum of discounted transfers which k receives minus the sum of discounted costs must at least equalize the benefits of non-compliance. On the other hand, country k takes into account that i and j cannot commit themselves credibly to pay compensations for already introduced reduction measures. Therefore, country k knows that it receives no transfers for an already realized degree of reductions. (16) gives the compliance constraint which takes into account that the costs of a certain measure are forever.

$\forall \tau \geq 1$:

$$\sum_{t=\tau}^{\infty} \delta_k^t X(t) - \sum_{t=\tau}^{\infty} \frac{\delta_k^t}{1-\delta_k} \Delta[\upsilon(t)] \geq \delta_k^\tau X(\tau) \Leftrightarrow \qquad (16)$$

$$\sum_{t=\tau+1}^{\infty} \delta_k^t X(t) - \sum_{t=\tau}^{\infty} \frac{\delta_k^t}{1-\delta_k} \Delta[\upsilon(t)] \geq 0$$

X, Δ and υ denote the transfers, the extra costs and the extra reduction measures, respectively, which the transfers imply. (16) specifies that the transfers in one period should not only cover the sum of discounted costs of the corresponding irreversible reduction measures but generally that the discounted value of a dynamic compensation schedule should not fall short of the benefits of non-compliance.

Because δ_k differs from δ, determining the division of bargaining gains raises a problem. One may circumvent this problem by assuming a specific compensation policy although this assumption is likely to conflict with the factual bargaining power of the donors but the mere interest in exploring the role of technology choices justifies this simplification. Except for the initial period 0, this section assumes that the cooperating countries are prepared to compensate the outsider for every *new* reduction measures on the basis of their Lindahlian utilities:

$$\forall t \geq 1:$$
$$X(t) = 2\delta\alpha\big[\upsilon(t) - \upsilon(t-1)\big] \tag{17a}$$

The reservation concerning transfers given in period 0 is due to potential switching costs which k has to carry when the irreversible technology incurs higher costs than the reversible one. Then, country k has to be compensated for the lower non-cooperative benefits which are due to a lower voluntary reduction level:

$$X(0) = \begin{cases} 2\delta\alpha\upsilon(0) \text{ if } \gamma \leq \beta \\ \left[\dfrac{3\alpha^2}{\beta} - \dfrac{3\alpha^2}{\gamma}\right]\dfrac{\delta_k}{1-\delta_k} + 2\delta\alpha\upsilon(0) \text{ if } \gamma > \beta \end{cases} \tag{17b}$$

Obviously, the switching costs do also influence the compliance constraint because the decision on compliance in the first period depends on the transfers in the following periods and on the costs in all following periods which include the switching costs. Since this section intends to show that the irreversible technology may be superior compared with the reversible technology even in the case of equal costs, one may assume for the moment that β is equal to γ such that switching costs do not exist.

One may now turn to the chances of a cooperative agreement between the donors and the recipient country. By means of a dynamic contract which is described by the function $h(t)$, the appendix proves that compensation policies can at best approach but never reach

$$\upsilon^{\infty} = (2\delta - 1)\frac{\alpha}{\gamma} \tag{18}$$

which requires a discount factor δ which surmounts 0.5. If $\delta < 0.5$, i and j will definitely refrain from any compensation policy. (18) shows that this limit of extra reduction efforts depends only on the discount factor of the paying countries. This limit gives only a first restriction which will turn out as useful when developing the compliance constraint in more detail. In order to compare both technology options, let l^t denote the specific dynamics of a dynamic compensation contract. The extra reduction level is given by

$$\upsilon(t) = \frac{\alpha}{\gamma} + (2\delta - 2)\frac{\alpha}{\gamma} - l^t(2\delta - 1)\frac{\alpha}{\gamma} = \big[1 - l^t\big]\big[2\delta - 1\big]\frac{\alpha}{\gamma}. \tag{19}$$

(19) and the specific compensation policy (17a) allow to compute the LHS of the compliance constraint (16):

$$\sum_{t=\tau+1}^{\infty} \delta_k^t X(t) = 2\delta\alpha \sum_{t=\tau+1}^{\infty} \delta_k^t \left[\upsilon(t) - \upsilon(t-1) \right] =$$

$$2\delta\alpha \sum_{t=\tau+1}^{\infty} \delta_k^t l^t \left[l^{-1} - 1 \right] \left[2\delta - 1 \right] \frac{\alpha}{\gamma} =$$

$$2\delta \frac{\alpha^2}{\gamma} \left[l^{-1} - 1 \right] \left[2\delta - 1 \right] \frac{\delta_k^{\tau+1} l^{\tau+1}}{1 - \delta_k l}$$

(19) produces extra costs according to

$$\Delta\left[\upsilon(\tau) \right] = \frac{\gamma}{2} \left\{ \left[\left(1 - l^\tau \right)(2\delta - 1)\frac{\alpha}{\gamma} \right]^2 - \left[\left(1 - l^{\tau-1} \right)(2\delta - 1)\frac{\alpha}{\gamma} \right]^2 \right\} =$$

$$\frac{(2\delta - 1)^2 \alpha^2}{2\gamma} \left[l^{-1} - 1 \right] l^\tau \left[2 - l^\tau \left(l^{-1} + 1 \right) \right]$$

(20)

and a compliance constraint according to

$$2\delta \frac{\delta_k l}{1 - \delta_k l} \geq \frac{2\delta - 1}{2(1 - \delta_k)} \left[\frac{2}{1 - \delta_k l} - \frac{l^\tau \left(l^{-1} + 1 \right)}{1 - \delta_k l^2} \right].$$

(21)

When τ grows infinitely, l^τ vanishes. Thus, the critical l^* of which the dynamic contract should not fall short is given by

$$l^* = \frac{2\delta - 1}{2\delta \delta_k (1 - \delta_k)}.$$

(22)

Since $\delta > 0.5$ for any joint transfer policy, the numerator is positive. Additionally, l^* should not exceed unity:

$$2\delta - 1 < 2\delta \delta_k (1 - \delta_k)$$

(23)

$$\Rightarrow \qquad \delta_k \in \emptyset \text{ if } \delta > \frac{2}{3}$$

$$\delta_k \in \left[\frac{1}{2} - \sqrt{\frac{1}{2\delta} - \frac{3}{4}}, \frac{1}{2} + \sqrt{\frac{1}{2\delta} - \frac{3}{4}} \right] \text{ if } \delta \le \frac{2}{3}$$

(23) describes the scope for joint transfer policies based on an arbitrary compensation policy rule which does not maximize the donors' bargaining gains. There are other contracts which are more favorable for i and j. The restriction imposed by δ is due to this compensation rule because a high δ implies high transfers which are more likely to violate the compliance constraint. Nevertheless (23) shows that discount factors of the recipient country k which are less than 0.5 do not exclude transfer policies for the introduction of an irreversible reduction technology.

Compensation policies which are based on a reversible technology are time-invariant because the reductions in the past do not play any role for the present extra reductions. The extra costs of reductions are given by:

$$\Phi(\omega) = \frac{\beta}{2} \left\{ \left[\frac{\alpha}{\beta} + \omega \right]^2 - \left[\frac{\alpha}{\beta} \right]^2 \right\} = \alpha\omega + \frac{\beta}{2}\omega^2. \tag{24}$$

ω denotes the extra reduction efforts which are based on a reversible technology and initiated by transfers. The compliance constraint is given by (25):

$$\frac{1}{1-\delta_k} X(\omega) - \frac{1}{1-\delta_k} \left[\alpha\omega + \frac{\beta}{2}\omega^2 \right] \ge X(\omega) \Leftrightarrow$$
$$X(\omega) \ge \frac{1}{\delta_k} \left[\alpha\omega + \frac{\beta}{2}\omega^2 \right] \tag{25}$$

Again, the compensations will never exceed $2\delta\alpha\omega$ because they are given in advance. For this policy, this section assumes that i and j are able to skim the maximum bargaining gains in the case of compensating for extra reductions based on a reversible technology. They just meet the compliance constraint by their transfers to k and maximize the Lindahlian utility:

$$\max_{\omega} \left\{ 2\delta\alpha\omega - \frac{1}{\delta_k} \left[\alpha\omega + \frac{\beta}{2}\omega^2 \right] \right\} \Rightarrow \omega^* = \begin{cases} 0 \text{ if } \delta\delta_k < 0.5 \\ \left(2\delta - \frac{1}{\delta_k} \right) \frac{\alpha}{\beta} \text{ if } \delta\delta_k \ge 0.5 \end{cases} \tag{26}$$

If $\delta < 0.5$ or $\delta_k < 0.5$, i and j will introduce no compensation policies. (26) demonstrates that there is no scope for joint transfer policies if δ_k falls short of 0.5. If δ_k exceeds 0.5, however, it is known from Section 2 that cooperation between i or j and k lead to first-best results as well. Then, it is not clear why k should be the recipient country but i or j could be as well. The irreversible technology option did not rule out $\delta_k < 0.5$. Hence, it can be seen from (23) and (26) that an arbitrary compensation policy for introducing an irreversible reduction technology may be more profitable for i and j. As the support for introducing reversible reduction measures was able to skim the maximum bargaining gains, the scope for compensating for irreversible reduction measures is obviously larger.

The section has shown that the problem of technology choice is different for the cooperating countries and for the compensations given to a third country. If the cooperating countries in the coalition have an intertemporal preference which implies a discount factor which exceeds 0.5, they may introduce compensation policies. Discount factors which exceed 0.5 guarantee also that the full cooperative level in the inner coalition is reached. Unless the costs of the irreversible technology surmount the costs of the irreversible technology significantly, this cooperation is based on irreversible reduction measures if δ_k is below 0.5. The full cooperation of the coalition is a necessary and sufficient condition for any compensation policies. The compensation policies depends on the impatience of the country which is to be compensated for extra reductions and on the impatience of the paying countries which are assumed to face a time lag between compensations and realized extra reductions. Furthermore, the ambiguity with respect to the preferred technology for which compensations are paid may explain why impatient countries receive support for irreversible technologies which do not minimize costs. They may bear a strategic advantage for the donors which may overcompensate for higher costs. This strategic advantage can be explained by the discount factor of country k. A low discount factor does not only determine the compliance incentive but also the sum of discounted costs which arise when an irreversible measure is introduced. If δ_k is not too high, these costs are not too high for the recipient country when deciding on compliance, and this determines the strategic advantage for the donors because irreversibility substitutes for commitment to behave compliantly in the future.

5.   SUMMARY AND CONCLUSIONS

This paper has demonstrated that partial cooperation with respect to the use of an international environmental resource may result in broader cooperation because two countries are able to pay a third country for extra reduction efforts. When addressing environmental problems which affect more than three countries, either this coalition may compensate further countries or other subcoalitions may be formed. Thus, although the starting coalition was assumed to comprise only two countries, broader cooperation is not restricted to coalitions which consist of two countries only.

The paper assumes identical benefits and costs and has demonstrated the crucial role of the discount factors in such a setting. The impatience of the donors decides on the degree of extra reductions whereas the impatience of the receiving country plays no role except for the switching costs. Exploring the implications of irreversible technologies, the paper has demonstrated that irreversibility may serve for commitment which may make these technologies superior. This result may also explain policies which compensate for the introduction of an obviously cost-inferior reduction technology which is very capital-intensive.

REFERENCES

Barrett, S. (1991), The Paradox of International Environmental Agreements, mimeo, London Business School.

Barrett, S. (1992), International Environmental Agreements as Games, in R. Pethig, *Conflicts and Cooperation in Managing Environmental Resources*, Springer: Berlin.

Bauer, A. (1992), International Cooperation over Environmental Goods, Münchener Wirtschaftswissenschaftliche Beiträge Nr. 92-17.

Carraro, C., D. Siniscalco (1993), Strategies for the International Protection of the Environment, *Journal of Public Economics*, 52: 309-328.

Damme, E. van (1989), Renegotiation-proof equilibria in repeated prisoner's dilemma, *Journal of Economic Theory*, 47: 206-207.

Farrell, J., E. Maskin (1989), Renegotiation in Repeated Games, *Games and Economic Behavior*, 1: 327-360.

Heal, G. (1992), International Negotiations on Emission Control, *Structural Change and Economic Dynamics*, 3: 223-240.

Stähler, F. (1996), "Reflections on Multilateral Environmental Agreements", in Xepapadeas, A. (Ed.), *Economic Policy for Natural Resources and the Environment*, Edward Elgar, Aldershot.

Stähler, F. (1998), Economic Games and Strategic Behaviour. Theory and Application, Edward Elgar, Aldershot.

APPENDIX

Computation of the limit of self-enforcing reduction efforts

Rearranging (10) and eliminating the benefit and costs parameters leads to a rewritten compliance constraint:

$$f(\tau-1)^2 - f(\tau)^2 + \delta f(\tau)^2 - \frac{1-\delta}{\delta\tau} \sum_{t=\tau+1}^{\infty} \delta^{\tau} f(\tau)^2 \geq 2\left[f(\tau-1)-f(\tau)\right] \Leftrightarrow$$

$$f(\tau-1)+f(\tau)+\frac{\delta f(\tau)^2 - \dfrac{1-\delta}{\delta\tau} \displaystyle\sum_{t=\tau+1}^{\infty} \delta^{\tau} f(\tau)^2}{f(\tau-1)-f(\tau)} \equiv \Omega(\tau) \leq 2$$

One may compute the limit by a linear approximation. Defining $f(\tau+1)=a$, $f(\tau)=a+b$, $f(\tau-1)=a+2b$, $f(\tau+2)=a-b,...$ and inserting this linear approximation into the sum term of the compliance constraint gives

$$\frac{1-\delta}{\delta\tau} \sum_{t=\tau+1}^{\infty} \delta^{\tau} f(t)^2 = (1-\delta)\sum_{n=1}^{\infty} \delta^n \left[a-(n-1)b\right]^2 =$$

$$\delta a^2 - \left\{ 2ab \sum_{n=1}^{\infty} 2\delta^n (n-1) - a^2b^2 \sum_{n=1}^{\infty} 2\delta^n (n-1)^2 \right\}(1-\delta) =$$

$$\delta a^2 - \left\{ \frac{2\delta^2 ab}{(1-\delta)^2} - a^2b^2 \sum_{n=1}^{\infty} 2\delta^n (n-1)^2 \right\}(1-\delta)$$

and leads to $\Omega(\tau) = 2a + 3b + 2\delta a + \delta b + \dfrac{2\delta^2 a}{1-\delta} - (1-\delta)a^2b \displaystyle\sum_{n=1}^{\infty} \delta^n (n-1)^2$.

Due to $\lim\limits_{n\to\infty} \left\{ \delta^n \left[n-1\right]^2 \right\} = 0$

(necessary condition for convergence) and

$$\lim_{n\to\infty}\left\{\frac{n^2\delta^{n+1}}{(n-1)^2\,\delta^n}\right\}=\delta\,\lim_{n\to\infty}\left\{\frac{n^2}{n^2-2n+1}\right\}=\delta<1$$

(sufficient condition for convergence), the sum term in $\Omega(\tau)$ converges when $n\to\infty$. This allows to compute the infinite limit of $\Omega(\tau)$ which is given for $b\to0$ and must not exceed 2:

$$\lim_{\tau\to\infty}\Omega(\tau)=\lim_{b\to0}\Omega(\tau)=\frac{2a}{1-\delta}\le2\Leftrightarrow a\le1-\delta\Rightarrow\theta=1-\delta.$$

This shows that a self-enforcing dynamic contract can maximally approach 1-δ.

Computation of υ^∞

Again, one may compute the limit by a linear approximation. Let $h(t)$ represent the dynamics of the contract:

$$\upsilon(t)=\frac{\alpha}{\gamma}-h(t)\frac{\alpha}{\gamma},h(0)=1,h'<0,0<h(t)\le1,\lim_{\tau\to\infty}h(\tau)=\psi.$$

The difference is defined by

$$\upsilon(t)-\upsilon(t-1)=\left[h(t-1)-h(t)\right]\frac{\alpha}{\gamma}.$$

A necessary (though not sufficient) condition for cooperation of the recipient country is that the sum of discounted transfers does not fall short of the sum of discounted costs of the *current* reduction measure:

$$2\delta\frac{\alpha^2}{\gamma}\sum_{t=\tau+1}^{\infty}\delta_k^t\left[h(t-1)-h(t)\right]\ge$$
$$\delta_k^{\tau+1}\frac{\frac{\alpha^2}{2\gamma}\left[h(\tau)^2-h(\tau-1)^2\right]+\frac{2\alpha^2}{\gamma}\left[h(\tau-1)-h(\tau)\right]}{1-\delta_k}$$

The linear approximation

$$h(\tau)=c,\ h(\tau+1)=c-d,h(\tau-1)=c+d,\ \dots$$

changes this condition into

$$2\delta + c + \frac{d}{2} - 2 \geq 0.$$

The condition is always met if this condition holds for a $d \to 0$ because a zero d gives the limit of strictly decreasing additional reductions:

$$2\delta + c - 2 \geq 0 \Leftrightarrow c \geq 2 - 2\delta \Rightarrow \psi = \begin{cases} 1 & \text{if } \delta \leq 0.5 \\ 2 - 2\delta & \text{if } \delta > 0.5 \end{cases}$$

This shows that a self-enforcing compensation policy can only be introduced if δ surmounts 0.5 and that h can at best approach 2-2δ.

9. Managing Global Pollution Problems by Reduction and Adaptation Policies

Frank Stähler

1. INTRODUCTION[1]

The previous paper in this volume considered the chances of international cooperation for environmental protection. Obviously, global problems like depleting the ozone layer, heating-up the atmosphere by emitting greenhouse gases and destroying biospheres require international cooperation. The previous paper has shown that international cooperation is sustainable only if every country is always at least not worse off by fulfilling the agreement than by breaking it.

This paper does not consider the chances of cooperative behavior but discusses the non-cooperative management of global pollution problems. Already the Earth Summit in 1992 has demonstrated that workable cooperation is obviously hard to achieve (Heister, Klepper, Stähler, 1992), and the first factual agreement reached recently in Kyoto is not more than a less ambitious starting-point. For these reasons, this paper considers international environmental policy still as a non-cooperative issue. Similar to the model of the previous paper, it assumes that two countries i and j use a global international environmental resource by emitting pollutants.

Contrary to the model of the previous paper, this paper will enlarge the analysis of a standard static non-cooperative game by two aspects which the literature has ignored so far. First, a country will be assumed to be able to

[1] This paper was a contribution to a research project on the stability of international environmental agreements supported by the Volkswagen Foundation. I am indebted to Johannes Heister and Peter Michaelis for useful comments on a first draft of this paper. The usual disclaimer applies.

improve the environmental quality not only by reducing emissions but also by adapting to changed environmental conditions. This paper will not assume that reduction and adaptation effects are strictly separable. On the contrary, it will assume that positive economies of scope exist between reduction and adaptation policies.

Second, managing environmental deterioration by adaptation policies can itself result in externalities for the other countries. Hence, this paper will add externality effects to the standard effects of adaptation policies. In doing so, it does not merely add an unchangeable suffer or benefit for either country but assumes that a country can influence the degree of externalities from which it suffers or which it enjoys. It may change its reduction efforts which influence the adaptation policy of the other country through the scope effect.

This paper will question the standard results of an international non-cooperative reduction game. Scope effects and externalities are likely to modify these results essentially. Thus, the ambiguity surrounding any theoretical forecast even in these static scenarios of this paper implies that the crucial parameters should be carefully investigated. The paper is organized as follows: Section 2 presents a model of interdependent reduction and adaptation policies. Section 3 compares the non-cooperative with the cooperative outcome, considers the slope of the reaction curves and discusses the role of different conjectures. Section 4 deals with corner solutions in the non-cooperative setting because sufficiently strong scope effects are able to violate the second-order-conditions for a joint reduction and adaptation policy. Section 5 summarizes the paper and concludes.

2.   A MODEL OF REDUCTION AND ADAPTATION POLICIES

Modelling interdependent reduction and adaptation policies means enlarging the standard static approach of global pollution problems. Let q_i (q_j) and x_i (x_j) denote the reduction efforts and investments for adaptation measures of country i (j), respectively. For the sake of simplicity, quadratic functions will give costs and benefits:

$$B_i = \alpha_i Q - \beta_i Q^2/2 + \gamma_i x_i - \delta_i x_i^2/2 + \varepsilon_i Q x_i - \omega_i x_i \qquad (1)$$
$$B_j = \alpha_j Q - \beta_j Q^2/2 + \gamma_j x_j - \delta_j x_j^2/2 + \varepsilon_j Q x_j - \omega_j x_j$$
$$\alpha_i, \ \beta_i, \ \gamma_i, \ \delta_i, \ \varepsilon_i, \alpha_j, \ \beta_j, \ \gamma_j, \ \delta_j, \ \varepsilon_j > 0,$$
$$Q = q_i + q_j < \min\{\alpha_i/\beta_i, \ \alpha_j/\beta_j\}, q_i, q_j > 0, x_i < \gamma_i/\delta_i, x_j < \gamma_j/\delta_j$$

Total benefits consist of benefits which depend on the degree of *total* reductions, of benefits which depend on the degree of *national* investments for adaptation measures, of the beneficial scope effects and of the externality effect. Scope and externality effects enter the benefit functions linearly which will simplify the discussion of conjectures and second-order-conditions in the following sections significantly. Restricting the relevant ranges of Q, of x_i and of x_j ensures that the first derivatives are positive. $\varepsilon_i = \partial^2 B_i / \partial Q \partial x_i$ and $\varepsilon_j = \partial^2 B_j / \partial Q \partial x_j$ mirror the scope effects and indicate the positive marginal change of the marginal benefits of reductions (adaptations) by a change of adaptations (reductions).

Several specific policy options fit the presentation by scope effects. E.g., consider a country which faces the risks of droughts because the release of greenhouse gases heats up the atmosphere. In addition to reducing greenhouse gas emissions, the country may opt to install an irrigation infrastructure in order to avoid harvest losses. In this case, an increase in greenhouse gas reductions can improve the marginal productivity of irrigation measures because lower global change risks improve the insurance against famines which is provided by irrigation. Alternatively, adaptation policies may specify incentives to emigrate in order to preserve a certain living standard for the remaining population. This danger which troubles many politicians in industrialized countries can originate from adaptation policies because a decrease or non-increase of the domestic population can improve the success of reduction policies.

Both examples shed also some light on the externality effects of adaptation policies which are indicated by the sign of ω. The pressure of immigration illustrates the effect of adaptation policies on another country. Erecting an irrigation infrastructure can represent a negative externality, too, because it can shorten the water availability in the other country significantly. Both effects confirm that managing specific pollution issues in a certain manner merely transfers the pollution problem to another agent (Bird, 1987). However, also positive externalities are conceivable. E.g., erecting dikes and dams to protect lowland against a rising sea level can also protect the lowland of the other country behind. Hence, ω can be positive or negative.

Reductions and adaptations incur costs which are given by

$$C_i = \theta_i q_i^2 / 2, \quad C_j = \theta_j q_j^2 / 2 \tag{2}$$
$$\theta_i, \theta_j > 0$$

and

$$D_i = \kappa_i x_i^2 / 2, \quad D_j = \kappa_j x_j^2 / 2 \tag{3}$$
$$\kappa_i, \kappa_j > 0$$

The basic structure of this model implies that country i (j) is not helpless in influencing the degree of externalities which are linearly dependent on the adaptation policy of j (i). Any variation of i's (j's) reduction efforts changes the adaptation policy of j (i) through the economies of scope. Hence, a country fearing substantial negative externalities can mitigate these effects by changing its own reduction plans. The next section will take these effects into account when different conjectures are considered.

3.   COOPERATIVE AND NON-COOPERATIVE INTERNATIONAL POLICIES

This section assumes that the second-order-conditions are fulfilled for the cooperative and non-cooperative solution. The appendix deals with these conditions explicitly and the following section will discuss corner solutions which are relevant if the second-order conditions are violated. Let U denote the sum of the net welfare of both countries. If a cooperative agreement assigns equal weights to each country's net benefits, the maximization of U with respect to the four instrument variables gives the optimal cooperative solution:

$$(\alpha_i + \alpha_j) - (\beta_i + \beta_j)(q_i + q_j) + \varepsilon_i\,x_i + \varepsilon_j\,x_j - \theta_i\,q_i = 0 \qquad (4)$$
$$\gamma_i - \delta_i\,x_i + \varepsilon_i\,(q_i + q_j) - \omega_j - \kappa_i\,x_i = 0$$
$$(\alpha_i + \alpha_j) - (\beta_i + \beta_j)(q_i + q_j) + \varepsilon_i\,x_i + \varepsilon_j\,x_j - \theta_j\,q_j = 0$$
$$\gamma_j - \delta_j\,x_j + \varepsilon_j\,(q_i + q_j) - \omega_i - \kappa_j\,x_j = 0$$

The lack of a cooperative agreement implies that every country takes only the effects of its own policy instruments on its own net benefits into account. Section 2 has already mentioned that the reduction policy can vary the degree of externalities. Without going into detail now, let (5) represent the conjectures of i and j with respect to a change of x_j and x_i by a change of q_i and q_j, respectively:

$$x'_j \equiv \Omega_i(q_i), \qquad \frac{d\Omega_i}{dq_i} = \text{const.} \geq 0, \qquad (5)$$

$$x'_i \equiv \Omega_j(q_j), \qquad \frac{d\Omega_j}{dq_j} = \text{const.} \geq 0.$$

Hence, the first-order-conditions for i and j are

$$\alpha_i - \left(\beta_i + \theta_i\right)q_i - \beta_i q_j + \varepsilon_i x_i - \omega_i \frac{d\Omega_i}{dq_i} = 0, \tag{6}$$

$$\gamma_i - \left(\delta_i + \kappa_i\right)x_i + \varepsilon_i\left(q_i + q_j\right) = 0,$$

$$\alpha_j - \left(\beta_j + \theta_j\right)q_j - \beta_j q_i + \varepsilon_j x_j - \omega_j \frac{d\Omega_j}{dq_j} = 0,$$

$$\gamma_j - \left(\delta_j + \kappa_j\right)x_j + \varepsilon_j\left(q_i + q_j\right) = 0.$$

In the case of mutual negative externalities, comparing (6) and (4) demonstrates that foregone benefits due to ignoring the harmful impacts of one country's adaptation policies on the other country supplement the foregone benefits due to non-cooperative reduction policies. According to (7),

$$x_i = \frac{\gamma_i + \varepsilon_i\left(q_i + q_j\right)}{\delta_i + \kappa_i}, \qquad x_j = \frac{\gamma_j + \varepsilon_j\left(q_i + q_j\right)}{\delta_j + \kappa_j} \tag{7}$$

the adaptation policy does only depend on the reduction policies. Inserting (7) into the first and third line of (6) gives the reaction curves $q_i = R_i(q_j)$ and $q_j = R_j(q_i)$ of i and j:

$$\tag{8}$$

$$R_i\left(q_j\right) \equiv \frac{\alpha_i\left(\delta_i + \kappa_i\right) + \varepsilon_i \gamma_i + \left[\varepsilon_i^2 - \beta_i\left(\delta_i + \kappa_i\right)\right]q_j - \omega_i\left(\delta_i + \kappa_i\right)d\Omega_i/dq_i}{\left|H_i\right|}$$

$$R_j\left(q_i\right) \equiv \frac{\alpha_j\left(\delta_j + \kappa_j\right) + \varepsilon_j \gamma_j + \left[\varepsilon_j^2 - \beta_j\left(\delta_j + \kappa_j\right)\right]q_i - \omega_j\left(\delta_j + \kappa_j\right)d\Omega_j/dq_j}{\left|H_j\right|}$$

$|H_k| = (\beta_k + \theta_k)(\delta_k + \kappa_k) - \varepsilon_k^2$, $k = i, j$, denotes the determinant of the Hessian which must be positive in order to fulfil the second-order-conditions.[2] Both reaction curves have a linear slope:

---

2   A positive $|H_k|$ guarantees a global maximum which may be a too strict condition. However, a local optimum requires only a non-negative $|H_k|$ which includes a zero $|H_k|$. A zero $|H_k|$ is ruled out here for reasons of better tractability.

$$\frac{dR_i}{dq_j} = -1 + \frac{\theta_i(\delta_i + \kappa_i)}{|H_i|} := \Phi_i > -1, \tag{9}$$

$$\frac{dR_j}{dq_i} = -1 + \frac{\theta_j(\delta_j + \kappa_j)}{|H_j|} := \Phi_j > -1.$$

Interestingly, there exists a range of positive ε_i's and ε_j's which implies positively sloped reaction curves while leaving $|H_i|$ and $|H_j|$ still positive. The condition for the determinant of the Hessians and (9) determine this range as

$$\sqrt{\delta_i(\delta_i + \kappa_i)} < \varepsilon_i < \sqrt{(\delta_i + \theta_i)(\delta_i + \kappa_i)}, \tag{10}$$
$$\sqrt{\delta_j(\delta_j + \kappa_j)} < \varepsilon_j < \sqrt{(\delta_j + \theta_j)(\delta_j + \kappa_j)}.$$

The higher the second derivatives of the reduction cost functions, i.e. θ_i and θ_j, are the larger is the range of ε_i and ε_j which fulfil (10). However, large θs do not imply a steep inclination of the reaction curve because they dominate the numerator and the denominator of the quotients in (9). These quotients approach unity as θ increases which results in a negligibly positive slope.

(10) demonstrates that a sufficiently strong scope effect is able to imply positive reactions. In such a case, if country i (j) increases its reduction efforts, country j (i) will react by increasing its reduction efforts, too, because the change in benefits via the scope term is so strong that own reduction efforts must be increased to balance the cost-weighted marginal benefits of reductions and adaptations. This effect deserves careful attention because the positive reaction is due to non-cooperative maximization. An increase of q_j increases the marginal productivity of x_i which must be compensated by an increase of q_i in order to maximize net benefits. A marginal balancing of x_i and q_i is necessary to adjust optimally to an external productivity shift. If this partial effect overcompensates the partial free-rider-effect, the reaction curve will be sloped upwards.

In order to determine the equilibrium values of q_i and q_j, defining some new terms is convenient:

$$\Sigma_i = \frac{\alpha_i(\delta_i + \kappa_i) + \varepsilon_i\gamma_i}{|H_i|}, \Sigma_j = \frac{\alpha_j(\delta_j + \kappa_j) + \varepsilon_j\gamma_j}{|H_j|},$$
$$T_i = \omega_i(\delta_i + \kappa_i), T_j = \omega_j(\delta_j + \kappa_j)$$

This model assumes that Σ_i and Σ_j are non-negative because negative reductions do not make sense even for zero reductions of the other country. Inserting these terms into (8) and solving for the equilibrium values gives

$$q_i^* = \frac{\Sigma_i + \Phi_i \Sigma_j - \Phi_i T_j \left. d\Omega_j \middle/ dq_j \right. - T_i \left. d\Omega_i \middle/ dq_i \right.}{1 - \Phi_i \Phi_j}, \tag{11}$$

$$q_j^* = \frac{\Sigma_j + \Phi_j \Sigma_i - \Phi_j T_i \left. d\Omega_i \middle/ dq_i \right. - T_j \left. d\Omega_j \middle/ dq_j \right.}{1 - \Phi_i \Phi_j}.$$

(11) assumes that a unique Nash solution always exists, i.e. that the equation system is non-singular. The standard assumption concerning the comparative statics' properties of non-cooperative game theory, i.e. $\Phi_i \Phi_j < 1$, meets this condition.

One may now introduce three different types of conjectures concerning the ability of a country to assess the influence of own reduction policies on the degree of externalities. There has been an extensive discussion about the potential role of conjectures in economics, especially in the theory of industrial organization (for an overview, see Martin, 1993, p. 24-30). Since a proper choice of conjectures can lead to every possible outcome, the relevance of conjectures which take the reaction of an opponent into account has been questioned. In the empirical literature, however, conjectures are used to model dynamic behavior in a basically static framework without introducing an explicit dynamic model. It is this approach which is adopted here because global pollution problems are obviously long-run policy issues. The conjectures employed in this model reflect also different degrees of a country's "policy sophistication":

- The case of *ignorance* assumes no influence on the externalities:

$$\frac{d\Omega_k}{dq_k} = 0 \tag{C1}$$

- The case of *partial integration* recognizes that, due to (5), an increase of reductions causes an increase of externalities:

$$\frac{d\Omega_i}{dq_i} = \frac{\varepsilon_j}{\delta_j + \kappa_j}, \qquad \frac{d\Omega_j}{dq_j} = \frac{\varepsilon_i}{\delta_i + \kappa_i} \tag{C2}$$

- The case of *total integration* recognizes additionally the variation of the other reduction level because an increase in q modifies also the other country's reduction level according to (8):

$$\frac{d\Omega_i}{dq_i} = \frac{\varepsilon_j}{\delta_j + \kappa_j}\left(1 + \Phi_j\right), \quad \frac{d\Omega_j}{dq_j} = \frac{\varepsilon_i}{\delta_i + \kappa_i}\left(1 + \Phi_i\right) \tag{C2}$$

Starting with discussing the case of ignorance for both countries, it is evident that the existence of economies of scope - measured by ε_i and ε_j - unambiguously mitigates the free-rider-effect which standard models observe. The introduction of non-negative ε's increases Σ_i, Σ_j, Φ_i and Φ_j and thus the equilibrium values q_i^* and q_j^*. For the case of ignorance, this result holds independent of the signs of T_i and T_j.

Conjectures C2 and C3 change the equilibrium values dependent on the signs of T_i and T_j. Table 1 summarizes the nine possible combinations of equilibrium values. The table reveals that determining the equilibrium values depends on a complex interplay among the slopes of the reaction curves, the signs of T_i and T_j and the different conjectures. Even if attention is restricted to the diagonal of Table 1 because other combinations imply asymmetric conjectures, the change of equilibrium values is by no means clear when compared to C1/C1. E.g., if both countries suffer from adaptations of each other, i.e. T_i, $T_j < 0$, the conjecture combination C2/C2 does only lead to lower equilibrium values if the slopes of the reaction curves Φ_i and Φ_j are negative. In such a case, C3/C3 is a damper on this effect.

The roles of ε_i and ε_j remain decisive for the interior solutions because they determine the slopes of the reaction curve and determine the changes which C2 and C3 induce. Hence, it should be interesting to know how a

Table 1: Equilibrium values for different conjecture combinations

	C1(i)	C2(i)	C3(i)
C1(j)	$q_i^* = \dfrac{\Sigma_i + \Phi_i\Sigma_j}{1-\Phi_i\Phi_j}$ $q_j^* = \dfrac{\Sigma_j + \Phi_j\Sigma_i}{1-\Phi_i\Phi_j}$	$q_i^* = \dfrac{\Sigma_i + \Phi_i\Sigma_j - T_i\varepsilon_j/(\delta_j+\kappa_j)}{1-\Phi_i\Phi_j}$ $q_j^* = \dfrac{\Sigma_j + \Phi_j\Sigma_i - \Phi_i T_i\varepsilon_j/(\delta_j+\kappa_j)}{1-\Phi_i\Phi_j}$	$q_i^* = \dfrac{\Sigma_i + \Phi_i\Sigma_j + T_i\varepsilon_j(1-\Phi_j)/(\delta_j+\kappa_j)}{1-\Phi_i\Phi_j}$ $q_j^* = \dfrac{\Sigma_j + \Phi_j\Sigma_i - \left(\Phi_i T_i\varepsilon_j + T_i\varepsilon_j\right)/(\delta_i+\kappa_i)}{1-\Phi_i\Phi_j}$
C2(j)	$q_i^* = \dfrac{\Sigma_i + \Phi_i\Sigma_j - \Phi_i T_j\varepsilon_i/(\delta_i+\kappa_i)}{1-\Phi_i\Phi_j}$ $q_j^* = \dfrac{\Sigma_j + \Phi_j\Sigma_i - T_j\varepsilon_i/(\delta_i+\kappa_i)}{1-\Phi_i\Phi_j}$	$q_i^* = \dfrac{\Sigma_i + \Phi_i\Sigma_j - \left(\Phi_i T_j\varepsilon_i + T_i\varepsilon_j\right)/(\delta_j+\kappa_j)}{1-\Phi_i\Phi_j}$ $q_j^* = \dfrac{\Sigma_j + \Phi_j\Sigma_i - \left(\Phi_j T_j\varepsilon_j + T_j\varepsilon_i\right)/(\delta_i+\kappa_i)}{1-\Phi_i\Phi_j}$	$q_i^* = \dfrac{\Sigma_i + \Phi_i\Sigma_j - \left(\Phi_i T_j\varepsilon_i + T_i\varepsilon_j(1+\Phi_i)\right)/(\delta_j+\kappa_j)}{1-\Phi_i\Phi_j}$ $q_j^* = \dfrac{\Sigma_j + \Phi_j\Sigma_i - \left(\Phi_j T_j\varepsilon_j + T_j\varepsilon_i(1+\Phi_j)\right)/(\delta_i+\kappa_i)}{1-\Phi_i\Phi_j}$
C3(j)	$q_i^* = \dfrac{\Sigma_i + \Phi_i\Sigma_j - \Phi_i T_j\varepsilon_i(1+\Phi_i)/(\delta_i+\kappa_i)}{1-\Phi_i\Phi_j}$ $q_j^* = \dfrac{\Sigma_j + \Phi_j\Sigma_i + T_j\varepsilon_i(1-\Phi_i)/(\delta_i+\kappa_i)}{1-\Phi_i\Phi_j}$	$q_i^* = \dfrac{\Sigma_i + \Phi_i\Sigma_j - \left(\Phi_i T_j\varepsilon_i(1+\Phi_i) + T_i\varepsilon_j\right)/(\delta_j+\kappa_j)}{1-\Phi_i\Phi_j}$ $q_j^* = \dfrac{\Sigma_j + \Phi_j\Sigma_i - \left(\Phi_j T_j\varepsilon_j + T_j\varepsilon_i(1+\Phi_i)\right)/(\delta_i+\kappa_i)}{1-\Phi_i\Phi_j}$	$q_i^* = \dfrac{\Sigma_i + \Phi_i\Sigma_j - \left(\Phi_j T_i\varepsilon_i + T_j\varepsilon_i(1+\Phi_i)\right)/(\delta_j+\kappa_j)}{1-\Phi_i\Phi_j}$ $q_j^* = \dfrac{\Sigma_j + \Phi_j\Sigma_i - \left(\Phi_j T_j\varepsilon_i(1+\Phi_i) + T_j\varepsilon_i(1+\Phi_i)\right)/(\delta_i+\kappa_i)}{1-\Phi_i\Phi_j}$

change in ε_i or ε_j will alter the equilibrium values q_i^* and q_j^*. This change can be due to new scientific results or from the availability of new adaptation measures which both emphasize the interdependence between reductions and adaptations. Taking ε_i as an example, differentiations (which have been carried out in the appendix) yield predominantly ambiguous results. Assuming that C1 holds for both countries, Table 2 summarizes the different combinations.

Table 2:   *Differentiations with respect to ε_i in the case of C1/C1*

	$\dfrac{\partial q_i^*}{\partial \varepsilon_i}$	$\dfrac{\partial q_j^*}{\partial \varepsilon_i}$
$\Phi_i, \Phi_j < 0$	ambiguous	ambiguous
$\Phi_i > 0, \Phi_j < 0$	ambiguous	ambiguous
$\Phi_i, \Phi_j > 0$	positive	positive
$\Phi_i < 0, \Phi_j > 0$	ambiguous	positive

The appendix proves that the ambiguity in signs cannot be removed if both countries anticipate the effects of their policies according to C2 or C3.

4.   CORNER SOLUTIONS IN THE NON-COOPERATIVE SETTING

The previous chapter has ruled out corner solutions by assuming negative definiteness. However, scope effects are apt to conflict with negative definiteness. Thus, this section will address non-cooperative corner solutions and compare them with the cooperative outcome. Whenever this chapter will use second-order conditions, the reader is referred to the appendix for details.

First observe that $d^2\Omega_k/dq_k^2 = d^2\Omega_k/dq_kdq_l = 0$ for any $k,l \in \{i,j\}$. Hence, conjectures are not relevant for the second-order-conditions *in this model*. Taking country i as an example, suppose that

$$(\beta_i + \theta_i)(\delta_i + \kappa_i) - \varepsilon_i^2 \left(= \left|E_2^i\right|\right) < 0 \qquad (12)$$

holds. (12) indicates that the first-order-conditions now represent a saddle point. The scope effects are so strong that an interior solution cannot be optimal for i. But (12) does not necessarily imply that one of the conditions of negative semi-definiteness for the cooperative solution is also violated.

$$\left(\beta_i + \beta_j + \theta_i\right)\left(\delta_i + \kappa_i\right) - \varepsilon_i^2\left(= \left|D_2^i\right|\right) \geq 0 \tag{13}$$

can still be fulfilled. A corner solution in the cooperative setting implies a corner solution in the non-cooperative setting, but not vice versa. There exists a range which depends on β_j and in which cooperation requires reduction *and* adaptation policies but non-cooperation stipulates either policy.[3] If country i concentrates on reduction policies, it sets x_i equal to zero:

$$\max_{q_i}\left[\alpha_i\left(q_i + q_j\right) - \frac{\beta_i\left(q_i + q_j\right)^2}{2} - \frac{\theta_i q_i^2}{2} - \omega_i x_j\right] \tag{14}$$

which leads to the optimal reduction level denoted by q_i^c:

$$q_i^c = \frac{\alpha_i - \beta_i q_j + \omega_i {d\Omega_i}/{dq_i}}{\beta_i + q_i}. \tag{15}$$

If country i concentrates on adaptation policies, it sets q_i equal to zero:

$$\max_{x_i}\left[\alpha_i q_j - \frac{\beta_i q_j^2}{2} - \gamma_i x_i - \frac{\delta_i x_i^2}{2} + \varepsilon_i q_j x_i - \omega_i x_j\right] \tag{16}$$

which leads to the optimal adaptation level denoted by x_i^c:

$$x_i^c = \frac{\gamma_i - \varepsilon_i q_j}{\beta_i + \kappa_i}. \tag{17}$$

Thus, if (12) is valid, the solution is given by

$$q_i \in \left\{0, \frac{\alpha_i - \beta_i q_j + \omega_i {d\Omega_i}/{dq_i}}{\beta_i + q_i}\right\}, x_i \in \left\{0, \frac{\gamma_i - \varepsilon_i q_j}{\beta_i + \kappa_i}\right\}, \tag{18}$$

---

[3]   The functional form rules out the no-policy-variant.

$$q_i x_i = 0, \qquad \max \{q_i, x_i\} > 0.$$

The parameters determine the superiority of the relevant policy option. The positive externalities implied by reductions make a preference for adaptation probable when (12) holds. To determine the factual preference, (17) and (15) must be inserted into the benefit functions and compared with each other. No superiority of a specific policy can be confirmed on purely theoretical grounds but both optimal levels depend on q_j. It is interesting to explore how a change in q_j changes the difference between the net benefits of an exclusive reduction policy and those of an exclusive adaptation policy. Define $\Delta_i(q_j) :=$ $U_i(q_i^c, q_j) - U_i(x_i^c, q_j)$:

$$\Delta_i\left(q_j\right) = \alpha_i q_i^c - \frac{\left(\beta_i + \theta_i\right) q^{c2}}{2} - \gamma_i x_i^c + \frac{\left(\delta_i + \kappa_i\right) x^{c2}}{2} - q_j\left(\beta_i q_i^c + \varepsilon_i x_i^c\right). \tag{19}$$

Using (15) and (17) to determine $\partial q_i^c/\partial q_j = -\beta_i/(\beta_i + \theta_i)$ and $\partial x_i^c/\partial q_j = \varepsilon_i/(\delta_i + \kappa_i)$ gives

$$\frac{d\Delta_i}{dq_j} = -\frac{\alpha_i \beta_i}{\beta_i + \theta_i} - \frac{\gamma_i \varepsilon_i}{\delta_i + \kappa_i} - q_j \left[\frac{\varepsilon_i^2}{\delta_i + \kappa_i} - \frac{\beta_i^2}{\beta_i + \theta_i} \right]. \tag{20}$$

The sign of $d\Delta_i/dq_j$ depends on the sign of the last term. Recall that $\varepsilon_i^2 > (\beta_i + \theta_i)(\delta_i + \kappa_i)$. Hence,

$$\frac{\varepsilon_i^2}{\delta_i + \kappa_i} - \frac{\beta_i^2}{\beta_i + \theta_i} > \frac{\left(\beta_i + \theta_i\right)\left(\delta_i + \kappa_i\right)}{\delta_i + \kappa_i} - \frac{\beta_i^2}{\beta_i + \theta_i}$$

$$= \frac{2\theta_i \beta_i + \theta_i^2}{\beta_i + \theta_i} > 0$$

Thus, the last term is also negative and

$$\frac{d\Delta_i}{dq_j} < 0$$

holds.[4] This result proves that, when adaptation policies are superior in the case of no reductions of j, i.e. $U_i(x_i^c,0) > U_i(q_i^c,0)$, they are also superior for any positive q_j. But if $U_i(x_i^c,0) < U_i(q_i^c,0)$, there may exist a break even-level in the relevant range of q_j. These results demonstrate also that concentrating on adaptive investments is the more profitable the higher j's reduction efforts are because the benefits of the scope effects can only be realized in the case of adaptation policies. Table 3 summarizes the different possible scenarios of corner solutions.

Table 3:   Different scenarios of corner solutions

I. $|E^i{}_2| < 0, |E^j{}_2| > 0$	II. $|E^i{}_2| < 0, |E^j{}_2| < 0$
a) $U_i(x_i^c,0) > U_i(q_i^c,0)$ $x_i^c > 0, q_i = 0, x_j, q_j > 0$ b$_1$) $U_i(x_i^c,0) < U_i(q_i^c,0), q_j < q_j^{\#}$ $q_i > 0, x_i^c = 0, x_j, q_j > 0$ b$_2$) $U_i(x_i^c,0) < U_i(q_i^c,0), q_j > q_j^{\#}$ $x_i^c > 0, q_i = 0, x_j, q_j > 0,$	a) $U_i(x_i^c,0) > U_i(q_i^c,0),$ $U_j(x_j^c,0) > U_j(q_j^c,0)$ $q_i = q_j = Q = 0$ $x_i, x_j > 0$ b) $U_i(x_i^c,0) > U_i(q_i^c,0),$ $U_j(x_j^c,0) < U_j(q_j^c,0)$ $q_i = 0 \Rightarrow x_j = 0, q_j > 0$ c) $U_i(x_i^c,0) < U_i(q_i^c,0),$ $U_j(x_j^c,0) < U_j(q_j^c,0)$ all combinations possible

$q_j^{\#}$ denotes the critical reductions of j. Reductions of j which fall short of $q_j^{\#}$ imply a concentration on reduction policies and reductions which surmount $q_j^{\#}$ imply a concentration on adaptation policies, causing a jump along the reaction curves.

---

4   Note that the D_i-function is concave because

$$\frac{d^2\Delta_i}{dq_j^2} = -\left[\frac{\varepsilon_i^2}{\delta_i + \kappa_i} - \frac{\beta_i^2}{\beta_i + \theta_i}\right] < 0.$$

This section has demonstrated that the chances for reduction policies are low if the second-order-conditions are not fulfilled. Assuming no reductions of the other country, one may expect adaptation policies because the *individual* marginal benefits of reductions are likely to fall short of the marginal costs. If this result holds, it holds also for any positive reductions of the other country. Therefore, very strong economies of scope imply no reductions whereas the standard results which guarantee an interior solution result in too low, but still positive reduction efforts.

5. SUMMARY AND CONCLUSIONS

This paper has shown that scope and externality effects introduce a good deal of ambiguity surrounding any attempt of a theoretical forecast about the non-cooperative management of global pollution problems. Scope effects can induce positively sloped reaction curves with respect to reduction efforts. When strong economies of scope exist which a country has not yet taken into account, increased reduction efforts may increase the net benefits. These effects can explain increased reduction efforts of a country which have been also considered as irrational "commitments" of a country to reduce unilaterally (Hoel, 1991). This paper has shown that these strategies can be due to efficient behavior which exploits dominant economies of scope.

The different conjectures shed some light on managing externalities which are due to the other country's adaptation policy in the long run. They increase the degree of ambiguity with respect to the equilibrium values significantly even if asymmetric conjecture combinations are ruled out. Different conjectures set the stage for strategic policy variants. They can serve as a basis to discuss long-run features of global pollution problems.

Strong scope effects are also able to violate the second-order-conditions. Whenever an exclusive adaptation policy is superior for zero reductions of the other country, it is superior also for all positive reductions of the opponent. Hence, scope effects can even conflict with the pessimistic standard non-cooperative results which show that reduction efforts are too low, but at least strictly positive. Their strength must be carefully taken into consideration when discussing international reduction games.

REFERENCES

Bird, P. (1987), The Transferability and Depletability of Externalities, *Journal of Environmental Economics and Management*, 14: 54-57.

Heister, J., G. Klepper, F. Stähler (1992), Strategien globaler Umweltpolitik. Die UNCED-Konferenz aus ökonomischer Sicht, *Zeitschrift für angewandte Umweltpolitik*, 5: 455-465.

Hoel, M. (1991), Global Environmental Problems: The Effects of Unilateral Actions Taken by One Country, *Journal of Environmental Economics and Management*, 20: 55-70.

Martin, S. (1993), Advanced Industrial Economics, Blackwell, Cambridge, Mass.

APPENDIX

Conditions for semi-definiteness

The Hessian for the cooperative outcome is given by

$$H = \begin{bmatrix} U_{q_i q_i} & U_{q_i q_j} & U_{q_i x_i} & U_{q_i x_j} \\ U_{q_j q_i} & U_{q_j q_j} & U_{q_j x_i} & U_{q_j x_j} \\ U_{x_i q_i} & U_{x_i q_j} & U_{x_i x_i} & U_{x_i x_j} \\ U_{x_j q_i} & U_{x_j q_j} & U_{x_j x_i} & U_{x_i x_j} \end{bmatrix}$$

and the second-order-conditions require

$$U_{q_i q_i}, U_{q_i q_i}, U_{x_i x_i}, U_{x_i x_j} \leq 0,$$

$$\left| D_2^1 \right| := U_{q_i q_i} U_{q_j q_j} - U_{q_i q_j}^2 \geq 0,$$

$$\left| D_2^2 \right| := U_{q_i q_i} U_{x_i x_i} - U_{q_i x_i}^2 \geq 0,$$

$$\left| D_2^3 \right| := U_{q_i q_i} U_{x_j x_j} - U_{q_i x_j}^2 \geq 0,$$

$$\left| D_2^4 \right| := U_{q_j q_j} U_{x_i x_i} - U_{q_j x_i}^2 \geq 0,$$

$$\left| D_5^5 \right| := U_{q_j q_j} U_{x_j x_j} - U_{q_j x_j}^2 \geq 0,$$

$$\left| D_2^6 \right| := U_{x_i x_i} U_{x_j x_j} - U_{x_i x_j}^2 \geq 0,$$

$$\left| D_3^1 \right| := 2 U_{q_i q_j} U_{q_i x_i} U_{q_j x_i} - U_{q_j q_j} U_{q_i x_i}^2 - U_{q_i q_i} U_{q_i x_i}^2 + U_{x_i x_i} \left| D_2^1 \right| \leq 0,$$

$$\left| D_3^2 \right| := 2 U_{q_i q_j} U_{q_i x_j} U_{q_j x_j} - U_{q_j q_j} U_{q_i x_j}^2 - U_{q_i q_i} U_{q_i x_j}^2 + U_{x_j x_j} \left| D_2^1 \right| \leq 0,$$

$$\left|D_3^3\right| := 2U_{q_i x_i} U_{q_i x_j} U_{x_i x_j} - U_{x_i x_i} U_{q_i x_j}^2 - U_{q_i q_i} U_{x_i x_j}^2 + U_{x_j x_j}\left|D_2^2\right| \le 0,$$

$$\left|D_3^4\right| := 2U_{q_j x_i} U_{q_j x_j} U_{x_i x_j} - U_{x_i x_i} U_{q_j x_j}^2 - U_{q_j q_j} U_{x_i x_j}^2 + U_{x_j x_j}\left|D_2^4\right| \le 0,$$

$$\left|D^4\right| = \left|H\right| \ge 0.$$

The model of the paper produces the Hessian H

$$|H| = \begin{bmatrix} -(\beta_i+\beta_j+\theta_i) & -(\beta_i+\beta_j) & \varepsilon_i & \varepsilon_j \\ -(\beta_i+\beta_j) & -(\beta_i+\beta_j+\theta_j) & \varepsilon_i & \varepsilon_j \\ \varepsilon_i & \varepsilon_i & -(\delta_i+\kappa_i) & 0 \\ \varepsilon_j & \varepsilon_j & 0 & -(\delta_j+\kappa_j) \end{bmatrix}$$

$U_{q_i q_i}, U_{q_j q_j}, U_{x_i x_i}, U_{x_j x_j} \le 0$ is always fulfilled. The other determinants are given by

$$\left|D_2^1\right| = (\beta_i+\beta_j+\theta_i)(\beta_i+\beta_j+\theta_j) - (\beta_i+\beta_j)^2 > 0,$$

$$\left|D_2^2\right| = (\beta_i+\beta_j+\theta_i)(\delta_i+\kappa_i) - \varepsilon_i^2,$$

$$\left|D_2^3\right| = (\beta_i+\beta_j+\theta_i)(\delta_j+\kappa_j) - \varepsilon_j^2,$$

$$\left|D_2^4\right| = (\beta_i+\beta_j+\theta_j)(\delta_i+\kappa_i) - \varepsilon_i^2,$$

$$\left|D_2^5\right| = (\beta_i+\beta_j+\theta_j)(\delta_j+\kappa_j) - \varepsilon_i^2,$$

$$\left|D_2^6\right| = (\delta_i+\kappa_i)(\delta_j+\kappa_j) > 0,$$

$$\left|D_3^1\right| = \varepsilon_i^2\theta_j - \varepsilon_i\varepsilon_j\theta_i - (\delta_i+\kappa_i)\left|D_2^1\right|,$$

$$\left|D_3^2\right| = \varepsilon_j^2(\theta_i-\theta_j) - (\delta_j+\kappa_j)\left|D_2^1\right|,$$

$$\left|D_3^3\right| = \varepsilon_j^2(\delta_i+\kappa_i) - (\delta_j+\kappa_j)\left|D_2^2\right|,$$

$$\left|D_3^4\right| = \varepsilon_j^2(\delta_i+\kappa_i) - (\delta_j+\kappa_j)\left|D_2^4\right|,$$

$$\left|D^4\right| = |H| = -\varepsilon_j^2(\theta_i-\theta_j)(\delta_i+\kappa_i) - (\delta_j+\kappa_j)\left|D_3^1\right|.$$

The second-order-conditions for the non-cooperative outcome embrace only two quadratic matrices. Let V denote the functional which is maximized non-cooperatively:

$V_{qiqi} = -(\beta_i + \theta_i) \leq 0, \; V_{xixi} = -(\delta_i + \kappa_i) \leq 0, \; V_{qjqj} = -(\beta_j + \theta_j) \leq 0,$
$V_{xjxj} = -(\delta_j + \kappa_j) \leq 0,$
$\left| E_2^i \right| = (\beta_i + \theta_i)(\delta_i + \kappa_i) - \varepsilon_i^2 \geq 0, \; \left| E_2^j \right| = (\beta_j + \theta_j)(\delta_j + \kappa_j) - \varepsilon_j^2 \geq 0.$

The last two determinants must be compared with $|D^2{}_2|$ and $|D^5{}_2|$, respectively, to determine the set of parameters β_i and β_j which fulfil the second-order-conditions in the cooperative but not in the non-cooperative setting.

Differentiations with respect to ε_i

$$\frac{\partial q_i^*}{\partial \varepsilon_i} = \frac{\dfrac{\partial \left(\Sigma_i + \Phi_i \Sigma_j \right)}{\partial \varepsilon_i}\left(1 - \Phi_i \Phi_j \right) - \dfrac{\partial \left(1 - \Phi_i \Phi_j \right)}{\partial \varepsilon_i}\left(\Sigma_i + \Phi_i \Sigma_j \right)}{\left(1 - \Phi_i \Phi_j \right)^2}$$

Disentangling the terms gives:

$$\frac{\partial \left(\Sigma_i + \Phi_i \Sigma_j \right)}{\partial \varepsilon_i} = \frac{\gamma_i\left[(\beta_i + \theta_i)(\delta_i + \kappa_i) - \varepsilon_i^2 \right] + 2\varepsilon_i\left[\alpha_i(\delta_i - \kappa_i) + \varepsilon_i \gamma_i \right]}{\left[(\beta_i + \theta_i)(\delta_i + \kappa_i) - \varepsilon_i^2 \right]^2}$$

$$+ \frac{2\varepsilon_i\left[(\beta_i + \theta_i)(\delta_i + \kappa_i) - \varepsilon_i^2 \right] + 2\varepsilon_i\left[\varepsilon_i^2 - \beta_i(\delta_i + \kappa_i) \right]}{\left[(\beta_i + \theta_i)(\delta_i + \kappa_i) - \varepsilon_i^2 \right]^2} \Sigma_j > 0$$

which is unambiguously positive,

$$\frac{\partial \left(1 - \Phi_i \Phi_j \right)}{\partial \varepsilon_i} = -\Phi_j \frac{2\varepsilon_i\left[(\beta_i + \theta_i)(\delta_i + \kappa_i) - \varepsilon_i^2 \right] + 2\varepsilon_i\left[\varepsilon_i^2 - \beta_i(\delta_i + \kappa_i) \right]}{\left[(\beta_i + \theta_i)(\delta_i + \kappa_i) - \varepsilon_i^2 \right]^2}$$

which depends on the sign of Φ_j:

$$\Phi_j \underset{>}{\overset{<}{}} 0 \Leftrightarrow \frac{\partial \left(1 - \Phi_i \Phi_j \right)}{\partial \varepsilon_i} \underset{<}{\overset{>}{}} 0.$$

$\Sigma_i + \Phi_i\Phi_j$ is positive if the slopes of the reaction curves have an equal sign and can be negative if they have opposite ones. Hence, $\partial q_i^*/\partial\varepsilon_i$ is only unambiguously positive if Φ_i and Φ_j are both positive. The signs of all other combinations depend on the parameters.

$$\frac{\partial q_j^*}{\partial\varepsilon_i} = \Phi_j \frac{\gamma_i\left[(\beta_i+\theta_i)(\delta_i+\kappa_i)-\varepsilon_i^2\right]+2\varepsilon_i\left[\alpha_i(\delta_i+\kappa_i)+\varepsilon_i\gamma_i\right]}{\left[(\beta_i+\theta_i)(\delta_i+\kappa_i)-\varepsilon_i^2\right]^2(1-\Phi_i\Phi_j)}$$

$$+\frac{\Sigma_i\Phi_j^2 \dfrac{2\varepsilon_i\left[(\beta_i+\theta_i)(\delta_i+\kappa_i)-\varepsilon_i^2\right]+2\varepsilon_i\left[\varepsilon_i^2-\beta_i(\delta_i+\kappa_i)\right]}{\left[(\beta_i+\theta_i)(\delta_i+\kappa_i)-\varepsilon_i^2\right]^2(1-\Phi_i\Phi_j)}}{(1-\Phi_i\Phi_j)^2}$$

The quotients in the numerator are both positive. Hence, if $\Phi_j > 0$, the sign is positive whereas it is ambiguous if $\Phi_j < 0$.

Taking possible conjectures into account requires to supplement $\partial q_i^*/\partial\varepsilon_i$ and $\partial q_j^*/\partial\varepsilon_i$. In the case of both countries evaluating its policy responds according to partial integration, $\partial q_i^*/\partial\varepsilon_i$ must be supplemented by

$$\mathrm{suppl}(C2,i):=T_j(1+\Phi_i\Phi_j)\frac{\dfrac{\partial\Phi_i}{\partial\varepsilon_i}\dfrac{\varepsilon_i}{\delta_i+\kappa_i}+\dfrac{\Phi_i}{\delta_i+\kappa_i}}{(1-\Phi_i\Phi_j)^2}$$

$$+\frac{\partial(1-\Phi_i\Phi_j)}{\partial\varepsilon_i}\frac{\Phi_iT_j\dfrac{\varepsilon_i}{\delta_i+\kappa_i}+T_i\dfrac{\varepsilon_j}{\delta_j+\kappa_j}}{(1-\Phi_i\Phi_j)^2}$$

whereas $\partial q_j^*/\partial\varepsilon_i$ must be supplemented by

$$\mathrm{suppl}(C2,j):=\frac{\dfrac{T_j(1-\Phi_i\Phi_j)}{\delta_i+\kappa_i}+\dfrac{T_j\varepsilon_i}{\delta_i+\kappa_i}\dfrac{\partial(1-\Phi_i\Phi_j)}{\partial\varepsilon_i}}{(1-\Phi_i\Phi_j)^2}.$$

Both supplements are ambiguous in sign and responsible for an overall ambiguity. In the case of total integration, the suppl(C2)'s themselves must be modified. Straightforward calculations show that the suppl(C3)'s do not remove ambiguity because they neither add the first summand nor substract the second one.

Contributions to Economics

Hagen Bobzin
Indivisibilities
1998. ISBN 3-7908-1123-8

Helmut Wagner (Ed.)
Current Issues in Monetary Economics
1998. ISBN 3-7908-1127-0

Druck: Strauss Offsetdruck, Mörlenbach
Verarbeitung: Schäffer, Grünstadt